BLESSED *from on High*

DAILY INSPIRATION FROM THE
DOCTRINE & COVENANTS

BLESSED *from on High*

DAILY INSPIRATION FROM THE
DOCTRINE & COVENANTS

ED J. PINEGAR & RICHARD J. ALLEN

Covenant Communications, Inc.

Published by Covenant Communications, Inc.
American Fork, Utah

Printed in Canada
First Printing: October 2008

14 13 12 11 10 09 08 10 9 8 7 6 5 4 3 2 1

ISBN 10: 1-59811-582-0
ISBN 13: 978-1-59811-582-6

Preface

Throughout the ages, God has continually commanded His children to live by every word that proceedeth forth from His mouth (see D&C 84:43–46).

As President Howard W. Hunter taught, the Doctrine and Covenants "contains more direct quotations from the Lord than any other existing book of scripture. It is not a translation of an ancient document, but is of modern origin. It is a book of revelation for our day. It is a unique and divinely inspired selection of revelations that came through prophets of God in our day in answer to questions, concerns, and challenges they and others faced. It contains divine answers to real-life problems involving real people. The Doctrine and Covenants contains the word and will of the Lord as revealed to men and women in this dispensation of time. It is a book of scripture specifically for our day. It is a book for the entire world" (Howard W. Hunter, *The Teachings of Howard W. Hunter,* ed. Clyde J. Williams [Salt Lake City: Bookcraft, 1997], 55).

With this clarion call concerning this great and magnificent scripture, it behooves us to diligently study the Doctrine and Covenants. Nephi has taught us that we are to liken the scriptures and their teachings to ourselves for our profit and learning (see 1 Nephi 19:23). Doing so will change our lives as we internalize the word of God and convert it into action.

This little book of quotes and scriptures can help us apply the word of God to our lives. In it, you will find on each page:

- A scripture with an identifiable principle or practice,
- A quote from a General Authority or noteworthy person that magnifies or brings a better understanding to the process of applying the principle or practice to our daily living, and
- A list of ideas for daily living—either for personal application or further study

We hope you will feel the spirit of this work and find joy in living the word of God.

—The Authors

JANUARY

ꟹ

And inasmuch as they were humble
they might be made strong, and blessed
from on high, and receive knowledge
from time to time.

—DOCTRINE & COVENANTS 1:28

A VOICE OF WARNING

And the voice of warning shall be unto all people, by the mouths of my disciples, whom I have chosen in these last days. And they shall go forth and none shall stay them, for I the Lord have commanded them.

D&C 1:4–5

The Author of the Doctrine and Covenants is the Lord Jesus Christ, speaking through the instrumentality of the Prophet Joseph Smith. The Doctrine and Covenants is unique among the standard works of the Church not only because it contains a divinely authored preface, but also because it is a modern book of scripture. The introduction of the preface includes an invitation to all mankind, especially members of His Church, to heed the revelations, for the "voice of warning" shall be unto all people.

(Ezra Taft Benson, "A Voice of Warning," *Ensign,* July 1986, 3)

Daily Living

DO WE LISTEN TO THE LORD, THE SPIRIT, AND OUR LEADERS?

- Are we easily entreated?—Alma 7:23
- Receive peace as we listen to the Lord—D&C 19:23
- Remember the Spirit is given to those who keep the commandments—D&C 20:77–79
- The Spirit will show us all things to do—2 Nephi 32:5
- Do we hearken to our leaders?—3 Nephi 28:34–35
- We are blessed when we believe in the words of our prophets and leaders—3 Nephi 12:2

INCREASE YOUR FAITH

That faith also might increase in the earth.
D&C 1:21

My constant prayer in behalf of the entire Church is this: Lord, increase our faith to rise above the feeble detractors of this Thy great and holy work. Strengthen our will. Help us to build and expand Thy kingdom according to Thy great mandate, that this gospel may be preached in all the world as a witness unto all nations.

(Gordon B. Hinckley, "Lord, Increase Our Faith," *Ensign,* November 1987, 51)

How can I touch a life with faith? A place to begin your pondering is with the Savior. . . . The word of God will be heard by people with hearts softened by love and by grief and so more likely to choose living it more fully. And from doing that, faith will increase and the changes will come in people which move them toward eternal life.

(Henry B. Eyring, "To Touch a Life with Faith," *Ensign,* November 1995, 37)

Daily Living

SEEK TO INCREASE YOUR FAITH IN THE LORD JESUS CHRIST.

- We can increase our faith by hearing and searching the word of God—Romans 10:17
- Fasting and prayer will cause our faith to be firm and immovable—Helaman 3:35
- Our faith is expressed through love—Galatians 5:6

WE CAN PROCLAIM THE GOSPEL

That the fulness of my gospel might be proclaimed by the weak and the simple unto the ends of the world, and before kings and rulers. Behold, I am God and have spoken it; these commandments are of me, and were given unto my servants in their weakness, after the manner of their language, that they might come to understanding.

D&C 1:23–24

When the Church was organized, they accepted most literally the revelation that its mission should be to preach the gospel ". . . unto every nation, and kindred, and tongue, and people." (D&C 133:37). . . . Their faith and confidence were marvelous. They trusted God, and they did not trust in vain. They knew that he had said that "The weak things of the world shall come forth and break down the mighty and strong ones" (D&C 1:19), and that "the fulness of my gospel might be proclaimed by the weak and the simple unto the ends of the world, and before kings and rulers" (D&C 1:23). With this assurance our forebears went forth.

(Stephen L. Richards, in Conference Report, October 1945, 53)

Daily Living

THOUGH WEAK WE CAN PREACH IN THE STRENGTH OF THE LORD.

- When we acknowledge our weaknesses we are humbled and then the Lord can and will strengthen us—Ether 12:27
- We can do all things through faith in the Lord Jesus Christ—Moroni 7:33
- We preach in the strength of the Lord—Alma 26:11–12

COME TO AN UNDERSTANDING

Behold, I am God and have spoken it; these commandments are of me, and were given unto my servants in their weakness, after the manner of their language, that they might come to understanding.
D&C 1:24

If we can help people first understand the plan, they will find a deeper and more permanent motivation to keep the commandments. . . . When we understand the great plan of happiness, we are gaining an eternal perspective, and the commandments, ordinances, covenants, and the experiences, trials, and tribulations can be seen in their true and eternal light."

(Jay E. Jensen, "Keep an Eternal Perspective," *Ensign*, May 2000, 27)

Daily Living

UNDERSTAND AND APPRECIATE, AND YOU WILL CHANGE.

- Understanding to the point that we comprehend and appreciate the doctrine or principle will fill us with gratitude to such degree that we will change our attitude and behavior. Understanding is the key to learning and change—Psalms 111:10; Proverbs 4:7; 15:21; Alma 17:2
- Gratitude becomes the catalyst of change, hence the value of being appreciative through understanding; this helps us give thanks for all our blessings from our Heavenly Father and our Savior and keep the commandments—Romans 6:17; Ether 6:9; D&C 59:7, 15, 21

ALLOWANCE FOR THE SINNER WHO REPENTS

For I the Lord cannot look upon sin with the least degree of allowance; Nevertheless, he that repents and does the commandments of the Lord shall be forgiven
D&C 1:31–32

If the time comes when you have done all that you can to repent of your sins, whoever you are, wherever you are, and have made amends and restitution to the best of your ability; if it be something that will affect your standing in the Church and you have gone to the proper authorities, then you will want that confirming answer as to whether or not the Lord has accepted of you. In your soul-searching, if you seek for and you find that peace of conscience, by that token you may know that the Lord has accepted of your repentance. [Mosiah 4:2–3.] . . . The miracle of forgiveness is available to all of those who turn from their evil doings and return no more.

(Harold B. Lee, in Conference Report, April 1973, 177–78)

Daily Living

Repent and be forgiven . . . or suffer the consequences.

- Through the grace of God and the infinite and eternal Atonement of our Savior Jesus Christ, we are provided the opportunity to repent. Through repentance we can make the Atonement efficacious in our lives and can be forgiven of our sins. If we don't repent, we must suffer for our sins—D&C 19:15–19
- Repent and the Lord will forgive you and remember the sin no more—D&C 58:42–43

THE WORD WILL BE FULFILLED

What I the Lord have spoken, I have spoken, and I excuse not myself; and though the heavens and the earth pass away, my word shall not pass away, but shall all be fulfilled, whether by mine own voice or by the voice of my servants, it is the same.
D&C 1:38

The need of every generation is to take the prophets' counsel, past and present, and apply it in our lives. There is safety and security in following the prophets, particularly those of our own day. . . . Those who were spared in the great Nephite destruction were saved because they "received the prophets" (3 Ne. 10:12). . . . In the words of President James E. Faust, Second Counselor in the First Presidency: *"We have been promised that the President of the Church will receive guidance for all of us as the revelator for the Church. Our safety lies in paying heed to that which he says and following his counsel."*

(Clyde J. Williams, "Following the Prophets: A Book of Mormon Perspective," *Ensign*, July 2000, 19)

Daily Living

THE PROPHETS SPEAK FOR THE LORD.

- When we hearken to the living prophets we are hearkening to Christ—3 Nephi 12:1–3; D&C 21:4–6
- If we fail to hearken to the prophets we are brought under condemnation—3 Nephi 28:34–35
- We are blessed when we receive the prophets—3 Nephi 10:12

FAMILY KEYS RESTORED

Behold, I will reveal unto you the Priesthood, by the hand of Elijah the prophet, before the coming of the great and dreadful day of the Lord. And he shall plant in the hearts of the children the promises made to the fathers, and the hearts of the children shall turn to their fathers. If it were not so, the whole earth would be utterly wasted at his coming.

D&C 2:1–3

Remember that turning our hearts to our children and our fathers refers to both the living and the dead. Elder Ballard reminds us, "We warn that individuals . . . who fail to fulfill family responsibilities will one day stand accountable before God. Further, we warn that the disintegration of the family will bring upon individuals, communities, and nations the calamities foretold by ancient and modern prophets."

(Elder M. Russell Ballard, "Let Our Voices Be Heard," *Ensign,* November 2003, 16)

Daily Living

FAMILY ROLES, RELATIONSHIPS, AND RESPONSIBILITIES ARE ETERNAL.

ꝏ Family is our first and primary priority. Families are eternal. Families are the basic unit of the Church and kingdom of God. The plan of exaltation and happiness is centered in the salvation of the family and its individual members. What are we doing to magnify our eternal roles and serve each other within the family unit—fathers and mothers, husbands and wives, brothers and sisters, and sons and daughters?—The Family: A Proclamation to the World

GOD'S WORK CANNOT BE FRUSTRATED

The works, and the designs, and the purposes of God cannot be frustrated, neither can they come to naught. For God doth not walk in crooked paths, neither doth he turn to the right hand nor to the left, neither doth he vary from that which he hath said, therefore his paths are straight, and his course is one eternal round. Remember, remember that it is not the work of God that is frustrated, but the work of men.

D&C 3:1–3

God works with man within the framework of human agency and responsibility, and He fulfils His obligations without deviating from His word. Failures thus result from the actions of men, and they are accounted unto men. Having explained this principle of responsible agency and having chastised Joseph for giving way to "the persuasions of men," the revelation assured him that by sincere repentance he could "again be called to the work."

(Hyrum L. Andrus, *God, Man, and the Universe* [Salt Lake City: Bookcraft, 1968], 88)

Daily Living

THE WORK OF GOD CANNOT BE FRUSTRATED.

- The responsibility of each individual in regard to their calling is to build up the kingdom of God—3 Nephi 12:33
- We are accountable—Article of Faith 1:2
- The way we use our agency will determine our success—2 Nephi 2:27
- The work will go forward. The question is—will we have done our part?—D&C 4; 107:99–100; 123:17

REMEMBER . . . TAKE COUNSEL FROM THE LORD

For although a man may have many revelations, and have power to do many mighty works, yet if he boasts in his own strength, and sets at naught the counsels of God, and follows after the dictates of his own will and carnal desires, he must fall and incur the vengeance of a just God upon him.

D&C 3:4

Every day I review scores of letters from members of the Church. They are writing for counsel regarding a myriad of personal problems. As I consider these matters, returning most to our local leaders, where they can best be dealt with, I am reminded that most of us have personal and family problems. We all have challenges, heartaches, and experience success and failures. It is from these that we grow, gain strength and experience while in mortality. But when they take on serious proportions, it sometimes means we have not been fully obedient to counsel . . . both that of the Lord through his Spirit and that of our appointed leaders.

(President Spencer W. Kimball, "The Fruit of Our Welfare Services Labors," *Ensign*, November 1978, 74)

Daily Living

PRAY FOR STRENGTH, RECEIVE COUNSEL, AND SUBMIT YOUR WILL.

- Will you remember?—Helaman 5:9–12
- Will you pray for strength?—1 Nephi 7:17; Alma 2:28
- Will you receive counsel?—2 Nephi 9:28–29; Jacob 4:10
- Will you yield to the Lord?—Mosiah 3:19; Helaman 3:35

TRUST IN GOD . . . FEAR NOT MAN

For, behold, you should not have feared man more than God. Although men set at naught the counsels of God, and despise his words—Yet you should have been faithful; and he would have extended his arm and supported you against all the fiery darts of the adversary; and he would have been with you in every time of trouble.

D&C 3:7–8

As leaders in Israel, we must seek to dispel fear from among our people. A timid, fearing people cannot do their work well. The Latter-day Saints have a divinely assigned world-mission so great that they cannot afford to dissipate their strength in fear. The Lord has repeatedly warned His people against fear. Many a blessing is withheld because of our fears. He has expressly declared that men cannot stop his work on earth, therefore, they who are engaged in the Lord's latter-day cause and who fear, really trust man more than God, and thereby are robbed of their power to serve.

(Elder John A. Widtsoe, in Conference Report, April 1942, 33)

Daily Living

TRUST IN THE LORD IN ALL THINGS.

- Trust in the Lord—Proverbs 3:5–6
- Do not trust in the arm of the flesh—2 Nephi 4:34
- You learn to trust in the Lord as you come to know and love Him, learn and live His doctrine, and increase your faith through the knowledge of His goodness and perfection—2 Nephi 4:19, 34; John 7:17; 17:3; Alma 36:3

THE PROMISES OF GOD ARE FULFILLED

And for this very purpose are these plates preserved, which contain these records—that the promises of the Lord might be fulfilled, which he made to his people;
And that the Lamanites might come to the knowledge of their fathers, and that they might know the promises of the Lord, and that they may believe the gospel and rely upon the merits of Jesus Christ, and be glorified through faith in his name, and that through their repentance they might be saved. Amen.
D&C 3:19–20

The very title page of the Book of Mormon states the same purpose [as that stated in D&C 3:19-20] and in many other places throughout the book it is reiterated. As "Gentiles" who have been greatly blessed by the Book of Mormon, members of the Church should recognize that they have a great obligation to help bring about the great promises of the Lord to his people.

(Gerald N. Lund, The Coming of the Lord {Salt Lake City: Bookcraft, 1971], 150)

Daily Living

GOD KNOWS ALL AND HIS WORDS WILL BE FULFILLED.

- The Book of Mormon is the word of God and will bring man closer to God—Introduction to the Book of Mormon, paragraph 6

A MARVELOUS WORK

Now behold, a marvelous work is about to come forth among the children of men.
D&C 4:1

This "marvelous work and a wonder" has come to pass and has spread all over the world where there has been religious liberty; and from every land and from every clime honest, faithful, God-fearing men and women have heard the sound of the true voice of the shepherd through his servants who have gone forth to proclaim the Gospel. And men of great influence have been gathered into this Church. Men like John Taylor who presided over the Church, heard the Gospel in a foreign land; the parents of George Q. Cannon, and many other leaders in this Church, heard the sound of this Gospel and embraced it and gathered to Zion, and labored with all the power and ability that they possessed for the advancement of God's kingdom. Year by year this great and wonderful work has rolled on and we are becoming known as a God-fearing people, as a people with a destiny that is sure to be fulfilled.

(Heber J. Grant, in Conference Report, October 1929, 9)

Daily Living

THE MARVELOUS WORK IS TO SHARE THE RESTORATION OF THE GOSPEL.

- The Book of Mormon is true and is the great converter of the soul—D&C 18;34–36
- You must feast upon the word of God—2 Nephi 32:3
- Don't treat lightly the Book of Mormon—D&C 84:54–57
- Share the gospel—D&C 4; 31:5; 33:8–11; 88:81; Mosiah 18:9; Mormon 9:22

January 13

SERVICE IN THE KINGDOM OF GOD

Therefore, O ye that embark in the service of God, see that ye serve him with all your heart, might, mind and strength, that ye may stand blameless before God at the last day.
D&C 4:2

This principle of service is reaffirmed in the fourth section of the Doctrine and Covenants: . . . Here we learn that it is not enough to serve God with all of our might and strength. He who looks into our hearts and knows our minds demands more than this. In order to stand blameless before God at the last day, we must also serve him with all our heart and mind. Self-effacing service with all of our heart and mind is a high challenge for all of us. Such service must be motivated solely by the pure love of Christ. Those who forget themselves and give service in this manner can look up to God "with a pure heart and clean hands" (Alma 5:19).

(Dallin H. Oaks, *Pure in Heart* [Salt Lake City: Bookcraft, 1988], 48)

Daily Living

SERVE WITH ALL YOUR HEART, MIGHT, MIND AND STRENGTH.

ჯ How do you serve with all your heart, might, mind, and strength? With love and concern, with your whole soul (give it your all), with your decisions and priorities governed by your call to serve, with all your physical strength and power, with all your intellectual and spiritual discernment, and with the strength of Lord through which you can do all things—Romans 12:1; 2 Nephi 2:3; Mosiah 2:11, 21; 7:33; 18:10, 13; Helaman 10:4–5

DESIRE TO SERVE THE LORD

Therefore, if ye have desires to serve God ye are called to the work.
D&C 4:3

Actually, everything depends—initially and finally—on our desires. These shape our thought patterns. Our desires thus precede our deeds and lie at the very cores of our souls, tilting us toward or away from God (see D&C 4:3). God can "educate our desires." Others seek to manipulate our desires. But it is we who form the desires, the "thoughts and intents of [our] hearts" (Mosiah 5:13). The end rule is "according to [our] desires . . . shall it be done unto [us]" (D&C 11:17), "for I, the Lord, will judge all men according to their works, according to the desire of their hearts" (D&C 137:9; see also Alma 41:5; D&C 6:20, 27). A person's individual will thus remains uniquely his. God will not override it or overwhelm it. Hence we'd better want the consequences of what we want! . . . But we must desire and provide it.

(Neal A. Maxwell, *If Thou Endure It Well* [Salt Lake City: Bookcraft, 1996], 51)

Daily Living

MOTIVATION TO SERVE, A DESIRE TO DO GOOD.

- Righteous desire is the seedbed for action—Proverbs 11:23; Mosiah 28:3
- Your desires to serve increase when you have faith, hope, and charity in Christ—Alma 7:24
- Gratitude and love of God help us keep the commandments—John 14:15

THE FIELD IS WHITE ALREADY TO HARVEST

For behold the field is white already to harvest; and lo, he that thrusteth in his sickle with his might, the same layeth up in store that he perisheth not, but bringeth salvation to his soul.
D&C 4:4

It is our responsibility to give all other men the opportunity of hearing and receiving [the] gospel if they desire. . . . No man ever puts out his hand to help another without gaining for himself the right to a merited salvation because of his willingness to help others. Now, keep in mind that all of us are our Father's children, whether presently members of the Church or not. It is these others of our Father's children about whom we must be much concerned. They are just as dear to Him as those who are presently members of the Church. If any one of us sets himself to the task of bringing others into the fold, the Lord says he brings salvation to his own soul.

(Harold B. Lee, *The Teachings of Harold B. Lee*, ed. Clyde J. Williams [Salt Lake City: Bookcraft, 1996], 594)

Daily Living

THE FIELD IS WHITE . . . SO THRUST IN YOUR SICKLES.

ꕥ Now is the time, and we are the ones to thrust in our sickles that we might bring souls unto Christ. The Lord needs full-time missionaries now. Young elders and sisters and senior sisters and couples, go ahead and submit your papers. Think of the joy—Alma 29:9–10; 36:24; D&C 15:6; 18:10–16

QUALIFYING FOR THE WORK

And faith, hope, charity, and love, with an eye single to the glory of God, qualify him for the work.
D&C 4:5

In the Church and kingdom of God there is no unimportant office or calling or service (see 1 Corinthians 12:12–25). We are all in it together and the Lord has a way of magnifying us. (San Diego California South Stake Conference, 6 December 1969). It is essential to all we do in our ministry that it be done with "an eye single to the glory of God" (D&C 4:5). That should be our primary motive. We have not been called to build up ourselves, but to build the kingdom of God. We shall be instrumental in achieving this momentous goal as we magnify our callings and honor the Lord (Salt Lake City, Utah, 19 January 1977).

(Ezra Taft Benson, *The Teachings of Ezra Taft Benson* [Salt Lake City: Bookcraft, 1988], 453–454)

Daily Living

Seek to do His will with an eye single to His glory.

- Increase your faith—Romans 10:17; Helaman 3:35
- Hope comes through our Savior Jesus Christ and His infinite and eternal Atonement—Jeremiah 17:7; 1 Corinthians 15:19; 2 Nephi 31:20; Ether 12:4, 32
- Pray for charity—Moroni 7:48
- Our eye is single to the glory of God when our will is swallowed up in the will of God—D&C 88:67
- Our desires are to build up the kingdom of God—3 Nephi 12:33

DIVINE CHARACTERISTICS

Remember faith, virtue, knowledge, temperance, patience, brotherly kindness, godliness, charity, humility, diligence.
D&C 4:6

The Lord provides two lists of characteristics that qualify a person for missionary work. The first list (faith, hope, charity, love) appears to be general and inclusive, while the second list (faith, virtue, knowledge, temperance, patience, brotherly kindness, godliness, charity, humility, diligence) seems to be more specific, although two terms, *faith* and *charity*, are common to both groups.

(Daniel H. Ludlow, *A Companion to Your Study of the Doctrine and Covenants,* 2 vols. [Salt Lake City: Deseret Book, 1978], 1:69)

Daily Living

TAKE UPON YOU THE DIVINE NATURE OF CHRIST.

℘ Faith, the foundation of all righteousness; virtue, the righteousness and power of God; knowledge, the truths and doctrines of God; temperance, the self-control and self-mastery of the soul; patience, the bedrock and constancy of charity and the antithesis of all the negative attributes; brotherly kindness, the showing forth of love and concern for all mankind; godliness, the qualities of a godly walk and talk like unto our Savior; charity, the pure love of Christ which never fails for Christ never fails . . . with humility and diligence—2 Peter 1:3–10; Galatians 5:5; D&C 121:45; Alma 7:23; D&C 67:13; Proverbs 19:22; 1 Timothy 4:8; Moroni 7:44–48; D&C 112:10; Mosiah 7:33

THE PRINCIPLE OF INQUIRY

Ask, and ye shall receive; knock, and it shall be opened unto you. Amen.
D&C 4:7

"If ye will not harden your hearts, and ask me in faith, believing that ye shall receive, with diligence in keeping my commandments, surely these things shall be made known unto you" (1 Nephi 15:11).

"Yea, I know that God will give liberally to him that asketh." (2 Nephi 4:35).

"Counsel with the Lord in all thy doings, and he will direct thee for good" (Alma 37:37). . . .

"And whatsoever ye shall ask the Father in my name, which is right, believing that ye shall receive, behold it shall be given unto you" (3 Nephi 20:18). . . .

". . . O Lord, thou hast given us a commandment that we must call upon thee, that from thee we may receive according to our desires" (Ether 3:2). . . .

"Therefore, he that lacketh wisdom, let him ask of me, and I will give him liberally and upbraid him not" (D&C 42:68).

(quoted in Boyd K. Packer, *Teach Ye Diligently* [Salt Lake City: Deseret Book, 1975], 16)

Ask!

- Ask in sincerity of heart—Mosiah 4:10
- Ask in the name of Jesus Christ—3 Nephi 27:28

January 19

THE WORD OF GOD THROUGH THE PROPHET

But this generation shall have my word through you.
D&C 5:10

When the Lord opened up this dispensation, he chose and appointed the Prophet Joseph Smith through whom to reveal his will. And the peoples of the earth were put under obligation to hear him. . . . The Lord said to the Prophet: ". . . this generation shall have my word through you" (D&C 5:10). . . . As long as the Prophet lived, the Lord revealed his will to that generation through him. . . . Since the Prophet's martyrdom, the will of the Lord has been given through succeeding prophets . . . who each in his turn has presided over the Church, and, like unto Moses, has guided the people of his generation on the issues of their day by the spirit of revelation. (See Doc. & Cov. 107:9; 8:2–3.) During the administrations of all these leaders, those who have accepted them as prophets . . . they are the ones who have been comforted and who have had peace in their souls.

(Marion G. Romney, in Conference Report, April 1945, 89–90)

Daily Living

THE PROPHETS SPEAK FOR THE LORD.

- Follow the counsel of the living prophets—D&C 1:38
- Followership is the essence of discipleship—1 Thessalonians 1:6
- Laws given by the prophets—D&C 58:18
- When we receive His servants, we receive Christ—D&C 84:36
- They speak by the power of the Holy Ghost—D&C 68:3

THE LAW OF WITNESSES

And in addition to your testimony, the testimony of three of my servants, whom I shall call and ordain, unto whom I will show these things, and they shall go forth with my words that are given through you. Yea, they shall know of a surety that these things are true, for from heaven will I declare it unto them. I will give them power that they may behold and view these things as they are; . . . And the testimony of three witnesses will I send forth of my word.

D&C 5:11–15

The divine law of witnesses indicates that "in the mouth of two or three witnesses shall every word be established" (2 Cor. 13:1; see also Deut. 17:6; Matt. 18:15–16; John 8:12–29). . . . The Book of Mormon has several modern witnesses to its authenticity: Joseph Smith, the three special witnesses, and the eight special witnesses. Such witnesses were provided by the Lord so that every word of his gospel might be established according to the divine law of witnesses.

(Daniel H. Ludlow, *A Companion to Your Study of the Doctrine and Covenants* [Salt Lake City: Deseret Book, 1978], 2:330)

Daily Living

WE ARE WITNESSES OF THE TRUTH TODAY.

ℰ Now it is our turn to bear witness of our Heavenly Father, our Savior Jesus Christ, the gospel, the Book of Mormon, the Prophet Joseph and the restoration of the Church and kingdom of God and of living prophets—Mosiah 18:9

BELIEVE IN THE WORD—BE BORN AGAIN

And behold, whosoever believeth on my words, them will I visit with the manifestation of my Spirit; and they shall be born of me, even of water and of the Spirit.
D&C 5:16

The Savior promised that those who would believe his words would be "born of me, even of water and of the spirit" (D&C 5:16). . . . The phrase *born of me* is elsewhere rendered as "born again" (John 3:1–8), "born of him" (Mosiah 5:7), "born of the Spirit" (Mosiah 27:24), and "born of God" (Alma 5:14). . . . To be born again is to be "spiritually begotten" of Christ and become "his sons and his daughters" (Mosiah 5:7). It is to have "the image of God engraven upon your countenance" (Alma 5:14–19), thus reflecting a godly image in everything one thinks, says, or does. . . . The Prophet Joseph Smith added this inspired thought: "Whosoever is born of God doth not continue in sin; for the Spirit of God remaineth in him; and he cannot continue in sin, because he is born of God, having received that holy Spirit of promise" (JST, 1 John 3:9).

(Hoyt W. Brewster, Jr., *Doctrine and Covenants Encyclopedia* [Salt Lake City: Bookcraft, 1996], 57)

Daily Living

BE BORN AGAIN . . . BE BORN OF GOD.

೫ Be born of God through the Atonement of the Lord and Savior Jesus Christ by obedience to the principles and ordinances of the gospel—3 Nephi 27:19–20

SEEK FOR WISDOM

Seek not for riches but for wisdom, and behold, the mysteries of God shall be unfolded unto you, and then shall you be made rich. Behold, he that hath eternal life is rich.
D&C 6:7

The riches of eternal life we ought to seek, not the riches of the world. . . . We do not look upon wealth in itself as a curse. We believe that those who can handle means rightly can do much to bless their fellows. But he who is ruled by the love of money is tempted to commit sin. The love of money is the root of all evil. [1 Tim. 6:10.] There is hardly a commandment but is violated through this seeking for riches.

(Anthon H. Lund, in Conference Report, April 1903, 97)

Daily Living

SEEK THE WISDOM OF THE LORD IN ALL THINGS.

- Follow the counsel of Jacob; "But before ye seek for riches, seek ye for the kingdom of God. And after ye have obtained a hope in Christ ye shall obtain riches, if ye seek them; and ye will seek them for the intent to do good" —Jacob 2:17–18
- Learn wisdom in thy youth—Alma 37:35
- "O be wise; what can I say more?"—Jacob 6:12
- If you truly seek eternal life you will always seek to build up the kingdom of God—JST—Matthew 6:38
- Learn wisdom through humility—D&C 136:32
- Those who hearken unto my precepts learn wisdom—2 Nephi 28:30

BE ENLIGHTENED OF THE SPIRIT

Behold, thou knowest that thou hast inquired of me and I did enlighten thy mind; and now I tell thee these things that thou mayest know that thou hast been enlightened by the Spirit of truth.
D&C 6:15

In its most familiar forms, revelation comes by means of words or thoughts or feelings communicated to the mind. "Behold," the Lord told Oliver Cowdery, "I will tell you in your mind and in your heart, by the Holy Ghost" (D&C 8:2). . . . We often refer to these most familiar forms of revelation as *inspiration.* Inspired thoughts or promptings can take the form of enlightenment of the mind (D&C 6:15), positive or negative feelings about proposed courses of action. . . . The experience of revelation is available to everyone. President Lorenzo Snow declared that it is "the grand privilege of every Latter-day Saint . . . to have the manifestations of the spirit every day of our lives."

(Dallin H. Oaks, *The Lord's Way* [Salt Lake City: Deseret Book, 1991], 23)

Daily Living

INQUIRE OF THE LORD AND BE ENLIGHTENED BY THE SPIRIT.

- Sometimes we fail to recognize the fruits of the Spirit. "But the fruit of the Spirit is love, joy, peace, longsuffering, gentleness, goodness, faith, meekness, temperance: against such there is no law."—Galatians 5:22–23
- Trust in the Spirit that you may be directed in all things pertaining to righteousness—D&C 11:12–13

THE WITNESS OF PEACE TO YOUR SOUL

Verily, verily, I say unto you, if you desire a further witness, cast your mind upon the night that you cried unto me in your heart, that you might know concerning the truth of these things. Did I not speak peace to your mind concerning the matter? What greater witness can you have than from God?

D&C 6:22–23

President Marion G. Romney taught, "Sometimes the Lord puts thoughts in our minds in answer to prayers. . . . [He] gives us peace in our minds" (Taiwan Area Conference, 1975, 7). . . . The peace God speaks to our minds will let us know when decisions we have made are right, when our course is true. It can come as personal inspiration and guidance to assist us in our daily life—in our homes, in our work. It can provide us with courage and hope to meet the challenges of life. The miracle of prayer, to me, is that in the private, quiet chambers of our mind and heart, God both hears *and* answers prayers.

(Rex D. Pinegar, "Peace through Prayer," *Peace* [Salt Lake City: Deseret Book, 1998], 73)

Daily Living

SEEK PEACE OF THE LORD IN ALL THINGS.

ℰ Sometimes we seek and desire the grandiose exhibits of miraculous spiritual manifestations to answers to our prayers—and in this we do err. The sweet whisperings of the Spirit to our heart and mind are witness enough. The blessing of peace is most delicious and brings calmness and serenity to the soul; what could be more cherished and treasured?—D&C 19:23

YOU REAP WHAT YOU SOW

Fear not to do good, my sons, for whatsoever ye sow, that shall ye also reap; therefore, if ye sow good ye shall also reap good for your reward.

D&C 6:33

"There is a law, irrevocably decreed in heaven before the foundations of this world, upon which all blessings are predicated—And when we obtain any blessing from God, it is by obedience to that law upon which it is predicated" (D&C 130:9, 20–21). . . . I should like to pause long enough to say to you that the most arresting declaration that you can make to the youth of your wards and stakes and missions is that there is a law which applies to them; it is inexorable, immutable; it is known as the law of the harvest. "As ye sow, so shall ye reap."

(Hugh B. Brown, *Continuing the Quest* [Salt Lake City: Deseret Book, 1961], 176)

Daily Living

WHAT GOES AROUND, COMES AROUND.

ꕥ What are you sowing? What goals and plans have you made? What has been your preparation to be successful in things that really matter? What price have you paid to increase in your faith, hope, and charity? Is your fasting and prayer with real intent? Do you sow seeds of gossip and judgment or supportive praise and patience? Do you seek to receive the love of God by holding to the iron rod? We all need to improve, and that is why we are here on earth. Let's make each day a better day than yesterday by sowing seeds of love, service to our fellowman, and by being obedient in all things—D&C 130:20–21

BRING SOULS UNTO CHRIST

And I said unto him: Lord, give unto me power over death, that I may live and bring souls unto thee.
D&C 7:2

John the Beloved asked to be a missionary here on earth, saying, "Lord, give unto me power over death, that I may live and bring souls unto thee." The Savior, much impressed with John's response, turned to Peter and said, in effect: You want a good thing, but John has desired a greater thing. In other words, in the view of the Savior, it is greater to be a missionary on earth, bringing souls unto him, than to be in heaven worshiping at his feet. What a lesson for us!

(Robert E. Wells, *The Mount and the Master* [Salt Lake City: Deseret Book, 1991], 104)

Daily Living

SEEK TO BRING SOULS UNTO CHRIST.

- Souls are precious. "Remember the worth of souls is great in the sight of God"—D&C 18:10
- "And how great is his [the Lord's] joy in the soul that repenteth!"—D&C 18:13
- The thing that will be of most worth is "that you may bring souls unto me"—D&C 15:6
- The desire of those who are truly converted is for the welfare of the souls of all mankind—Mosiah 28:3
- Alma's joy was to help others come unto Christ and taste of the joy of the gospel of Jesus Christ—Alma 36:24
- And this is our joy too . . . to bring souls unto Christ—D&C 18:14–16

THE SPIRIT OF REVELATION

Yea, behold, I will tell you in your mind and in your heart, by the Holy Ghost, which shall come upon you and which shall dwell in your heart. Now, behold, this is the spirit of revelation.
D&C 8:2–3

Revelation may be given to every member of the Church. The Prophet said that every man should be a prophet; that the testimony of Jesus is the spirit of prophecy. It is not only the privilege but the duty of each member of the Church to know the truth which will make him free. . . . But the members of the Church are entitled to receive revelation which is needful for their progress, and if they will hearken to the Spirit of truth and walk humbly before the Lord, they will not fall short of this spiritual guidance.

(Joseph Fielding Smith, *Church History and Modern Revelation* [Salt Lake City: Deseret Book, 1947], 4:36)

Daily Living

SEEK REVELATION BY THE POWER OF THE HOLY GHOST.

Remember, "A person may profit by noticing the first intimation of the spirit of revelation; for instance, when you feel pure intelligence flowing unto you, it may give you sudden strokes of ideas, so that by noticing it, you may find it fulfilled the same day or soon; (i.e.) those things that were presented into your minds by the Spirit of God [D&C 85:6; Enos 1], will come to pass; and thus by learning the Spirit of God and understanding it, you may grow into the principle of revelation, until you become perfect in Christ Jesus."—Joseph Smith, *History of the Church,* 3:381

ANSWERS TO PRAYERS

Behold, you have not understood; you have supposed that I would give it unto you, when you took no thought save it was to ask me. But, behold, I say unto you, that you must study it out in your mind; then you must ask me if it be right, and if it is right I will cause that your bosom shall burn within you; therefore, you shall feel that it is right. But if it be not right you shall have no such feelings, but you shall have a stupor of thought that shall cause you to forget the thing which is wrong; therefore, you cannot write that which is sacred save it be given you from me.

D&C 9:7–9

President Benson suggests the following in the decision-making process: "1. From my youth I have searched the scriptures. 2. I have tried to honestly face the challenge or question presented with a sincere desire to solve it as Jesus would solve it. 3. I have, through diligent study and prayer, sought to weigh alternatives in light of what I knew about gospel principles. 4. I have made a decision in my own mind. 5. I have then taken the matter to the Lord, told him the problem, told him that I wanted to do what was right in his view, and asked him to give me peace of mind if I have made the right decision."

(Ezra Taft Benson, *Come unto Christ* [Salt Lake City: Deseret Book, 1983], 45)

Daily Living

DECISION MAKING AND GETTING ANSWERS TO OUR PRAYERS.

ꟾ Follow the above counsel of President Ezra Taft Benson.

January 29

PRAY ALWAYS

Pray always, that you may come off conqueror; yea, that you may conquer Satan, and that you may escape the hands of the servants of Satan that do uphold his work.

D&C 10:5

Prayer, in fact, is to be a reflection of our attitude toward God and life. In this sense, we can always be praying (Luke 18:1). Clearly, however, since praying is a part of living, if we are not living righteously the quality of our prayers will be affected. Likewise, routine personal prayers will scarcely reflect the unevenness of life, especially those moments when we are in deep need. When in deep need, we, as did He, "being in agony" will need to pray "more earnestly" (Luke 22:44). . . . It should not surprise us as we grow if we are sometimes less than fully comprehending of prayer. . . . There are no Christlike prayers, however, that do not include, as did the Lord's Prayer, deep expressions of gratitude and appreciation to our Father in heaven along with a submittal to Him.

(Neal A. Maxwell, *All These Things Shall Give Thee Experience* [Salt Lake City: Deseret Book, 1979], 93)

Daily Living

CONSIDER YOUR PRAYERS . . . PRAY WITH REAL INTENT.

- Pray for all things—Alma 34:17–27
- Pray to increase in humility and faith—Helaman 3:35
- Pray for those who know not God—Alma 6:6
- Pray to overcome temptation—3 Nephi 18:18
- Pray for charity—Moroni 7:48

THE DEVIL SEEKS TO DESTROY THE SOULS OF MEN

And thus he [the devil] goeth up and down, to and fro in the earth, seeking to destroy the souls of men.
D&C 10:27

President Harold B. Lee has warned us, "Satan seeks to destroy our agency. Don't have any mistaken ideas about the devil. . . . You cannot tell me that there isn't such a thing as a devil possessing the body of a person who allows himself to take a course that makes that possible. If you forget everything else I have said today, please remember, young people, that the prince of this world, Satan, is going to try to trap every one of you. That is his program. He is trying to destroy our agency. If he can get you going along the path of taking a smoke, taking a drink, listening to sensuous music, or accepting in any degree an invitation that leads downward, he will take you to the bottom of the canyon on that road of sin to a place where no sunlight can be seen."
(Harold B. Lee, *The Teachings of Harold B. Lee*, ed. Clyde J. Williams, 41)

Daily Living

REMEMBER THE DEVIL IS REAL AND SEEKS TO DESTROY YOU.

- He seeks to lead us carefully down to hell—2 Nephi 28:21
- The devil seeks you to be miserable like him—2 Nephi 2:27
- To withstand all the temptations of the devil:

  –Hold to the iron rod, the word of God—1 Nephi 15:24

  –Lay hold to the word of God—Helaman 3:29

  –Pray with all your heart—3 Nephi 18:18

January 31

REMEMBER THE WORDS OF CHRIST

And now, remember the words of him who is the life and light of the world, your Redeemer, your Lord and your God. Amen.
D&C 10:70

Read in the scriptures; in them is life and light and the power that leads back unto God, our Father. A short time ago, I asked the branch presidents and conference presidents and each missionary in the Central States mission, to take up a labor with the members of their branches, and with every member of the Church with whom they came in contact, encouraging them to read the scriptures, not only in preparation for their lessons for auxiliary organizations, but separate and apart from that—to read the scriptures one-half hour a day. I tell you if men and women will do this the Lord's truth will come into their minds and into their hearts, and they will remember constantly the word of God.

(Elder Samuel O. Bennion, in Conference Report, April 1922, 140)

Daily Living

FEAST AND PONDER ON THE WORD OF GOD.

- We are to live by every word that proceedeth forth from the mouth of God—D&C 84:43–46
- The word of God has the greatest power to lead us to do that which is good—Alma 31:5
- Feast upon the word of God, for it will tell us all things what we should do—2 Nephi 32:3

FEBRUARY

Wherefore, the blessings which I give unto you are above all things.

—Doctrine & Covenants 18:45

PREACH REPENTANCE

Say nothing but repentance unto this generation. Keep my commandments, and assist to bring forth my work, according to my commandments, and you shall be blessed.
D&C 11:9

If there be any here who have . . . sinned, there is repentance and there is forgiveness, provided there is "godly sorrow." (See 2 Cor. 7:10.) All is not lost. Each of you has a bishop, who has been ordained and set apart under the authority of the holy priesthood and who, in the exercise of his office, is entitled to the inspiration of the Lord. He is a man of experience, he is a man of understanding, he is a man who carries in his heart a love for the youth of his ward. He is a servant of God who understands his obligation of confidentiality and who will help you with your problem. Do not be afraid to talk with him.

(Gordon B. Hinckley, *Teachings of Gordon B. Hinckley* [Salt Lake City: Deseret Book, 1997], 545–546)

Daily Living

PREACH, TEACH, AND LIVE REPENTANCE.

- Preach nothing save it be repentance—Mosiah 18:20
- All need to repent, for all have sinned—1 John 1:8–10
- Repentance is a process of becoming, through the grace of God, and not made by announcement or confession alone; it requires healing and good works—Helaman 12:24
- When we truly repent, the Lord forgives us and remembers our sins no more—D&C 58:42–43

TRUST IN THE HOLY SPIRIT

And now, verily, verily, I say unto thee, put your trust in that Spirit which leadeth to do good—yea, to do justly, to walk humbly, to judge righteously; and this is my Spirit. Verily, verily, I say unto you, I will impart unto you of my Spirit, which shall enlighten your mind, which shall fill your soul with joy.

D&C 11:12–13

We should try to learn the nature of this spirit, that we may understand its suggestions, and then we will always be able to do right. This is the grand privilege of every Latter-day Saint. We know that it is our right to have the manifestations of the spirit every day of our lives. . . . We have a friend, if we do not drive it from us by doing wrong. That friend is the Holy Spirit, the Holy Ghost, which partakes of the things of God and shows them unto us. This is a grand means that the Lord has provided for us, that we may know the light, and not be groveling continually in the dark.

(Lorenzo Snow, in Conference Report, April 1899, 52)

Daily Living

REMEMBER TO BE WORTHY OF THE SPIRIT.

- We must live worthy of and be prepared to receive the Spirit through increased faith in the Lord—1 Nephi 10:17
- Possess and express an abundance of love and be purified before the Lord—D&C 76:116
- Keep the commandments—D&C 20:77, 79
- Pray for Spirit in our lives—3 Nephi 19:9

SEEK TO OBTAIN THE WORD

Seek not to declare my word, but first seek to obtain my word, and then shall your tongue be loosed; then, if you desire, you shall have my Spirit and my word, yea, the power of God unto the convincing of men.
D&C 11:21

Scripture study brings an outpouring of the Spirit. Brothers and sisters, we urge each of you to carefully consider how much time you are currently giving to prayerful pondering of the scriptures. As one of the Lord's servants, I challenge you to do the following: 1. Read, ponder and pray over the scriptures daily as individual members of the Church. 2. Hold family scripture reading on a regular basis. We commend those of you who are already doing this and urge those of you who have not yet started to begin doing so without delay. 3. Seek the Spirit to know better how to learn and teach by the Spirit. The Lord has said, "The Spirit shall be given unto you by the prayer of faith" (D&C 42:14).

(Howard W. Hunter, *The Teachings of Howard W. Hunter,* ed. Clyde J. Williams [Salt Lake City: Bookcraft, 1997], 52)

Daily Living

FEAST UPON, PONDER, AND LIVE THE WORD OF GOD.

- Set some goals and make some plans to search, ponder, and apply the scriptures in your life. You will need a time, a place, and a way, and you will achieve your goals.
- Feast upon the word—2 Nephi 32:3
- Ponder the word—D&C 138:11
- Live the word—D&C 84:43–46

BECOMING WORTHY TO ASSIST IN THE WORK

And no one can assist in this work except he shall be humble and full of love, having faith, hope, and charity, being temperate in all things, whatsoever shall be entrusted to his care.
D&C 12:8

Humility does not mean weakness. It does not mean timidity; it does not mean fear. A man can be humble and also fearless. A man can be humble and also courageous. Humility is the recognition of our dependence upon a higher power, a constant need for the Lord's support in His work. . . . We must develop a love for people. Our hearts must go out to them in the pure love of the gospel, in a desire to lift them, to build them up, to point them to a higher, finer life and eventually to exaltation in the celestial kingdom of God.

(Ezra Taft Benson, *Come unto Christ* [Salt Lake City: Deseret Book, 1983], 94–95)

Daily Living

PREPARE TO ASSIST IN THE WORK OF THE LORD.

- The power to bless lives and assist in building up the kingdom of God is not a passive thought, nor is it to be taken lightly. This is the challenge of becoming an instrument in the hands of God.
- Seek humility as the beginning virtue—Helaman 3:35
- Seek charity and love and express it through concern and service for others—Moroni 7:44–48; John 13:34–35
- Increase in faith in Jesus Christ—Romans 10:17; Alma 32; Ether 12; Moroni 7
- Live with hope—Romans 15:13; Ether 12:4; Moroni 7:41

AARONIC PRIESTHOOD RESTORATION

Upon you my fellow servants, in the name of Messiah I confer the Priesthood of Aaron, which holds the keys of the ministering of angels, and of the gospel of repentance, and of baptism by immersion for the remission of sins; and this shall never be taken again from the earth, until the sons of Levi do offer again an offering unto the Lord in righteousness.

D&C 13:1

Preparing young men to receive and advance in the priesthood is a sacred trust. We trust that young men are being properly tutored before receiving the Aaronic Priesthood at the age of twelve and that their parents and advisors are preparing them to advance within the priesthood at the appropriate age and then be ordained to the Melchizedek Priesthood at the proper time.

(Howard W. Hunter, *The Teachings of Howard W. Hunter*, ed. Clyde J. Williams [Salt Lake City: Bookcraft, 1997], 216)

Daily Living

APPRECIATE THE BLESSINGS OF THE AARONIC PRIESTHOOD.

ཆ Ponder and meditate upon the power and blessings of the Aaronic Priesthood and its holders: the ministering of angels, the gospel of repentance, baptism and all the associated commitments . . . All these things, including the blessing and administration of the sacrament to the members of the Church—D&C 20:38–64

THE GREATEST GIFT OF GOD

And, if you keep my commandments and endure to the end you shall have eternal life, which gift is the greatest of all the gifts of God.
D&C 14:7

Keep my commandments and endure to the end. We have entered into the bond of that new and everlasting covenant agreeing that we would obey the commandments of God in all things whatsoever he shall command us. This is an everlasting covenant even unto the end of our days. . . . It is upon this principle that we keep in touch with God, and remain in harmony with his purposes. It is only in this way that we can consummate our mission, and obtain our crown and the gift of eternal lives, which is the greatest gift of God. Can you imagine any other way?

(Joseph F. Smith, in Conference Report, April 1898, 68)

Daily Living

SEEK ETERNAL LIFE . . . THE GREATEST GIFT OF GOD.

- When the trials, tribulations, and the vicissitudes of life seem to overwhelm you . . . stop. Ponder the things that matter most and your quest to obtain the blessings of eternal life. If we do this we can always keep life in its true perspective. Enduring to the end is indeed the finale of mortality—2 Nephi 31:20
- Never give up. Never give in. Never give out, and, of course, cheerfully do all that lies within your power—D&C 123:17

THE THING OF MOST WORTH

And now, behold, I say unto you, that the thing which will be of the most worth unto you will be to declare repentance unto this people, that you may bring souls unto me, that you may rest with them in the kingdom of my Father. Amen.

D&C 15:6 OR 16:6

One of the happiest moments for a missionary is when he converts an honest investigator to the gospel. Thousands of missionaries have declared this experience to be the climax of missionary work. Every missionary hopes to have this soul-satisfying experience at least once during his career in the ministry.

Why shouldn't conversion of a truth seeker be a thrilling experience? The Master has made plain that bringing souls unto him is the most worth while work one can pursue. Since it is the greatest work, it will bring the greatest joy to those who faithfully engage in it.

(*Improvement Era*, vol. 56 "Priests Under 21," November 1953, No.11)

Daily Living

REMEMBER THAT THE SOULS OF ALL MANKIND ARE WHAT MATTERS.

- Souls matter most—Moses 1:39
- Have concern for the welfare of every soul—Mosiah 28:3
- Pray for all those who know not God—Alma 6:6
- Open your mouth—D&C 33:8–11; 68:3–7; 84:85
- Invite and persuade all to come unto Christ—Jacob 1:7
- Stand as a witness at all times—Mosiah 18:9
- Bear your testimony—D&C 62:3

BY FAITH YOU CAN SEE

And it is by your faith that you shall obtain a view of them, even by that faith which was had by the prophets of old. And after that you have obtained faith, and have seen them with your eyes, you shall testify of them, by the power of God.
D&C 17:2–3

Daily faith helps us endure the seeming repetitiveness of life. As an example, faith permits us to see opportunities for service which might not appear as such to the casual glance or which the unfaithful see as mere repetition. Faith also helps us to endure the repeated lessons of life with gratitude for God's long-suffering, which persists in providing fresh opportunities to overcome our shortcomings. Even though we seem to have been through some of the experiences before, faith permits us to accept what is thus freshly allotted to us along with seeing life's vexations as being "but for a small moment" (D&C 122:4).

(Neal A. Maxwell, *Lord, Increase Our Faith* [Salt Lake City: Bookcraft, 1994], 102)

Daily Living

INCREASE IN YOUR FAITH IN JESUS CHRIST.

- Faith in Jesus Christ is the founding principle of all righteousness and is the way the Lord works with His children—2 Nephi 26:13
- Are we fasting and praying that we might increase in our faith?—Helaman 3:35
- Faith in the Lord Jesus Christ is the power by which all things are done—Ether 12:4–30

BUILD UP THE CHURCH

Wherefore, if you shall build up my church, upon the foundation of my gospel and my rock, the gates of hell shall not prevail against you.
D&C 18:5

Elder Delbert L. Stapley reminds us that the Church is built upon the gospel of Jesus Christ (see 3 Ne. 27:7–8, 10). "My brothers and sisters, I testify that the Church of Jesus Christ of Latter-day Saints is built upon the true gospel of Jesus Christ. It does bear his name and does show forth the works of God in it. . . . Its missionaries bear the gospel message to all nations. It is set up after the organization of the primitive Church, with prophets, apostles, evangelists, etc., and with authority divinely bestowed through the priesthood of God to officiate in all the saving ordinances of the gospel to perfect and exalt man."

(Elder Delbert L. Stapley, in Conference Report, April 1954, 136–137)

Daily Living

BUILD UP THE CHURCH ON THE FOUNDATION OF THE GOSPEL.

- The gospel of Jesus Christ is the foundation of the Church—3 Nephi 27:8–14
- The gospel is centered in the infinite and eternal Atonement of the Lord Jesus Christ—3 Nephi 27:13–14
- We must seek to understand and appreciate the gospel so as to better make it part of our lives and build upon our Savior Jesus Christ—Helaman 5:12

THE SAVIOR'S JOY IN REPENTANT SOULS

Remember the worth of souls is great in the sight of God; . . .
And how great is his joy in the soul that repenteth!
D&C 18:10–13

There is no greater joy than helping to save a soul. This isn't just bringing the gospel to a nonmember or helping perfect a Saint. Sometimes we can bring someone to Christ through a very small thing, such as encouraging someone, visiting someone who is sick, sharing a smile or an embrace, being a good listener, cheering up a child, and so on. Each little act of kindness, in my judgment, is part of bringing a soul to Christ.

As you act as Christ did in relation to other people, those people will see Christ in you and desire to follow your leadership and teachings. Truly there is no greater joy than bringing happiness to others and helping them save their own souls. This basic principle of love must be paramount in our teachings and our example to our children if we desire to raise them up to the Lord.

(Gene R. Cook, *Raising Up a Family to the Lord* [Salt Lake City: Deseret Book, 1993], 310–311)

Daily Living

WE BRING JOY TO OUR SAVIOR AS WE ALL REPENT.

- Repentance brings joy, great delight, and happiness to the soul—Alma 36:19–21
- Helping others repent and taste of this joy also brings us great joy—Alma 29:9–10; 36:24
- This is the joy of life—2 Nephi 2:25; D&C 18:10–16

LABORING IN THE KINGDOM BRINGS JOY

And if it so be that you should labor all your days in crying repentance unto this people, and bring, save it be one soul unto me, how great shall be your joy with him in the kingdom of my Father!

D&C 18:15–16

We must not worry about being successful. We *will* be successful—there is no doubt about it. The Lord has sent us to the earth at the time of harvest. He does not expect us to fail. He has called no one to this work to fail. He expects us to succeed. The Prophet Joseph Smith said, "After all that has been said, the greatest and most important duty is to preach the Gospel" (*History of the Church,* 2:478). . . . Missionary work provides us the happiest years of our lives. I know whereof I speak. I have tasted the joy of missionary work. There is no work in all the world that can bring an individual greater joy and happiness. Like Ammon of old, our joy can be full because of seeing others come into the kingdom of God.

(Ezra Taft Benson, *Come unto Christ* [Salt Lake City: Deseret Book, 1983], 95)

Daily Living

JOY COMES FROM BRINGING SOULS UNTO CHRIST.

- When we understand and appreciate the oft-repeated statement, "It was the happiest two years of my life," we too will understand Alma's joy—Alma 29:9–10; 36:24
- Appreciate the Lord's joy—D&C 18:13; 3 Nephi 17:20
- Then our thoughts and priorities will be aligned with the values and purposes of God—Moses 1:39

FAITH, HOPE, AND CHARITY ARE INDISPENSABLE

And if you have not faith, hope, and charity, you can do nothing.
D&C 18:19

Elder Neal A. Maxwell reminds us, "Of course, faith, hope, and charity are not exclusive, but are mutual and interacting gifts. . . . This scriptural insistence on the interactiveness of these virtues deserves real pondering; its recurrence is not accidental. If one is hopeless, he cannot for long remain sinless, for he will have given up and slackened his resolve; futility fosters vulnerability. The prophets, therefore, say that "without faith there cannot be any hope" (Moroni 7:42). Faith, hope, and charity draw to them other needed virtues, such as patience and temperance. We will be abounding in good works if we have faith, hope, and charity (Alma 7:24), because, knowing that there is divine purpose in life and personal accountability, we also know that what we do really matters."

(Neal A. Maxwell, *Notwithstanding My Weakness* [Salt Lake City: Deseret Book, 1981], 48–49)

Daily Living

SEEK FAITH, HOPE, AND CHARITY.

- The cardinal principles and virtues of faith, hope, and charity empower us to live and serve our Heavenly Father and Savior here upon the earth. Search the scriptures—1 Corinthians13; Hebrews 11; James 2; Alma 32: Ether 12; Moroni 7
- Liken the scriptures to your life and you will want to do the things you have read, pondered, and prayed about—1 Nephi 19:23

SAVED ONLY THROUGH JESUS CHRIST

Behold, Jesus Christ is the name which is given of the Father, and there is none other name given whereby man can be saved.
D&C 18:23

James E. Talmage has written, "I rejoice in the testimony of the Savior that he is verily the Christ and we proclaim him as such. . . . There are volumes of recent publications dealing with the Christ of literature, the Christ of history, the Christ of reason, the Christ of experience. . . . But the tendency is to view him from this angle or that and not to look with direct vision. I am thankful that the Church to which I belong preaches Christ and him crucified, and resurrected, the Christ that ascended into heaven, the Christ that was the offspring in the flesh, as well as in the spirit, of the very eternal Father, Christ who is the Savior and Redeemer of mankind, beside whom there is none, beside whose name there is no name under heaven whereby mankind may be saved."
(James E. Talmage, in Conference Report, April 1916, 131)

Daily Living

THE ONLY NAME WHEREBY MAN CAN BE SAVED.

- After all you do you can only be saved but through the merits and grace of the Lord Jesus Christ—2 Nephi 25:23
- The Lord does everything for us—Psalms 23; Alma 26:11–12; D&C 84:88; Alma 7:11–12
- Gratitude should fill our hearts as the sufferings of the Lord draw us to Him—3 Nephi 27:13–14

THE WORD FROM THE LORD

These words are not of men nor of man, but of me; wherefore, you shall testify they are of me and not of man; For it is my voice which speaketh them unto you; for they are given by my Spirit unto you, and by my power you can read them one to another; and save it were by my power you could not have them; Wherefore, you can testify that you have heard my voice, and know my words.

D&C 18:34–36

Do you want your children to hear the voice of God and know his words? Such is made possible through the scriptures. This is what the Lord promised . . . [see D&C 18:34–36]. Scripture reading is like a daily interview with the Lord, providing the reader studies with real intent and listens to the whisperings of the Holy Spirit. The voice of the Lord came into the mind of Enos, whereby Enos received intelligence and truth that changed the course of his life. The same can happen to us and our children by feasting upon the word of God (Enos 1:1–10).

(Carlos E. Asay, *Family Pecan Trees: Planting a Legacy of Faith at Home* [Salt Lake City: Deseret Book, 1992], 30)

Daily Living

REJOICE IN AND RECEIVE THE WORD OF GOD.

- Lest we forget, the words spoken by the power of the Holy Ghost, "shall be scripture, shall be the will of the Lord, shall be the mind of the Lord, shall be the word of the Lord, shall be the voice of the Lord, and the power of God unto salvation"—D&C 68:3–7

ENDLESS AND ETERNAL

For, behold, the mystery of godliness, how great is it! For, behold, I am endless, and the punishment which is given from my hand is endless punishment, for Endless is my name. Wherefore—Eternal punishment is God's punishment. Endless punishment is God's punishment.

D&C 19:10–12

Endless, used as a noun and not as an adjective, is one of the names of God and signifies his unending, eternal continuance as the supreme, exalted ruler of the universe . . . (See Moses 1:3; 7:35.) . . . Endless life means God's life. . . . One of the names of God is Eternal; to Enoch the Lord said, "Eternal is my name" (Moses 7:35), using this designation as a noun and not as an adjective. This name of Deity signifies that he is "infinite and eternal, from everlasting to everlasting the same unchangeable God" (D. & C. 20:17). . . . Thus the kind of life he lives (which, of course, is God's life) is called eternal life (meaning exaltation); and the kind of punishment which is dealt out to transgressors by him is called eternal punishment, a name having reference to the type and not the duration of the penalty imposed."

(Bruce R. McConkie, *Mormon Doctrine*, 2d ed. [Salt Lake City: Bookcraft, 1966], 226, 233)

Daily Living

SEEK ETERNAL LIFE, WHICH IS BOTH ENDLESS AND ETERNAL.

- Be steadfast, full of hope and love of all men, and endure to end, thus gaining eternal life—2 Nephi 31:20

REPENT—LEST YE SUFFER

Therefore I command you to repent—repent, lest I smite you by the rod of my mouth, and by my wrath, and by my anger, and your sufferings be sore—how sore you know not, how exquisite you know not, yea, how hard to bear you know not. For behold, I, God, have suffered these things for all, that they might not suffer if they would repent; But if they would not repent they must suffer even as I; Which suffering caused myself, even God, the greatest of all, to tremble because of pain, and to bleed at every pore, and to suffer both body and spirit—and would that I might not drink the bitter cup, and shrink—Nevertheless, glory be to the Father, and I partook and finished my preparations unto the children of men.

D&C 19:15–19

President Spencer W. Kimball admonishes us in regard to repentance: "The prophetic message has always carried the same penalty, for no one can reject with impunity the call from the God of law and justice. Hence the alternative the Lord has given—repent or perish! . . . That endless misery and suffering await the unrepentant sinner."

(Spencer W. Kimball, *The Miracle of Forgiveness* [Salt Lake City: Bookcraft, 1969], 133)

Daily Living

DAILY REPENTANCE IS VITAL TO OUR SALVATION.

- If we do not repent we must suffer the just judgment of God—D&C 101:78
- Allowance is made for the sinner that repents but not the sin—D&C 1:31–33

I COMMAND YOU AGAIN TO REPENT

Wherefore, I command you again to repent, lest I humble you with my almighty power; and that you confess your sins, lest you suffer these punishments of which I have spoken, of which in the smallest, yea, even in the least degree you have tasted at the time I withdrew my Spirit.

D&C 19:20

Repentance is essential to salvation; without it no accountable person can be saved in the kingdom of God. (D. & C. 20:29; Moses 6:52–53, 57; 3 Ne. 9:22). . . . It is a requirement made of every accountable person, that is of those "having knowledge" (D. & C. 29:49), and parents are obligated to teach repentance to their children to qualify them for baptism when they reach the years of accountability (D. & C. 68:25–27). . . . The very plan of salvation offered to the world is a "gospel of repentance" (D&C 13; 84:27). The elders of Israel go forth with the command, "Say nothing but repentance unto this generation" (D. & C. 6:9; 11:9; 14:8).

(Bruce R. McConkie, *Mormon Doctrine*, 2d ed. [Salt Lake City: Bookcraft, 1966], 630–631)

Daily Living

TO BECOME PERFECT, REPENT PERFECTLY.

- No doctrine is preached more than the doctrine of faith unto repentance—Mosiah 18:20; Alma 34:15–17
- Ponder the significance of the doctrine of repentance, for it is the key to forgiveness and perfection—D&C 138:1–2

PEACE IN THE LORD

Learn of me, and listen to my words; walk in the meekness of my Spirit, and you shall have peace in me.
D&C 19:23

These words [D&C 19:23] give me the feeling of such closeness to, such intimacy with the Savior, looking at him, listening to him, learning from him, walking with him, and feeling his peace like his very arms around me. Within each of us is an intense hunger for this intimacy with and closeness to him. I think we all want to feel his spirit around us. . . .

I find myself coming back to the same answer. It's more of an image than a concept. The image that comes to mind is one of light. Jesus calls himself the "light of the world" and promises, "he that followeth me shall not walk in darkness, but shall have the light of life" (John 8:12).

(Chieko N. Okazaki, *Lighten Up!* [Salt Lake City: Deseret Book, 1993], 199)

Daily Living

PEACE FROM THE LORD JESUS CHRIST.

- To be spiritually minded brings peace—Romans 8:6
- A fruit from the Spirit is peace—Galatians 5:22
- Righteousness is sown in peace—James 3:18
- Be a peacemaker—3 Nephi 12:9
- Seek peace of conscience—Mosiah 4:3
- The love of God stops contention and brings peace—4 Nephi 1:15

THOU SHALT NOT COVET

And again, I command thee that thou shalt not covet thy neighbor's wife; nor seek thy neighbor's life. And again, I command thee that thou shalt not covet thine own property, but impart it freely to the printing of the Book of Mormon, which contains the truth and the word of God.

D&C 19:25–26

Covetousness is contrary to the spirit of love and concern for others that is inherent in the gospel. . . . [Bruce R. McConkie said:] "To covet is to have an eager, extreme, and ungodly desire for something. The presence of *covetousness* in a human soul shows that such person has not overcome the world and is not living by gospel standards of conduct. Coveting is such a serious offense, and it is so imperative that man overcome all tendencies thereto, that the Lord condemned it in the Ten Commandments." (Ex. 20:17; Mosiah 13:24)." (Bruce R. McConkie, Mormon Doctrine, 156).

(quoted in Daniel H. Ludlow, *A Companion to Your Study of the Doctrine and Covenants*, vol. 2 [Salt Lake City: Deseret Book, 1982], 54)

Daily Living

ALIGN YOUR WILL WITH THE WILL OF GOD.

- Greed, lust, and pride spawn the sinful attitude of covetousness, which is idolatry—Colossians 3:5
- Ponder upon your priorities and values to be sure that they are aligned with the things of God, for lust will surely cause you to follow your own carnal desires—2 Peter 3:3

PRAYER

And again, I command thee that thou shalt pray vocally as well as in thy heart; yea, before the world as well as in secret, in public as well as in private.
Pray always, and I will pour out my Spirit upon you and great shall be your blessing—yea, even more than if you should obtain treasures of earth and corruptibleness to the extent thereof.
D&C 19:28, 38

My brethren and sisters, let us remember and call upon God and implore his blessings and his favor upon us. Let us do it, nevertheless, in wisdom and in righteousness, and when we pray we should call upon him in a consistent and reasonable way. . . . We should ask for that which we need, and we should ask in faith, "nothing wavering, for he that wavereth," as the Apostle said, "is like the wave of the sea, driven by the wind and tossed. For let not that man think that he shall receive anything of the Lord" [James 1:6]. But when we ask of God for blessings let us ask in the faith of the Gospel, in that faith that he has promised to give to those who believe in him and obey His commandments.

(Joseph F. Smith, in Conference Report, October 1914, 6–7)

Daily Living

PRAY CONTINUALLY THAT YOU MAY COMMUNE WITH GOD.

- Remember that in gratitude we pray for all things—morning, noon, and night, and with a prayer in our heart continually—Alma 34:17–27; 3 Nephi 20:1
- Never cease to call upon God lest we offend Him by not acknowledging His hand in all things—D&C 59:21

GOD IS THE SAME YESTERDAY, TODAY, AND FOREVER

Thereby showing that he is the same God yesterday, today, and forever. Amen.
D&C 20:12

The Lord has provided three sets of plates to establish his covenant with our dispensation. These three sets of plates show that God's plans are the same for both the Nephites and the Jaredites. The Book of Mormon is divinely designed to prove "to the world that the holy scriptures are true, and that God does inspire men and call them to his holy work in this age and generation, as well as in generations of old; Thereby showing that he is the same God yesterday, today, and forever" (D&C 20:11–12). The plates of Ether are divinely placed to establish the covenant with latter-day readers and to warn them away from a similar fall.

(Monte S. Nyman and Charles D. Tate, Jr., eds., *Fourth Nephi through Moroni: From Zion to Destruction* [Provo: BYU Religious Studies Center, 1995], 78)

Daily Living

HEAVENLY FATHER LOVES ALL OF HIS CHILDREN.

- All have the right to a relationship and communication with our Heavenly Father. He has commanded us to call upon His name in and through our Savior Jesus Christ. He will answer our prayers and never upbraid us—James 1:5–6
- The heavens are open and the work of God rolls forth. He knocks. . . . Will we open the door?—Revelations 3:20

LOVE AND SERVE GOD

And [He] gave unto them commandments that they should love and serve him, the only living and true God, and that he should be the only being whom they should worship.
D&C 20:19

How can we decrease our love for things not for our best good? We must examine our lives, see what services we are rendering and what sacrifices are being made, and then stop the expenditure of time and effort in these directions. . . . Our love should be channeled into sources that are eternally oriented. Our neighbors and families will respond to our love if we will but follow through with sustaining support and self-sharing. True love is as eternal as life itself. Some callings and assignments in the Church may seem insignificant and unimportant at the time, but with each willingly fulfilled assignment, love of the Lord will grow. We learn to love God as we serve and know Him.

(Elder Marvin J. Ashton, "We Serve That Which We Love," *Ensign*, May 1981, 22)

Daily Living

DEMONSTRATE YOUR LOVE OF GOD THROUGH SERVICE.

- The depth of our love is demonstrated by our obedience to Heavenly Father's commandments—John 14:15
- When we forget God, our attitudes and behavior are mercurial, and we are disobedient—Helaman 12:2
- Maybe our love is not deep enough. The solution is to love God and remember His goodness, and then we will always serve Him—Mosiah 4:11; 5:12; Alma 29:10

February 23

JUSTIFICATION AND SANCTIFICATION

And we know that justification through the grace of our Lord and Savior Jesus Christ is just and true; And we know also, that sanctification through the grace of our Lord and Savior Jesus Christ is just and true, to all those who love and serve God with all their mights, minds, and strength.

D&C 20:30–31

Justification directly opens the way to sanctification by establishing a "right" relationship of mortals with God. Thus, God, without denying justice, can bless them with the sanctifying power of the Holy Ghost (Mosiah 5:1–2; 3 Ne. 27:20). Justification starts the believer on the path toward righteousness (*Encyclopedia of Mormonism*, 1–4 vols., ed. Daniel H. Ludlow (New York: Macmillan, 1992), 776).

Thus, *sanctification is the process of becoming pure and spotless before God* through the power of the Sanctifier, who is the Holy Ghost . . . through the grace of Christ. . . . Sanctification is brought to those whose complete repentance and love of that which is good have whitened their garments through the blood of Christ's atonement.

(Hoyt W. Brewster, Jr., *Doctrine and Covenants Encyclopedia* [Salt Lake City: Bookcraft, 1996], 490)

Daily Living

SEEK TO BE JUSTIFIED AND SANCTIFIED.

ஐ Ponder justification and sanctification so as to be able to return to the presence of Heavenly Father—Titus 3:7; Mosiah 4:26; Alma 5:27; D&C 88:39

QUALIFYING FOR BAPTISM

And again, by way of commandment to the church concerning the manner of baptism—All those who humble themselves before God, and desire to be baptized, and come forth with broken hearts and contrite spirits, and witness before the church that they have truly repented of all their sins, and are willing to take upon them the name of Jesus Christ, having a determination to serve him to the end, and truly manifest by their works that they have received of the Spirit of Christ unto the remission of their sins, shall be received by baptism into his church.

D&C 20:37

Elder Joseph Fielding Smith has said, "Every person baptized into this Church has made a covenant with the Lord to keep his commandments. We are to serve the Lord with all the heart, and all the mind, and all the strength that we have, and that too in the name of Jesus Christ . . . that we would be obedient and humble, diligent in his service, willing to obey, to hearken to the counsels of those who preside over us and do all things with an eye single to the glory of God."

(Joseph Fielding Smith, *Doctrines of Salvation*, vol. 2 [Salt Lake City: Bookcraft, 1955], 328)

Daily Living

WE QUALIFY FOR THE SACRAMENT JUST LIKE BAPTISM.

- As we partake of the sacrament, we are renewing our covenants with the Lord, hence all the qualifications for baptisms apply to partaking of the sacrament—Moroni 6:1–4; Mosiah 18:8–9
- We partake of the sacrament that we may enjoy the blessings of the Holy Spirit!—Moroni 4:3, 5:2

MEETINGS TO BE CONDUCTED BY THE HOLY GHOST

The elders are to conduct the meetings as they are led by the Holy Ghost, according to the commandments and revelations of God.
D&C 20:45

Church meetings should assist us to live better lives. If our meetings are to be impressively meaningful in assisting those assembled to better live the Lord's law and commandments, meetings should be:

1. Well planned.
2. Conducted with reverence and dignity by one "led by the Holy Ghost." "The elders are to conduct the meetings as they are led by the Holy Ghost, according to the commandments and revelations of God" (D&C 20:45).

Our Church meetings should therefore be both instructional and inspirational. People should leave our meetings lifted up, motivated to walk more uprightly before the Lord and to feel more of the joy which comes through better living his commandments.
(Howard W. Hunter, *The Teachings of Howard W. Hunter*, ed. Clyde J. Williams [Salt Lake City: Bookcraft, 1997], 114)

Daily Living

THE SPIRIT SHOULD DIRECT ALL THINGS.

※ Preparation to conduct and participate in meetings is for all who attend, not just those that preside. All should pray that the Spirit might attend that all may be edified and blessed—D&C 43:8–10; Moroni 6:9

DUTIES OF THE AARONIC PRIESTHOOD BEARERS

The priest's duty is to preach, teach, expound, exhort, and baptize, and administer the sacrament, And visit the house of each member, and exhort them to pray vocally and in secret and attend to all family duties.
D&C 20:46–47

The teacher's duty is to watch over the church always, and be with and strengthen them; And see that there is no iniquity in the church, neither hardness with each other, neither lying, backbiting, nor evil speaking;
D&C 20:53–54

And is to be assisted always, in all his duties in the church, by the deacons, if occasion requires.
D&C 20:57

Daily Living

RESPECT AND HONOR THE AARONIC PRIESTHOOD.

- Priests: preach, teach, expound, exhort, administer the sacrament, visit members, ordain other Aaronic Priesthood bearers, baptize, and assist elders—D&C 20:46–52
- Teachers: watch over the Church and strengthen members—D&C 20:53–56
- Deacons assist the teachers—D&C 20:57
- Deacons and teachers are to warn, expound, exhort, teach, and invite all to come unto Christ—D&C 20:59

DUTIES OF THE MEMBERS OF THE CHURCH

And the members shall manifest before the church, and also before the elders, by a godly walk and conversation, that they are worthy of it, that there may be works and faith agreeable to the holy scriptures—walking in holiness before the Lord.

D&C 20:69

Again here we are involved: it is our duty as members of this Church, to serve the Lord our God with all our mights, with all our minds, with all our strength, and as it is stated in another revelation, with all our hearts. That is our duty—not to serve him half-heartedly, not to accept a portion of the commandments—only, not to receive only those things which appeal to us, and refuse to accept those principles which do not appeal to us. We should be converted in full to the gospel of Jesus Christ.

(Joseph Fielding Smith, *Take Heed to Yourselves!* [Salt Lake City: Deseret Book, 1966], 126)

Daily Living

THINGS TO REMEMBER AND DO AS MEMBERS OF THE CHURCH.

- Love one another—John 13:34–35
- Assist in building up the kingdom of God by proclaiming the gospel, redeeming the dead, and perfecting the Saints, that all might come unto Christ—JST—Matthew 6:38
- Strengthen others in all that we do—D&C 108:7
- Pray for all those who know not God—Alma 6:6
- Stand as witnesses for God at all times—Mosiah 18:9
- Keep the commandments—D&C 20:77, 79

SACRAMENTAL PRAYERS

O God, the Eternal Father, we ask thee in the name of thy Son, Jesus Christ, to bless and sanctify this bread to the souls of all those who partake of it, that they may eat in remembrance of the body of thy Son, and witness unto thee, O God, the Eternal Father, that they are willing to take upon them the name of thy Son, and always remember him and keep his commandments which he has given them; that they may always have his Spirit to be with them. Amen.

D&C 20:77 AND SEE ALSO VERSE 79

When the priest offers the scriptural prayer . . . he prays that all who partake may witness unto God, the Eternal Father, that they are willing to take upon them the name of thy Son (D&C 20:77; Moro. 4:3). . . . to renew the covenant we made in the waters of baptism . . . and serve him to the end. . . . Our willingness to take upon us his name signifies our willingness to take upon us the authority of Jesus Christ in the sacred ordinances of the temple, and to receive the highest blessings available through his authority when he chooses to confer them upon us. . . . That is what we should ponder as we partake of the sacred emblems of the sacrament.

(Elder Dallin H. Oaks, "Taking upon Us the Name of Jesus Christ," *Ensign*, May 1985, 80)

Daily Living

KEEP THE COMMANDMENTS AND ALWAYS HAVE THE SPIRIT.

ꢀ Blessings of the Spirit will help you in all things—1 Nephi 4:6; 2 Nephi 32:5; Moroni 10:5, 8–18; John 14:26; 15:26

MARCH

For the Lord God has spoken it; and we, the elders of the church, have heard and bear witness to the words of the glorious Majesty on high, to whom be glory forever and ever. Amen.

—Doctrine & Covenants 20:16

FOLLOW THE PROPHET

Wherefore, meaning the church, thou shalt give heed unto all his words and commandments which he shall give unto you as he receiveth them, walking in all holiness before me; For his word ye shall receive, as if from mine own mouth, in all patience and faith. For by doing these things the gates of hell shall not prevail against you; yea, and the Lord God will disperse the powers of darkness from before you, and cause the heavens to shake for your good, and his name's glory.

D&C 21:4–6

May each Church member seek to possess the inner spiritual strength which flows from faithfully heeding the words of the living prophets. Such loyalty and obedience will clothe us with the protective armor of God. . . . "We have been promised that the President of the Church will receive guidance for all of us as the revelator for the Church," taught Elder James E. Faust. "Our safety lies in paying heed to that which he says and following his counsel."

(Brent L. Top, Larry E. Dahl, and Walter D. Bowen, *Follow the Living Prophets* [Salt Lake City: Bookcraft, 1993], 199)

Daily Living

THE LORD WILL NEVER ALLOW THE PROPHET TO LEAD US ASTRAY.

- By following the prophets we are following our Savior, and we shall be blessed—Nephi 12:1–2; D&C 1:38; 21:4–6
- When we receive His servants we will receive Christ—D&C 84:36

BEWARE OF PRIDE

But beware of pride, lest thou shouldst enter into temptation.
D&C 23:1

One of Satan's greatest tools is pride: to cause a man or a woman to center so much attention on self that he or she becomes insensitive to their Creator or fellow beings. It is a cause for discontent, divorce, teenage rebellion, family indebtedness, and most other problems we face. In the scriptures there is no such thing as righteous pride. It is always considered as a sin. . . . Essentially, pride is a "my will" rather than "thy will" approach to life. The opposite of pride is humbleness, meekness, submissiveness, or teachableness (see Alma 13:28). . . . Pride is manifest in the spirit of contention. . . . Pride is characterized by "What do I want out of life?" rather than by "What would God have me do with my life?" . . . The proud do not change to improve, but defend their position by rationalizing. Repentance means change, and it takes a humble person to change. But we can do it.

(Ezra Taft Benson, *The Teachings of Ezra Taft Benson* [Salt Lake City: Bookcraft, 1988], 435–436)

Daily Living

THE ANTIDOTE FOR PRIDE IS HUMILITY.

- Consider your ways and seek humility at all costs. Recognize your nothingness before God—Mosiah 4:5
- Pray to be strong in humility—Helaman 3:35
- In humility you will be made strong—Ether 12:27

March 3

BE PATIENT IN AFFLICTIONS

Be patient in afflictions, for thou shalt have many; but endure them, for, lo, I am with thee, even unto the end of thy days.
D&C 24:8

I believe that lack of patience is a major cause of many difficulties and much unhappiness in the world today. Too often we are impatient with ourselves, with our family members and friends, and even with the Lord. . . . Perhaps the practice of patience is more difficult, yet more necessary, now than at any previous time. To the Latter-day Saints, the Lord gave patience as one of the divine attributes that qualifies a person for the ministry. (See D&C 4:6.) He counseled them to be patient in their afflictions (see D&C 24:8; 31:9; 54:10; 98:23–24), and to make their decisions in patience (see D&C 107:30). He taught us to be perfect (see Matthew 5:48; 3 Nephi 12:48) and said, "Ye are not able to abide the presence of God now, neither the ministering of angels; wherefore, continue in patience until ye are perfected" (D&C 67:13).

(Joseph B. Wirthlin, *Finding Peace in Our Lives* [Salt Lake City: Deseret Book, 1995], 203)

Daily Living

WE CAN LEARN PATIENCE THROUGH AFFLICTIONS.

- Remember afflictions are for our good—D&C 122:7
- Remember that one of the main virtues that make up charity is patience—Moroni 7:45

DECLARE THE GOSPEL—PRUNE THE VINEYARD

And at all times, and in all places, he shall open his mouth and declare my gospel as with the voice of a trump, both day and night. And I will give unto him strength such as is not known among men. . . .
For thou art called to prune my vineyard with a mighty pruning, yea, even for the last time; yea, and also all those whom thou hast ordained, and they shall do even according to this pattern.
D&C 24:12, 19

THE MISSIONARY SPIRIT—I rejoice in proclaiming this glorious gospel, because it takes root in the hearts of the children of men, and they rejoice with me to be connected with, and participate in, the blessings of the kingdom of God.

(John Taylor, *The Gospel Kingdom: Selections from the Writings and Discourses of John Taylor*, selected, arranged, and edited, with an introduction by G. Homer Durham [Salt Lake City: Desert Book, 1943], 234)

Daily Living

SEEK TO CULTIVATE A MISSIONARY SPIRIT IN YOUR LIFE.

- We are to warn our neighbors—D&C 88:81
- We open our mouths—D&C 33:8–11
- Stand as witnesses at all times—Mosiah 18:9
- Declare repentance that souls might repent and come unto Christ—D&C 15:6
- Invite all to taste of the joy of the gospel in their lives—Alma 36:24
- Joy together with those whom you assist in bringing into the kingdom of God—D&C 18:10–16

EMMA—AN ELECT LADY

Behold, thy sins are forgiven thee, and thou art an elect lady, whom I have called.
D&C 25:3

Emma Smith is remembered as the woman who faithfully stood by her husband during his life. Emma was a woman of great faith and courage. . . . The terminology of *elect* was defined by Joseph Smith on 17 March 1842 in Nauvoo, Illinois, when he told the sisters that "elect meant to be elected to a certain work . . . and that the revelation was then fulfilled by Sister Emma's election to the Presidency of the [Relief] Society." Her calling was to be the wife of a prophet. . . . She was also admonished to beware of pride (D&C 25:14). If Emma proved faithful, she was to receive "a crown of righteousness." (D&C 25:15.) Joseph Smith loved Emma, for she did comfort him, she increased her talents, and she heeded the Lord's admonitions. In his love for her, Joseph pleaded with the Lord on her behalf, "Have mercy, O Lord, upon [my] wife . . . , that [she] may be exalted in thy presence, and preserved by thy fostering hand" (D&C 109:69).

(Susan Easton Black et al., *Doctrines for Exaltation: The 1989 Sperry Symposium on the Doctrine and Covenants* [Salt Lake City: Deseret Book, 1989], 4–5)

Daily Living

BECOME AN ELECT PERSON THROUGH REPENTANCE.

ꝏ May we all remember that the key to exaltation, perfection, and eternal life is through repentance and forgiveness; thus, we become a just person—D&C 76:69

THE LAW OF COMMON CONSENT

And all things shall be done by common consent
in the church, by much prayer and faith,
for all things you shall receive by faith. Amen.
D&C 26:2

It was designed by the Almighty in the organization of this Church, that the voice of the people should respond to the voice of the Lord. It is the voice of the Lord and the voice of the people together in this Church that sanctions all things therein [Sec. 20:63–66]. In the rise of the Church the Lord gave a revelation which said that "all things shall be done by common consent." And the Lord designs that every individual member shall take an interest therein, shall bear a part of the responsibility, and shall take upon him or her the spirit of the Church, and be an active living member of the body.

(Charles W. Penrose, *JD,* 21:47–48)

Daily Living

THE LAW OF COMMON CONSENT MAKES ONE ACCOUNTABLE.

- When we raise our arms to the square, we covenant to sustain and support the action agreed to, thus making us accountable for which we must someday give a report—Romans 14:12
- Remember, this is a solemn and sacred duty; not a perfunctory action but rather an opportunity to become united in building up the kingdom of God and becoming one in purpose and action—John 17:11; Philippians 1:27; 2:2; D&C 38:27

March 7

THE EMBLEMS OF THE SACRAMENT

For, behold, I say unto you, that it mattereth not what ye shall eat or what ye shall drink when ye partake of the sacrament, if it so be that ye do it with an eye single to my glory—remembering unto the Father my body which was laid down for you, and my blood which was shed for the remission of your sins.

D&C 27:2

To the Saints of the latter days, the Lord has spoken authorizing the use of water in place of wine. . . . Consistent with the principle is the following comment: The New Testament churches used wine diluted with water. In our day the Lord has commanded the use of pure water instead of adulterated wine, and this is by no means contrary to the Scriptures. In their accounts of the institution of the Sacrament, Matthew, Mark, Luke, and Paul—the latter having received his information of the Lord Himself (1 Cor. 11:23) make it clear that it is the eating of the broken bread and the partaking of the common Cup—the contents are not once mentioned—that constitute the essential elements of the sacrament.

(Roy W. Doxey, *The Doctrine and Covenants Speaks* [Salt Lake City: Deseret Book, 1964], 1:135)

Daily Living

THE SACRAMENT IS FOR MAKING SACRED COVENANTS.

℘ Remembering our Savior and our sacred covenants, maintaining our personal righteousness, keeping the commandments, and having an appropriate attitude and pure motives make the difference as we partake of the sacrament—Mormon 9:29

ELIJAH TO RESTORE THE TURNING OF HEARTS

And also Elijah, unto whom I have committed the keys of the power of turning the hearts of the fathers to the children, and the hearts of the children to the fathers, that the whole earth may not be smitten with a curse.

D&C 27:9

If Elijah had not come, we are led to believe that all the work of past ages would have been of little avail, for the Lord said the whole earth, under such conditions, would be utterly wasted at his coming. Therefore his mission was of vast importance to the world. It is not the question of baptism for the dead alone, but also the sealing of parents and children to parents, so that there should be a "whole and complete and perfect union, and welding together of dispensations, and keys, and powers, and glories," from the beginning down to the end of time. . . . Why would the earth be wasted? Simply because if there is not a welding link between the fathers and the children—which is the work for the dead—then we will all stand rejected; the whole work of God will fail and be utterly wasted. Such a condition, of course, shall not be."

(Joseph Fielding Smith, *Doctrines of Salvation*, 2:121–122)

Daily Living

LET YOUR HEARTS TURN TO YOUR FAMILIES LIVING AND DEAD.

ꕤ Remember, our family is our primary responsibility in the Church. Then we must remember those who have gone before us, for they are depending upon us to do their temple work; it is exalting—D&C 128:15

RESTORATION OF THE KEYS OF THE KINGDOM

And also with Peter, and James, and John, whom I have sent unto you, by whom I have ordained you and confirmed you to be apostles, and especial witnesses of my name, and bear the keys of your ministry and of the same things which I revealed unto them; Unto whom I have committed the keys of my kingdom, and a dispensation of the gospel for the last times; and for the fulness of times, in the which I will gather together in one all things, both which are in heaven, and which are on earth.

D&C 27:12–13

These keys are the right of presidency; they are the power and authority to govern and direct all of the Lord's affairs on earth. Those who hold them have power to govern and control the manner in which all others may serve in the priesthood. All of us may hold the priesthood, but we can only use it as authorized and directed so to do by those who hold the keys. This priesthood and these keys were conferred upon Joseph Smith and Oliver Cowdery by Peter, James, and John, and by Moses and Elijah and others of the ancient prophets.

(Joseph Fielding Smith, "Eternal Keys and the Right to Preside," *Ensign,* July 1972, 87)

Daily Living

THE RESTORATION OF THE MELCHIZEDEK PRIESTHOOD AND KEYS.

- Magnify and keep the oath and covenant of the priesthood—D&C 84:33–42
- All priesthood bearers operate under the prophet, who holds all the keys of the priesthood—D&C 64:5; 81:2

PUT ON THE ARMOR OF GOD

Wherefore, lift up your hearts and rejoice, and gird up your loins, and take upon you my whole armor, that ye may be able to withstand the evil day. . . . Stand, therefore, having your loins girt about with truth, having on the breastplate of righteousness, and your feet shod with the preparation of the gospel of peace, which I have sent mine angels to commit unto you; Taking the shield of faith wherewith ye shall be able to quench all the fiery darts of the wicked; And take the helmet of salvation, and the sword of my Spirit, which I will pour out upon you, and my word which I reveal unto you, and be agreed as touching all things whatsoever ye ask of me, and be faithful until I come, and ye shall be caught up, that where I am ye shall be also. Amen.

D&C 27:15–18

Surely we must put on the whole armor of God, consisting, as Paul said, of truth, righteousness, peace, [and] faith with the helmet of salvation and the sword of the Spirit, which is the word of God. Because of our faith in a living, personal, and all powerful God, we do not fear the final outcome in our fight against the emissaries of Satan, though we must ever be alert, united, and on guard.

(Hugh B. Brown, *The Abundant Life* [Salt Lake City: Bookcraft, 1965], 155)

Daily Living

WE MUST PUT ON THE ARMOR OF GOD.

- Prepare every needful thing to be able to withstand the evil day—Ephesians 6:11–18; 1 Nephi 15:24; 3 Nephi 18:18

March 11

LED BY THE SPIRIT

And if thou art led at any time by the Comforter to speak or teach, or at all times by the way of commandment unto the church, thou mayest do it.
D&C 28:4

Nephi said, "And I was led by the Spirit, not knowing beforehand the things which I should do." . . . You will probably have the same thing happen to you. . . . You'll say, "Oh Father," and at that moment when you pray, "What should I do?" then all of a sudden the words will come. You'll find yourself saying, "And by the power of the Spirit, I testify to you." You will bear your testimony with power, and then you'll wonder, "How did I do that?" Remember, the Lord is in charge!

When you teach with power, you teach the mind and the will of God. . . . You speak by the Spirit, and the Spirit speaks the word of Christ.

(Ed J. Pinegar, *Especially for Missionaries,* 4 vols. [American Fork, UT: Covenant Communications, 1997], 3:4–5)

Daily Living

SEEK TO BE LED BY THE SPIRIT.

- The Spirit is the key to teaching, preaching, and testifying of gospel truths—Moroni 10:5; D&C 42:14; 50:17–22
- We should do all in our power to receive blessings of the Spirit in our lives—1 Nephi 10:17; D&C 20:77, 79; 76:116
- If we are worthy, we can even be led when we know not what to do—1 Nephi 4:6
- Seek the gifts of the Spirit—D&C 46:8–32; Moroni 10:8–18

THE LORD GATHERETH HIS PEOPLE

Listen to the voice of Jesus Christ, your Redeemer, the Great I AM, whose arm of mercy hath atoned for your sins; Who will gather his people even as a hen gathereth her chickens under her wings, even as many as will hearken to my voice and humble themselves before me, and call upon me in mighty prayer. Amen.

D&C 29:1–2

The Lord has promised to gather together in one all things which are in Christ, both which are in heaven and which are upon earth. . . . As soon as the Gospel was first preached to the people, they felt the spirit of gathering. . . . The spirit of the work was upon them. Thus the spirit of gathering comes upon the Saints wherever the Gospel is preached to them, and there arises within them an inclination to want to leave where they have become strangers, to go to people whose faith is like their own, with whom they are acquainted in the Lord and have fellowship together.

(Franklin D. Richards, in Conference Report, April 1899, 44)

Daily Living

SEEK TO ASSIST IN THE GATHERING OF THE LORD'S PEOPLE.

- The Lord's elect are those who hearken (listen and do) to His voice, and humble themselves before Him, and call upon Him in mighty prayer—D&C 29:7
- The Lord will seek after us to gather us in—3 Nephi 10:4–6
- Let us open our mouths—D&C 33:8–11
- Strengthen others—D&C 108:7
- Proclaim His gospel—D&C 30:9; 66:5; 75:2

THE LORD IS IN OUR MIDST

Lift up your hearts and be glad, for I am in your midst, and am your advocate with the Father; and it is his good will to give you the kingdom.

D&C 29:5

Now this Lord . . . is in our midst from time to time, and we as a people do not see him nearly as often as we should. We are not speaking of him being in our midst in the spiritual sense that he is here by the power of his Spirit. We are speaking of his personal literal presence. . . . "Verily, verily, I say unto you that mine eyes are upon you. I am in your midst and ye cannot see me; But the day soon cometh that ye shall see me, and know that I am; for the veil of darkness shall soon be rent, and he that is not purified shall not abide the day" (D&C 38:7–8).

(Bruce R. McConkie, *The Promised Messiah: The First Coming of Christ* [Salt Lake City: Deseret Book, 1978], 611)

Daily Living

REMEMBER, THE LORD IS WITH US.

- Our Savior Jesus Christ is not only our advocate but He nurtures us and helps us in our afflictions—Alma 7:11–12
- The Lord has said, "And whoso receiveth you, there I will be also, for I will go before your face. I will be on your right hand and on your left, and my Spirit shall be in your hearts, and mine angels round about you, to bear you up"—D&C 84:88
- We should have no fear and be full of gratitude knowing that the Lord is with us in all things—2 Nephi 4:19–26, 33–35

UNITED IN PRAYER

And, as it is written—Whatsoever ye shall ask in faith, being united in prayer according to my command, ye shall receive.
D&C 29:6

To be unified in prayer brings more strength. If you can get a number of people praying for you—a family, your brothers and sisters, friends, ward members—the unity in strength that results will help to bring increased power to your request. Over the years I've learned increasingly that when we have a serious problem that is not too personal, we should get all of our family to pray about it, especially the little ones. They may not understand all the details of what we need, but they can know enough to pray that Dad or Mom needs this. And when they pray, they seem to have a channel right into heaven. Not only can they help you receive an answer to your prayer, but the very process will teach them over and over again that the Lord does answer prayer.

(Gene R. Cook, *Receiving Answers to Our Prayers* [Salt Lake City: Deseret Book, 1996], 68)

Daily Living

BE UNITED IN PRAYER.

- The prayers of faith draw down the powers of heaven. In unity our prayers are magnified even like the righteous Nephites: "But it is by the prayers of the righteous that ye are spared"—Alma 10:23
- We are blessed and strengthened by the Lord when we are united in prayer—3 Nephi 27:1
- When we are one, we are the Lord's—D&C 38:27

THE ELECT WILL HEAR THE LORD'S VOICE

And ye are called to bring to pass the gathering of mine elect; for mine elect hear my voice and harden not their hearts.
D&C 29:7

They believe in Christ and hearken to his voice. (D&C 33:6.) They magnify their callings. (D&C 84:33.) They are on guard concerning their own lives and give diligent heed to the words of eternal life. (D&C 84:43.) They live by every word that comes forth from the mouth of God. (D&C 84:44.) The "elect" of God are sensitive to the word of the Lord which comes from his voice. They hear, and hearken, and heed, and live by the words which come from his mouth. . . . Of the "elect" in the last days the Lord declared, "They will hear my voice, and shall see me, and shall not be asleep, and shall abide the day of my coming; for they shall be purified, even as I am pure" (D&C 35:21).

(Susan Easton Black, et al., *Doctrines for Exaltation: The 1989 Sperry Symposium on the Doctrine and Covenants* [Salt Lake City: Deseret Book, 1989], 142–143)

Daily Living

SEEK TO BECOME AN ELECT PERSON.

- We can be an elect person through repentance and forgiveness—D&C 25:3
- Do we hearken to the voice of the Lord?—D&C 29:2
- Treasure the word of God and live by every word that comes forth from the mouth of God—D&C 84:43–46, 85

ALL LAWS ARE SPIRITUAL

Wherefore, verily I say unto you that all things unto me are spiritual, and not at any time have I given unto you a law which was temporal; neither any man, nor the children of men; neither Adam, your father, whom I created.

D&C 29:34

A contrast is frequently drawn between "spiritual things" and those of a temporal nature (D&C 29:31–34; 70:12). The Melchizedek Priesthood in particular is to administer in the "spiritual things" of the Church (D&C 107:8–12). . . . Of this statement, President Joseph Fielding Smith said: "All things to him are spiritual, or in other words *intended to be eternal.* The Lord does not think in temporal terms; his plan is to bring to pass the immortality and eternal life of man. In his eyes, therefore, all the commandments that have to do with our present welfare, are considered to be but steps on the way to his eternal salvation." (CHMR 1:307–8; italics added).

(Hoyt W. Brewster, Jr., *Doctrine and Covenants Encyclopedia* [Salt Lake City: Bookcraft, 1996], 556–557)

Daily Living

REMEMBER, ALL COMMANDMENTS ARE ETERNAL.

- Everything we do in mortality has eternal consequences: either eternal life or misery—2 Nephi 2:27
- Do we love God?—John 14:15
- Obedience to laws and ordinances of the gospel bring forth corresponding blessings now and in the hereafter—D&C 130:20–21

NECESSITY OF TEMPTATION

And it must needs be that the devil should tempt the children of men, or they could not be agents unto themselves; for if they never should have bitter they could not know the sweet.
D&C 29:39

The object of the Father's plan was "to bring to pass the immortality and eternal life" (sometimes called salvation) of all of his spirit children (Moses 1:39). He would create a world in which his children would receive mortality and exercise the agency (power of choice) he had given them (Moses 4:3). They would be tested "to see if they will do all things whatsoever the Lord their God shall command them" (Abr. 3:25). The choices the children of God would make in the exercise of their agency would be made in the face of opposition (2 Ne. 2:16; D&C 29:39).

(Dallin H. Oaks, *The Lord's Way* [Salt Lake City: Deseret Book, 1991], 7–8)

Daily Living

OPPOSITION AND TEMPTATION ARE PART OF THE TEST.

- Opposition and temptation are essential for the test of life to prove ourselves worthy—2 Nephi 2:11
- No one is without trials, tribulations, and afflictions here in mortality, and the Lord will bless us for enduring—Alma 7:11–12
- What will you do to overcome temptation? Feast upon the word of God—1 Nephi 15:24
- Pray always—3 Nephi 18:18
- Remember that the Spirit will show us all things which we should do—2 Nephi 32:5

THE WAGES OF SIN

And they that believe not unto eternal damnation; for they cannot be redeemed from their spiritual fall, because they repent not; For they love darkness rather than light, and their deeds are evil, and they receive their wages of whom they list to obey.
D&C 29:44–45

Those who sin and procrastinate the day of their repentance, "even until death . . . have become subjected to the spirit of the devil, and he doth seal you his; therefore, the Spirit of the Lord hath withdrawn from you" (Alma 34:35). The hell to which we will be consigned if we sin and repent not will be a "bright recollection of all our guilt" (Alma 11:43) for in the day of judgment "our words will condemn us . . . and our thoughts will also condemn us . . . and we would fain be glad if we could command the rocks and the mountains to fall upon us to hide us from his presence" (Alma 12:14).

Youth of today, by your conduct you become the servants of that power whom you thus serve. Your reward for a good life is to live in the sunburst of heavenly light and intelligence.

(Harold B. Lee, *Decisions for Successful Living* [Salt Lake City: Deseret Book, 1973], 90)

Daily Living

BE BELIEVING AND ALWAYS SEEK FORGIVENESS.

- Pray always and be believing—D&C 90:24
- Be easily entreated and humble and diligent in keeping the commandments—Alma 7:23
- Doubt not and be believing—Mormon 9:27

LABOR FOR ZION

And your whole labor shall be in Zion, with all your soul, from henceforth; yea, you shall ever open your mouth in my cause, not fearing what man can do, for I am with you. Amen.
D&C 30:11

In these latter days we are commanded to "seek to bring forth and establish the cause of Zion" (D&C 6:6). . . . Service that is ostensibly for God or fellowmen but is really for the sake of the server's riches or honor surely comes within the Savior's condemnation. . . . Such service earns no gospel reward. All Latter-day Saints should remember Nephi's warning: "But the laborer in Zion shall labor for Zion; for if they labor for money they shall perish" (2 Nephi 26:31). In contrast to those who complete their service for selfish reasons, such as to be seen of men, those who serve quietly, even "in secret," qualify for the Savior's promise that "thy Father who seeth in secret, himself shall reward thee openly" (3 Nephi 13:4; Matthew 6:4).

(Dallin H. Oaks, *Pure in Heart* [Salt Lake City: Bookcraft, 1988], 40)

Daily Living

LABOR FOR ZION AS YOU BUILD UP THE KINGDOM OF GOD.

- As disciples of Christ and Saints in the Church and kingdom of God, our whole duty is to build up the kingdom of God and to help establish Zion—3 Nephi 12:33
- Bless and serve your fellow man with purity of heart by helping them come unto Christ—Jacob 1:7

BLESSINGS OF MISSIONARY SERVICE

Lift up your heart and rejoice, for the hour of your mission is come; and your tongue shall be loosed, and you shall declare glad tidings of great joy unto this generation. You shall declare the things which have been revealed to my servant, Joseph Smith, Jun. You shall begin to preach from this time forth, yea, to reap in the field which is white already to be burned. Therefore, thrust in your sickle with all your soul, and your sins are forgiven you, and you shall be laden with sheaves upon your back, for the laborer is worthy of his hire. Wherefore, your family shall live.

D&C 31:3–5

Said President Kimball, "Missionary work, like the tithing, will pour out blessings . . . so many blessings that there'll hardly be room enough to receive them." I believe that.

(Carlos E. Asay, *The Seven M's of Missionary Service: Proclaiming the Gospel as a Member or Full-time Missionary* [Salt Lake City: Bookcraft, 1996], 131)

Daily Living

CONSIDER THE BLESSINGS OF MISSIONARY WORK.

- Bearing testimony brings forgiveness of sins—D&C 62:3
- You will have glory and joy in being an instrument in the hands of God—Alma 29:9–10
- You will come to understand charity and the worth of souls—Mosiah 28:3; D&C 18:10–16
- You will find your life—Matthew 10:39; 16:25
- You will do that which is of most worth by bringing souls to Christ—D&C 15:6

PRAY TO OVERCOME TEMPTATION

*Pray always, lest you enter into temptation
and lose your reward.*
D&C 31:12

It is not a difficult thing to lose the Spirit of the Lord and turn away from the truth into darkness. The Lord gave the warning to the members of the Church at the time of its organization, in these words: "And we know also, that sanctification through the grace of our Lord and Savior Jesus Christ is just and true, to all those who love and serve God; with all their mights, minds, and strength. But there is a possibility that man may fall from grace and depart from the living God; therefore let the Church take heed and pray always, lest they fall into temptation; yea and even let those who are sanctified take heed also" (D. & C. 20:31–34). How does apostasy come about? By neglect of duty, failing to keep in our souls the spirit of prayer, of obedience to the principles of the Gospel.

(Joseph Fielding Smith, *Church History and Modern Revelation*, 4 vols. [Salt Lake City: The Church of Jesus Christ of Latter-day Saints, 1946–1949], 3:150)

Daily Living

PRAY WITH GREAT DESIRE AND FAITH TO OVERCOME TEMPTATION.

- Remember that without the word of God and the guidance of the Holy Ghost, we are left to ourselves—D&C 30:2–3
- Pray always, for Satan desires to have you—3 Nephi 18:18
- Faith is your shield to protect you—D&C 27:17
- The word of God directs you as you give heed to it and are faithful and diligent—Alma 37:41, 44

PRAY FOR UNDERSTANDING

And they shall give heed to that which is written, and pretend to no other revelation; and they shall pray always that I may unfold the same to their understanding.
D&C 32:4

"Therefore," the Lord said, "if you will ask of me you shall receive; if you will knock it shall be opened unto you" (D&C 6:5; see also 88:63). Seek for wisdom, the Lord said, "and behold, the mysteries of God shall be unfolded unto you, and then shall you be made rich" (D&C 6:7). "And if thou wilt inquire, thou shalt know mysteries which are great and marvelous" (D&C 6:11). . . .

Each of us should pray that the Lord will unfold the scriptures to our understanding (D&C 32:4). God has promised that if we ask him, we will "receive revelation upon revelation, knowledge upon knowledge, that [we may] know the mysteries and peaceable things—that which bringeth joy, that which bringeth life eternal" (D&C 42:61).

(Dallin H. Oaks, *The Lord's Way* [Salt Lake City: Deseret Book, 1991], 34)

Daily Living

PRAY TO UNDERSTAND ALL THINGS.

- When you come to understand and appreciate the word, you will be filled with gratitude, thus resulting in a change of your attitude and behavior—Alma 31:5; 36:26
- Pray to understand—Daniel 9:13; Mosiah 2:40
- The word of God will enlighten your understanding—Alma 32:28
- Remember, understanding brings wisdom—Proverbs 10:23

THE GATHERING

And even so will I gather mine elect from the four quarters of the earth, even as many as will believe in me, and hearken unto my voice.

D&C 33:6

We look upon this as the land of Zion, and the principle of gathering, though a unique one, has been one that has pervaded the teachings and belief of the Latter-day Saints from the beginning. Even before the Elders in their missionary labors have said anything about a Zion, the Spirit of God has witnessed to the spirits of those who have received the Gospel that there would be a gathering, but that God would have a people of his own and that they would be gathered in one place. From the very beginning of the Gospel being sent to England we have evidence to prove this. I have seen in my administrations how quickly this spirit has taken possession of the Saints. And while we do not urge gathering today, feeling that the work will be strengthened by most of the Saints remaining in the branches for a time and helping the Elders carry the warning message of the Gospel, yet the principle of gathering is just as true as ever it has been.

(Anthon H. Lund, in Conference Report, October 1899, 13)

Daily Living

We are responsible for the last pruning of the vineyard.

ꕥ In the dispensation of the fullness of times, we have been given the responsibility to gather Israel and all those who will accept the gospel of Jesus Christ. This is the last time the vineyard will be pruned—Jacob 5:70–71

OPEN YOUR MOUTH

Open your mouths and they shall be filled. . . . Yea, open your mouths and spare not, and you shall be laden with sheaves upon your backs, for lo, I am with you. Yea, open your mouths and they shall be filled, saying: Repent, repent, and prepare ye the way of the Lord, and make his paths straight; for the kingdom of heaven is at hand.

D&C 33:8–10

The Lord reveals that one of the principal purposes of the restoration is to proclaim the gospel—to bring truth and priesthood authority back to the earth so that missionary work can be organized and carried out as a mighty effort upon the earth in the last days. . . . Each of us has the sacred responsibility to proclaim the gospel. The Savior's commandment applies to all members of the Church, not just to full-time missionaries or to returned missionaries. We each have the responsibility to follow the Spirit when it prompts us to share the gospel so that others can come to follow the Savior.

(Joseph B. Wirthlin, *Finding Peace in Our Lives* [Salt Lake City: Deseret Book, 1995], 241)

Daily Living

IN SHARING THE GOSPEL WE MUST EVENTUALLY OPEN OUR MOUTHS.

- The courage and faith to open your mouth is always accompanied by the blessing of being given what you should say at that very moment—D&C 84:85; 100:5–6
- The Lord will even put the words you should say into your heart—Helaman 13:4–5

LIVING THE GOSPEL

Yea, repent and be baptized, every one of you, for a remission of your sins; yea, be baptized even by water, and then cometh the baptism of fire and of the Holy Ghost. Behold, verily, verily, I say unto you, this is my gospel; and remember that they shall have faith in me or they can in nowise be saved; And upon this rock I will build my church; yea, upon this rock ye are built, and if ye continue, the gates of hell shall not prevail against you.

D&C 33:11–13

A truly committed person does not falter in the face of adversity. . . . If we profess to be Latter-day Saints, let us be committed to living like Latter-day Saints, using Jesus Christ as our master teacher. It is not too late to commit ourselves to living the gospel totally while here on earth. Each day we must be committed to lofty Christian performance because commitment to the truths of the gospel of Jesus Christ is essential to our eternal joy and happiness. The time to commit and recommit is now.

(Marvin J. Ashton, *Be of Good Cheer* [Salt Lake City: Deseret Book, 1987], 51, 53)

Daily Living

LIVING THE GOSPEL IS REWARDED WITH ETERNAL LIFE.

ཱ Living the gospel embraces every doctrine, principle, and commandment given by God for the exaltation of His children; yea we must live by every word that proceedeth forth from the mouth of God—D&C 84:44–46

THE BOOK OF MORMON AND THE HOLY SCRIPTURES

And the Book of Mormon and the holy scriptures
are given of me for your instruction;
and the power of my Spirit quickeneth all things.
D&C 33:16

Now, the Lord has revealed unto us in these modern scriptures as well as in scriptures that were given in ancient times, the necessary articles and covenants by which we may be guided and directed in church government and understand the truth of the Gospel. Through the faith, diligence and heed we give to these instructions, we may know that the Lord and Savior of this world is indeed our Redeemer and the Son of God. We may know this provided our studies and faithfulness are guided by prayer.

(Anthony W. Ivins, in Conference Report, October 1918, 54)

Daily Living

THE SCRIPTURES ARE MADE ALIVE BY THE HOLY SPIRIT.

- Do you realize that the scriptures are indeed the word of God and are given that we might have the knowledge of things pertaining to eternal life? The word of God is the true panacea for life. Yet sometimes we take lightly the commandment to search and feast upon the word of God—D&C 84:53–57; 2 Nephi 32:3
- When we liken the scriptures to our lives, our intellect is quickened, and the words are made alive by the power of the Holy Ghost—1 Nephi 19:23
- All things given and spoken by the power of the Holy Ghost are the word of God—D&C 68:3

PREPARE FOR THE SECOND COMING

Wherefore, be faithful, praying always, having your lamps trimmed and burning, and oil with you, that you may be ready at the coming of the Bridegroom.
D&C 33:17

The Doctrine and Covenants uses the verbs *coming, come,* and *cometh* extensively to express Christ's return to the earth. For instance, the Lord invites the faithful to pray for his coming: "Calling upon the name of the Lord day and night, saying: O that thou wouldst rend the heavens, that thou wouldst come down, that the mountains might flow down at thy presence" (D&C 133:40). . . . And he promises those who overcome the world that they will accompany Christ, "when he shall come in the clouds of heaven to reign on the earth over his people" (D&C 76:63).

Sinners receive a different message. The Lord warns that the unrepentant will be "utterly destroyed by the brightness of my coming" (D&C 5:19).

(Donald W. Parry and Jay A. Parry, *Understanding the Signs of the Times* [Salt Lake City: Deseret Book, 1999], 382–383)

Daily Living

EVERY DAY IS A DAY TO PREPARE TO MEET GOD.

- Prepare for the coming of the Lord with oil in our lamps. Be watchful that you will not be overcome—D&C 61:38
- Our meeting of the Lord and Savior Jesus Christ can be at death, so now is the time to prepare to meet God—Alma 34:32

LIFT UP YOUR VOICE

To lift up your voice as with the sound of a trump, both long and loud, and cry repentance unto a crooked and perverse generation, preparing the way of the Lord for his second coming. Wherefore, lift up your voice and spare not, for the Lord God hath spoken; therefore prophesy, and it shall be given by the power of the Holy Ghost. And if you are faithful, behold, I am with you until I come.

D&C 34:6, 10–11

So far as you may have opportunity I wish you to improve yourself to the utmost in studying good books and in associating with, and listening to, and profiting by, the conversation and experience of good persons, that when you speak to the people, they may be persuaded that they are not only listening to one having authority, but also to one appreciating and preaching the good, sound, saving doctrines and precepts he teaches. Cease not to lift up your voice in all faithfulness, teaching the people the way of life and salvation, which you know.

(Brigham Young, *Letters of Brigham Young to His Sons,* edited and introduced by Dean C. Jessee [Salt Lake City: Deseret Book, 1974], 28)

Daily Living

OPEN YOUR MOUTH—LIFT UP YOUR VOICE AND BE A WITNESS.

ꕥ A good example is so important, but eventually the word, even the word of God, must be spoken that people might be invited to come unto Christ. Be not afraid; the Lord will help—Alma 26:11–12; D&C 84:85, 88; 100:5–6

FAITH PRECEDES THE MIRACLE

For I am God, and mine arm is not shortened; and I will show miracles, signs, and wonders, unto all those who believe on my name. And whoso shall ask it in my name in faith, they shall cast out devils; they shall heal the sick; they shall cause the blind to receive their sight, and the deaf to hear, and the dumb to speak, and the lame to walk.

D&C 35:8–9

In faith we plant the seed, and soon we see the miracle of the blossoming. Men have often misunderstood and have reversed the process. They would have the harvest before the planting, the reward before the service, the miracle before the faith. . . . If we could only realize, as Moroni writes: "For if there be no faith among the children of men God can do no miracle among them. . . . And neither at any time hath any wrought miracles until after their faith; wherefore they first believed in the Son of God" (Ether 12:12, 18).

(Spencer W. Kimball, *Faith Precedes the Miracle* [Salt Lake City: Deseret Book, 1972], 4)

Daily Living

THROUGH FAITH IN JESUS CHRIST YOU CAN DO ALL THINGS.

- Seek to increase your faith, for all things are done by faith in the Lord Jesus Christ—Moroni 10:23
- Faith leads to repentance—Alma 34:15–17; Enos 1:8
- Be cleansed from iniquity and thus qualify to perform miracles, "and there was not any man who could do a miracle in the name of Jesus save he were cleansed every whit from his iniquity"—3 Nephi 8:1

THE LORD KNOWS ALL THINGS

Thus saith the Lord your God, even Jesus Christ, the Great I AM, Alpha and Omega, the beginning and the end, the same which looked upon the wide expanse of eternity, and all the seraphic hosts of heaven, before the world was made; The same which knoweth all things, for all things are present before mine eyes.
D&C 38:1–2

Omniscience consists in having unlimited knowledge. God knows all things (2 Ne. 9:20; D. & C. 38:1–2; 88:7–13); possesses "a fulness of truth, yea, even of all truth" (D. & C. 93:11, 26); "has all power, all wisdom, and all understanding" (Alma 26:35); is infinite in understanding (Ps. 147:4–5); comprehends all things (Alma 26:35; D. & C. 88:41); and "hath given a law unto all things" (D. & C. 88:42). . . . Joseph Smith said: "Without the knowledge of all things God would not be able to save any portion of his creatures; . . . and if it were not for the idea existing in the minds of men that God had all knowledge it would be impossible for them to exercise faith in him" (Lectures on Faith, 44).

(Bruce R. McConkie, *Mormon Doctrine*, 2d ed. [Salt Lake City: Bookcraft, 1966], 545)

Daily Living

GOD KNOWS ALL THINGS, THUS OUR FAITH AND HOPE INCREASE.

- When we realize that God has all knowledge, all power and is all loving, we have faith in Him, are filled with hope, love Him, and seek to obey the commandments—Moroni 7:42; 2 Corinthians 10:15; John 14:15

TEACH ONE ANOTHER

But, verily I say unto you, teach one another according to the office wherewith I have appointed you.
D&C 38:23

President Harold B. Lee has stated, "He commanded that they should "teach one another the doctrine of the kingdom . . . in all things that pertain [to] the kingdom of God. . . ." (D&C 88:77–78). . . . "Seek learning, even by study and also by faith." (D&C 88:118). . . . First, one must arouse his faculties and experiment on the words of the Lord and desire to believe. . . . Then, like a planted seed, it must be cultivated and not resist the Spirit of the Lord . . . it must be good, for it enlarges your soul and enlightens your understanding and, like the fruit of the tree in Lehi's vision, it becomes delicious to the taste (see Alma 32)."

(Harold B. Lee, *Stand Ye in Holy Places* [Salt Lake City: Deseret Book, 1974], 358)

Daily Living

SEEK TO LEARN AND TEACH FROM ONE ANOTHER.

- You can teach by the Spirit if you are worthy and have a prayer of faith—D&C 42:14
- We are to teach one another the doctrine of the kingdom and to do it diligently, and the grace of the Lord will attend us—D&C 88:77–78
- The leaders of quorums are to teach their quorum members—D&C 107:89
- All have a right to speak in appropriate settings that all might be edified; all are learners and teachers—D&C 88:122; Alma 1:26

APRIL

&

Hearken and hear, O ye my people, saith the Lord and your God, ye whom I delight to bless with the greatest of all blessings.

—DOCTRINE & COVENANTS 41:1

LOVE ONE ANOTHER

And let every man esteem his brother as himself, and practise virtue and holiness before me. And again I say unto you, let every man esteem his brother as himself.

D&C 38:24–25

Sister Elaine Jack has taught us concerning the love of God when it dwells in the hearts of the people: "'There was no contention in the land, because of the love of God which did dwell in the hearts of the people. . . . And surely there could not be a happier people among all the people who had been created by the hand of God' (4 Nephi 1:15–16). . . . Do you see a pattern? I do, and I am grateful for these ideas: 1. The people of God love him. 2. They love each other. 3. They are greatly changed by their love. 4. They deal justly with one another. 5. They hold all things in common. 6. They are pure in heart. 7. They live peacefully together."

(Elaine L. Jack, *Eye to Eye, Heart to Heart* [Salt Lake City: Deseret Book, 1992], 84)

Daily Living

LOVE ONE ANOTHER—ESTEEM YOUR BROTHER AS YOURSELF.

- Concerning the great commandment of love, the Lord reminds us that this commandment fulfills all the law and the prophets—Matthew 22:36–40
- In love is the motive of every righteous action. Those truly and deeply converted to the gospel of Jesus Christ will, by their change of nature, have overwhelming concern for their fellow man, which is a sign of their love—John 13:34–35; Mosiah 28:3; Alma 36:24

UNITY—IF YE ARE NOT ONE YE ARE NOT MINE

Behold, this I have given unto you as a parable,
and it is even as I am. I say unto you, be one;
and if ye are not one ye are not mine.
D&C 38:27

The Lord desires to have us a united people, the people that will listen to his voice. And what does this mean? Does it mean tyranny? Does it mean oppression? Does it mean the taking away of any human being's rights? Does it encroach upon the liberty of any soul? No, it does not. It never has. It never will, because the Priesthood of the Son of God is not a tyrant. The operations of that Priesthood are beneficent under all circumstances. Look at the prosperity of this people. See how God has blessed them when they have listened to counsel and been guided aright. All our prosperity is traceable to this. Our misfortunes are traceable to our disobedience and neglect. Everyone knows this that has any faith whatever in the work of God. There is nothing asked of any man that he cannot do with the utmost pleasure and with the freest exercise of his agency. It has been so from the beginning, and it will be so to the end.

(George Q. Cannon, in Conference Report, April 1898, 35)

Daily Living

UNITY AND ONENESS BRINGS PEACE IN YOUR LIFE.

ꝏ The key to unity with God and man is to have the same values. You could say, "agreed-upon values brings unity or oneness" to the family, the group or the cause—Acts 1:14; Romans 12:5; Galatians 3:28; 2 Nephi 1:21; 3 Nephi 27:1

BE PREPARED

Ye hear of wars in far countries, and you say that there will soon be great wars in far countries, but ye know not the hearts of men in your own land. I tell you these things because of your prayers; wherefore, treasure up wisdom in your bosoms, lest the wickedness of men reveal these things unto you by their wickedness, in a manner which shall speak in your ears with a voice louder than that which shall shake the earth; but if ye are prepared ye shall not fear.

D&C 38:29–30

I believe it is time to review (perhaps with some urgency) the counsel we have received regarding our personal and family preparedness. We want to be found with oil in our lamps sufficient to endure to the end. . . . President Kimball said, "In our lives the oil of preparedness is accumulated drop by drop in righteous living." He also issued a warning: "The Lord will not translate one's good hopes and desires and intentions into works. Each of us must do that for himself." . . . Just as it is important to prepare ourselves spiritually, we must also prepare for our temporal needs. We all need to take the time to ask ourselves, What preparations should we make to care for our needs and the needs of our families?

(L. Tom Perry, *Living with Enthusiasm* [Salt Lake City: Deseret Book, 1996], 22–23)

Daily Living

IF YE ARE PREPARED, YE SHALL NOT FEAR.

℘ Prepare and organize every needful thing—D&C 88:119

PREACH WITH MILDNESS AND MEEKNESS

And let your preaching be the warning voice, every man to his neighbor, in mildness and in meekness.

D&C 38:41

I DO NOT believe that we need to be bombastic, loud, pushy, or insensitive in our approach [to missionary work]. Our personal missionary work should not be so threatening as to destroy our personal friendships and good will. There should be nothing approaching even a hint of a threat or ultimatum of any kind. Alma said we should "use boldness, but not overbearance" (Alma 38:12). The light of the gospel should show in our countenances as well as our actions. I do, however, believe that we need to be courageous, resourceful, and sensitive. The Lord counsels us, "And let your preaching be the warning voice, every man to his neighbor in mildness and in meekness" (D&C 38:41).

(James E. Faust and James Bell, *In the Strength of the Lord: The Life and Teachings of James E. Faust* [Salt Lake City: Deseret Book, 1999], 373)

Daily Living

PREACH WITH MILDNESS AND MEEKNESS.

- Be tender, gentle, and kindly in all your conversation. In meekness we submit to the divine will of God, hence we preach and teach according to the Spirit. For by the Spirit we preach and teach the gospel of Jesus Christ—D&C 42:14
- Remember, we must be bold but not overbearing—Alma 38:12

THE HOLY GHOST SHOWETH ALL THINGS

And verily, verily, I say unto you, he that receiveth my gospel receiveth me; and he that receiveth not my gospel receiveth not me. And this is my gospel—repentance and baptism by water, and then cometh the baptism of fire and the Holy Ghost, even the Comforter, which showeth all things, and teacheth the peaceable things of the kingdom.

D&C 39:5–6

The gift of the Holy Ghost adapts itself to all these organs or attributes. It quickens all the intellectual faculties, increases, enlarges, expands and purifies all the natural passions and affections, and adapts them, by the gift of wisdom, to their lawful use. It inspires, develops, cultivates and matures all the fine-toned sympathies, joys, tastes, kindred feelings and affections of our natures. It inspires virtue, kindness, goodness, tenderness, gentleness and charity. . . . It tends to health, vigor, animation and social feeling. It invigorates all the faculties of the physical and intellectual man. It strengthens and gives tone to the nerves. In short, it is as it were, marrow to the bone, joy to the heart, light to the eyes, music to the ears, and life to the whole being.

(Parley Pratt, *Key to the Science of Theology*, 1843, 101)

Daily Living

SEEK THE HOLY SPIRIT.

- Seek the Holy Spirit, for He will teach you the truth of all things—Moroni 10:5
- The Spirit will show you all things to do—2 Nephi 32:5

FEAR OF PERSECUTION

And he received the word with gladness, but straightway Satan tempted him; and the fear of persecution and the cares of the world caused him to reject the word.
D&C 40:2

Persecution is the heritage of the faithful. As long as mortal conditions prevail among men, the saints may rest assured that all that will live godly in Christ Jesus shall suffer persecution (2 Tim. 3:12). This persecution will consist in ill treatment and oppression, in acts of persistent and cruel hostility, heaped upon them because of their religious beliefs. . . . Persecution is a tool of Satan by which he continues among mortal men the war of rebellion he began in pre-existence. He recognizes the true Church, and in his open rebellion does all he can to persuade those who follow him to fight against the truth and to destroy those who believe it. The restored truth is always preached "in the midst of persecution and wickedness" (D. & C. 99:1), and "the fear of persecution and the care of the world" cause many "to reject the word" (D&C 40:2).

(Bruce R. McConkie, *Mormon Doctrine*, 2d ed. [Salt Lake City: Bookcraft, 1966], 569)

Daily Living

BE COURAGEOUS AND FAITHFUL.

- Be strong. Blessed are those who are persecuted for the Lord's sake—3 Nephi 12:10–12
- Faith can and will overcome all doubt and fear, so seek to increase your faith—Helaman 3:35

April 7

TRUE DISCIPLESHIP

He that receiveth my law and doeth it, the same is my disciple; and he that saith he receiveth it and doeth it not, the same is not my disciple, and shall be cast out from among you.
D&C 41:5

The commitment to become a disciple of Christ . . . centers a person's life on Christ, making Jesus the supreme law-giver, the frame of reference through which all else is viewed. Christ's influence then begins to direct a person's words, acts, and even thoughts, enabling that individual to become a partaker of the divine nature (2 Pet. 1:4). . . . The heart of this process is learning to educate and obey the conscience, the repository of the Spirit of Christ given to every person (John 1:9; Moro. 7:16). As individuals obey the general commandments given through his appointed prophets, they become more attuned to hear the "still small voice" of the Holy Ghost (1 Ne. 17:45) that communicates specific personal direction and leads individuals to full discipleship.

(Stephen R. Covey, *Encyclopedia of Mormonism*, 1–4 vols., ed. Daniel H. Ludlow [New York: Macmillan, 1992], 385)

Daily Living

PASS THE TEST OF DISCIPLESHIP.

- Whom do you follow?—Mark 6:1
- Do you have love for one another?—John 13:34–35
- Do you keep the commandments?—Matthew 21:6
- Do you forsake all?—Luke 14:33

A PURE HEART

And this because his heart is pure before me, for he is like unto Nathanael of old, in whom there is no guile.
D&C 41:11

A person is a true Latter-day Saint if he (or she) is so inwardly, if his conversion is that of the heart, in the spirit, whose praise is not from men for outward acts but from God for the inward desires of his heart.

As we seek to determine whether we have become true Latter-day Saints—inwardly as well as outwardly—it soon becomes apparent that the critical element is progress, not longevity. The question is not how much time we have logged, but how far we have progressed toward perfection. As Elder Neal A. Maxwell has said, "Life is not lineal, but experiential, not chronological, but developmental" (*Ensign*, December 1986, 23). The issue is not what we have done but what we have become. And what we have become is the result of more than our actions. It is also the result of our attitudes, our motives, and our desires. Each of these is an ingredient of the pure heart.

(Dallin H. Oaks, *Pure in Heart* [Salt Lake City: Bookcraft, 1988], 138)

Daily Living

SEEK TO HAVE A PURE HEART.

- A pure heart rejects vanity—Psalms 24:4
- Out of a pure heart can come charity—1 Timothy 1:5
- The pure in heart receive the word of God, shall see God, and are a Zion people—Jacob 3:1–3; D&C 97:16, 21

LIKE UNTO ANGELS OF GOD

And ye shall go forth in the power of my Spirit, preaching my gospel, two by two, in my name, lifting up your voices as with the sound of a trump, declaring my word like unto angels of God.
D&C 42:6

God will bestow his Spirit "on those who love him and purify themselves before him" (D&C 76:116). That is why the Lord has said that the basic qualification to serve in the kingdom is to "love the Lord thy God with all thy heart, with all thy might, mind, and strength" (D&C 59:5) and "to keep my commandments, yea, with all your might, mind and strength" (D&C 11:20). That prepares us to be in tune with the Holy Ghost. The Spirit is given to us "by the prayer of faith" (D&C 42:14). . . . "Pray always, and I will pour out my Spirit upon you" (D&C 19:38). The members of the Church are also promised that if they partake of the sacrament with the proper attitude, they will "always have his Spirit to be with them" (D&C 20:77). Therefore we who engage in the preaching of the gospel can, if we desire, have the Holy Ghost as our companion.

(Byron R. Merrill et al., comps., *The Heavens Are Open: The 1992 Sperry Symposium on the Doctrine and Covenants and Church History* [Salt Lake City: Deseret Book, 1993], 136)

Daily Living

POWER OF THE SPIRIT—LIKE UNTO ANGELS OF GOD.

- Missionaries, like angels, who are messengers for God, speak by the power of the Holy Ghost—2 Nephi 32:3

TEACH THE PRINCIPLES OF THE GOSPEL

And again, the elders, priests and teachers of this church shall teach the principles of my gospel, which are in the Bible and the Book of Mormon, in the which is the fulness of the gospel. And they shall observe the covenants and church articles to do them, and these shall be their teachings, as they shall be directed by the Spirit.

D&C 42:12–13

The ideal way to transform your home into a house of learning is to hold family home evening faithfully. The Church has reserved Monday evening for that purpose. In 1915, the First Presidency instructed local leaders and parents to inaugurate a home evening, a time when parents should teach their families the principles of the gospel. The Presidency wrote: "If the Saints obey this counsel, we promise that great blessings will result. Love at home and obedience to parents will increase. Faith will be developed in the hearts of the youth of Israel, and they will gain power to combat the evil influence and temptations which beset them."

(Joseph B. Wirthlin, *Finding Peace in Our Lives* [Salt Lake City: Deseret Book, 1995], 55)

Daily Living

TEACH THE GOSPEL AS DIRECTED BY THE SPIRIT.

℘ Teachers in the Church and especially parents in the home are responsible to be sure that the gospel of Jesus Christ is taught by the Spirit so that all might be nourished by the good word of God—Moroni 6:4

TEACH ONLY BY THE SPIRIT

And the Spirit shall be given unto you by the prayer of faith; and if ye receive not the Spirit ye shall not teach.
D&C 42:14

Jesus, who taught "as one having authority" (Matthew 7:29), was and ever will be the greatest teacher. He provides the perfect model for us to follow as we strive to improve our own teaching skills. We are to teach by the Spirit (see D&C 42:14 and 50:17–22), "according to the office wherewith I have appointed you," the Lord says (D&C 38:23). As we strive to do so, we will receive wondrous blessings of power and comprehension, far beyond our mortal capacities. "Teach ye diligently and my grace shall attend you, that you may be instructed more perfectly in theory, in principle, in doctrine, in the law of the gospel, in all things that pertain unto the kingdom of God, . . . that ye may be prepared in all things . . . to magnify the calling whereunto I have called you, and the mission with which I have commissioned you" (D&C 88:78, 80).

(Alexander B. Morrison, *Feed My Sheep: Leadership Ideas for Latter-day Shepherds* [Salt Lake City: Deseret Book, 1992], 67)

Daily Living

TEACH BY THE SPIRIT THAT ALL MIGHT BE EDIFIED.

- Teach by the Spirit of truth that all might be edified—D&C 50:17–22
- The Spirit will testify to the truth of all things—Moroni 10:5

THOU SHALT NOT LIE

Thou shalt not lie;
he that lieth and will not repent shall be cast out.
D&C 42:21

President Hinckley has admonished us, "Be strong . . . with the strength of simple honesty. How easy it is to 'lie a little, take the advantage of one because of his words, dig a pit for thy neighbor' (2 Ne. 28:8). Nephi so describes the people of his day, as he also describes so many of our day. How easy it is for us to say, 'We believe in being honest, true, chaste, benevolent' (A of F 1:13). But how difficult for so many to resist the temptation to lie a little, cheat a little, steal a little, bear false witness in speaking gossipy words about others. Rise above it, brethren. Be strong in the simple virtue of honesty. Simple honesty is so remarkable a quality. It is of the very essence of integrity. It demands that we be straightforward, unequivocal, in walking the straight and narrow line of what is right and true. It is so easy to cheat. At times it is so enticing to do so. Better a poor grade than a dishonest act."

(*Teachings of Gordon B. Hinckley* [Salt Lake City: Deseret Book, 1997], 269)

Daily Living

INTEGRITY AND HONESTY ARE THE PILLARS OF CHARACTER.

ꝏ The Lord commands us to be honest in our dealings. This is reiterated in the temple recommend interview. If we are not honest with our fellow men and with the Lord, we are not worthy to enter His house, for "wo unto the liar, for he shall be thrust down to hell"—2 Nephi 9:34

April 13

LOVE YOUR WIFE

Thou shalt love thy wife with all thy heart, and shalt cleave unto her and none else.
D&C 42:22

There are those married people who permit their eyes to wander and their hearts to become vagrant, who think it is not improper to flirt a little, to share their hearts and have desire for someone other than the wife or the husband. . . . And, when the Lord says *all* thy heart, it allows for no sharing nor dividing nor depriving. And, to the woman it is paraphrased: "Thou shalt love thy husband with *all* thy heart and shalt cleave unto him and none else." The words *none else* eliminate everyone and everything. The spouse then becomes preeminent in the life of the husband or wife, and neither social life nor occupational life nor political life nor any other interest nor person nor thing shall ever take precedence over the companion spouse. . . .

Marriage presupposes total allegiance and total fidelity. Each spouse takes the partner with the understanding that he or she gives totally to the spouse all the heart, strength, loyalty, honor, and affection, with all dignity. Any divergence is sin; any sharing of the heart is transgression.

(Spencer W. Kimball, *Faith Precedes the Miracle* [Salt Lake City: Deseret Book, 1972], 141–142)

Daily Living

LOVE THY WIFE WITH ALL THY HEART.

ℬ Love and commitment to your covenants in marriage is the only way to keep a marriage strong, else selfishness and all its trailing sins will destroy it—Ephesians 5:33

BEWARE OF LUST

And he that looketh upon a woman to lust after her shall deny the faith, and shall not have the Spirit; and if he repents not he shall be cast out. Thou shalt not commit adultery; and he that committeth adultery, and repenteth not, shall be cast out. But he that has committed adultery and repents with all his heart, and forsaketh it, and doeth it no more, thou shalt forgive.

D&C 42:23–25

Adultery stands next to the shedding of innocent blood and the sin against the Holy Ghost (see Alma 39:5). The Lord through His prophets has warned and counseled against "lustful desires." (see 1 Peter 2 :11; D&C 88:121). Brent Barlow gives some good advice, "It's true that sexual stimuli can come unsolicited to almost everyone in our sexually oriented society. But as one of my lifelong friends, David Despain, has noted, 'Just because a bird flies over your head, you don't have to let it build a nest in your hair.' Modern revelation admonishes us to 'let virtue garnish thy thoughts *unceasingly*; then shall thy confidence wax strong in the presence of God'" (D&C 121:45; italics added).

(Brent A. Barlow, *Worth Waiting For: Sexual Abstinence Before Marriage* [Salt Lake City: Deseret Book, 1995], 103–104)

Daily Living

BEWARE OF LUST LEST YOU AND YOUR FAMILY BE DESTROYED.

- Wanton eyes and partaking of pornographic material is a sure way to fall into Satan's trap, which will inevitably destroy your morality, virtue, and your family—James 1:14

SPEAK NO EVIL

Thou shalt not speak evil of thy neighbor,
nor do him any harm.
D&C 42:27

Love our Neighbor. After our love of God must come our love for our neighbor, whom we should love as ourselves (D. & C. 59:6). The very essence of life as a Latter-day Saint, as already implied, is love for our fellow men. . . . We must not speak evil of our neighbor, gossip about him, or do him any harm (D. & C. 42:27); on the contrary, we must learn to impart to each other of all the good we have (D. & C. 88:81, 123), and seek one another's interests and live together in love (D. & C. 42:45). By such neighborly love, Latter-day Saints must be distinguished among the peoples of earth.

(John A. Widtsoe, *Program of The Church of Jesus Christ of Latter-day Saints* [Salt Lake City: The Church of Jesus Christ of Latter-day Saints, 1937], 111–112)

Daily Living

SPEAK ONLY THAT WHICH IS KIND, JUST, AND TRUE.

- You can be defiled by your mouth—Matthew 15:11
- Never seek to contend, for it is of the devil—3 Nephi 11:29
- A soft answer turneth away wrath—Proverbs 15:1
- Never judge or seek to fault find or lay blame—Moroni 7:18
- Consider what you say—Is it kind? Is it true? Is it necessary? We may find ourselves a little short for words.

LOVE GOD—KEEP HIS COMMANDMENTS

If thou lovest me thou shalt serve me and keep all my commandments.
D&C 42:29

Obedience is the most genuine way to show our love for God. We need to keep the commandments of God, and we need to encourage all to do so. "If ye love me, keep my commandments" (John 14:15), the Savior taught.

Belief alone is not sufficient. When speaking to the multitudes [the Savior] said: "Not every one that saith unto me, Lord, Lord, shall enter into the kingdom of heaven; but he that doeth the will of my Father which is in heaven" (Matthew 7:21). As I read these words, it seems to me that the Lord is saying. . . . belief alone is not sufficient. Then he expressly adds, "but he that doeth the will of my Father." In other words, he that labors and prunes the vineyard that it may bring forth good fruit.

(Howard W. Hunter, *The Teachings of Howard W. Hunter*, ed. Clyde J. Williams [Salt Lake City: Bookcraft, 1997], 21)

Daily Living

LOVE GOD AS WE SERVE HIM AND KEEP HIS COMMANDMENTS.

- True love always has within its expressions a desire to serve and bless—Mosiah 2:17; Joshua 24:15
- The Lord blesses us more than what we do; hence, we are always unprofitable servants—Mosiah 2:21
- Remember, you cannot serve two masters—Matthew 6:24
- If we truly love God we will serve Him—D&C 42:29
- Remember that love is a verb.

April 17

REMEMBER THE POOR AND NEEDY

And behold, thou wilt remember the poor, and consecrate of thy properties for their support that which thou hast to impart unto them, with a covenant and a deed which cannot be broken. And inasmuch as ye impart of your substance unto the poor, ye will do it unto me.

D&C 42:30–31

President Hinckley has counseled us concerning our appearance before the judgment bar of God. He said, "I believe we will be examined on what we did to build the kingdom, to bring light and understanding of the eternal truths of the gospel to the eyes and minds of all who are willing to listen, to care for the poor and the needy, and to make of the world a better place as a result of our presence."

(Gordon B. Hinckley, "Questions and Answers," *Ensign,* November 1985, 52)

Daily Living

CONSIDER HOW YOU CAN HELP OTHERS IN NEED.

- Every good deed lasts forever. We give all credit to our Heavenly Father; all good comes from God—Alma 5:40
- Consider how you can help the poor and needy in regard to all of their needs, temporal, emotional, intellectual, spiritual, and social. All need help in some area—D&C 81:5; Alma 1:27; 4:13
- We can strengthen and serve others with our conversations, our prayers, and our exhortations and in all our doings—D&C 108:7

BLESS AND SERVE OTHERS—YE HAVE DONE IT UNTO CHRIST

For inasmuch as ye do it unto the least of these, ye do it unto me.
D&C 42:38

What is meant by "after all we can do"? "After all we can do" includes extending our best effort. "After all we can do" includes living His commandments. "After all we can do" includes loving our fellowmen and praying for those who regard us as their adversary. "After all we can do" means clothing the naked, feeding the hungry, visiting the sick and giving "succor [to] those who stand in need of [our] succor" (Mosiah 4:15)—remembering that what we do unto one of the least of God's children, we do unto Him (see Matthew 25:34–40; D&C 42:38). "After all we can do" means leading chaste, clean, pure lives, being scrupulously honest in all our dealings and treating others the way we would want to be treated.

(Ezra Taft Benson, *The Teachings of Ezra Taft Benson* [Salt Lake City: Bookcraft, 1988], 354)

Daily Living

DO IT UNTO THE LEAST OF THESE—YE HAVE DONE IT UNTO CHRIST.

- As we treat even the least of these our brothers and sisters, it is as if we have treated our Savior the same—Matthew 25:40
- This doctrine is transcending in how it encompasses the worth of souls as well as the ranking of goodness and righteousness. This demonstrates the ultimate and perfect love of our Heavenly Father and our Savior Jesus Christ for all of their children—John 3:16; 2 Nephi 26:24; Mosiah 2:17; Moses 1:39

IDLENESS OR WORK

Thou shalt not be idle; for he that is idle shall not eat the bread nor wear the garments of the laborer.
D&C 42:42

We shall have the joy of work, too, for man also is that he might work, he went forth from the innocence of Eden to the God-like knowledge of good and evil, with the Divine blessing—not curse—as it seems to me: "In the sweat of thy face shalt thou eat bread." And save in extremity, no man may rightfully violate that law by living by the sweat from the brow of his brother. It is the eternal, inescapable law that growth comes only from work and preparation, whether the growth be material, mental, or spiritual. Work has no substitute. Idleness brings neither profit, nor advantage, nor good—only a withering decay and death. The world is near to forgetting all this; I hope that we as a people shall keep it ever in remembrance, for in proportion as it is forgotten, evil will rule.

(J. Rueben Clarke, in Conference Report, April 1933, 102)

Daily Living

WORK WISELY, BE DILIGENT . . . TIME IS PRECIOUS.

- There is nothing quite so destructive to the soul and the feeling of well being as is the failure to be productive. Set goals, make plans, and be diligent—D&C 88:119
- Time is precious and can never be replenished or stored, therefore we must be diligent in our efforts—Hebrews 11:6; 2 Peter 1:5; 2 Nephi 31:20; Mosiah 7:33; Alma 17:2; Moroni 8:26; 9:6; D&C 6:20; 58:27; 75:29; 90:24

THE BLESSINGS OF FAITH

He who hath faith to see shall see. He who hath faith to hear shall hear. The lame who hath faith to leap shall leap.
D&C 42:49–51

"Thy faith hath made thee whole" or words like unto it occur throughout the scriptures. One of the gifts of the Spirit is faith to be healed (see D&C 46:19). And thus we gain insight as mentioned before why the early Apostles entreated the Lord to increase their faith (see Luke 17:5). President Hinckley has said, "If there is any one thing you and I need in this world it is faith, that dynamic, powerful, marvelous element by which, as Paul declared, the very worlds were framed (Hebrews 11:3). . . . Faith—the kind of faith that moves one to get on his knees and plead with the Lord and then get on his feet and go to work—is an asset beyond compare, even in the acquisition of secular knowledge.

(*Teachings of Gordon B. Hinckley* [Salt Lake City: Deseret Book, 1997], 186)

Daily Living

EXERCISE AND INCREASE YOUR FAITH IN JESUS CHRIST.

- Faith is not only the foundation of all righteousness but the power to all things—Moroni 7:33
- Faith, when exercised in the Lord Jesus Christ, brings miracles and blessings into our lives—Ether 12:12
- Remember, our faith must be tried—3 Nephi 26:9
- The witness comes after our trial of faith—Ether 12:6
- Strength is increased according to our faith—Alma 14:26
- Pray, and hear the word—Helaman 3:35, Romans 10:17

ASK AND YE SHALL RECEIVE

If thou shalt ask, thou shalt receive revelation upon revelation, knowledge upon knowledge, that thou mayest know the mysteries and peaceable things—that which bringeth joy, that which bringeth life eternal. Therefore, he that lacketh wisdom, let him ask of me, and I will give him liberally and upbraid him not.
D&C 42:61, 68

Too often we fail to ask and we do not listen with full anticipation of receiving an answer. Maybe we really don't even expect an answer. . . . Nephi understood how to talk and listen to the Lord. He explained, "I . . . did go into the mount oft, and I did pray oft unto the Lord; wherefore the Lord showed unto me great things" (1 Nephi 18:3). First we must desire to talk to our Heavenly Father and to listen to him, knowing that he in turn will talk to us in our minds and in our hearts (D&C 8:2) and will listen to us. There is no question about his promise to us.

(Ardeth Greene Kapp, *The Joy of the Journey* [Salt Lake City: Deseret Book, 1992], 123–127)

Daily Living

WE MUST ASK IN ORDER TO RECEIVE.

- Ask and ye shall receive occurs eighteen times in the scriptures.
- Asking or calling upon our Heavenly Father in prayer is a requirement in order to receive the blessings of God. People often are simply left to themselves and their limited knowledge and inadequate strength because they fail to ask—1 Nephi 15:7–9

CHOOSE TO NOT TAKE OFFENSE

And if thy brother or sister offend thee, thou shalt take him or her between him or her and thee alone; and if he or she confess thou shalt be reconciled.
D&C 42:88

Why is the initiative with the one who has been offended, when the natural tendency when we are offended is to say within ourselves, "He is the one at fault; therefore he should come to me." Oftentimes a person offends unknowingly. . . . If someone offends you unknowingly and continues to do so, you are responsible for the strain in the relationship if you do not take the initiative to clear it up. Often you'll find you made unrealistic expectations. You may discover you simply didn't understand the situation at all. . . .Obviously, therefore, it's better not to take offense, whether intended or not. It's best not to judge another at all but to forgive "seven times seventy," if need be. But if we are offended and we can't fully forgive or resolve it inside, we should go to the other shortly after the offense so reconciliation can take place.

(Stephen R. Covey, *How to Succeed with People* [Salt Lake City: Deseret Book, 1971], 51–53)

Daily Living

CHOOSE TO NEVER TAKE OFFENSE AND YOU SHALL BE BLESSED.

ꕥ Don't look to find fault and lay blame, but rather seek to praise and look for the good. Make a commitment to yourself to never take offense or judge another. For in judging and taking offense, we can become the offender, and with that judgment be judged as well—Matthew 7:1–2

April 23

CHURCH DISCIPLINE

And if thy brother or sister offend many, he or she shall be chastened before many. And if any one offend openly, he or she shall be rebuked openly, that he or she may be ashamed. And if he or she confess not, he or she shall be delivered up unto the law of God.

D&C 42:90–91

This revelation shows the interaction between two different purposes of punishment—protecting the good name and moral influence of the Church and facilitating repentance. When a serious sin is widely known or there were many victims . . . the purpose of church discipline concerned with the good name and influence of the Church dictates that the church discipline be widely known. He who "offend[ed] openly . . . shall be rebuked openly." On the other hand, where a sin is not known widely, repentance and church discipline can be a private affair. He who "offend[ed] in secret . . . shall be rebuked in secret." Similarly, when persons have not confessed or repented, they are delivered up to a meeting of elders who act for the Church "and that not before the world."

(Dallin H. Oaks, *The Lord's Way* [Salt Lake City: Deseret Book, 1991], 245)

Daily Living

CHURCH DISCIPLINE PROVIDES OPPORTUNITY TO REPENT.

ꝏ Church discipline is motivated by charity for all and the welfare of their souls. The purpose of Church discipline and the chastening of an individual is to provide an opportunity for people to repent—D&C 95:1–2

PURPOSE OF MEETINGS

And now, behold, I give unto you a commandment, that when ye are assembled together ye shall instruct and edify each other, that ye may know how to act and direct my church, how to act upon the points of my law and commandments, which I have given. And thus ye shall become instructed in the law of my church, and be sanctified by that which ye have received, and ye shall bind yourselves to act in all holiness before me—That inasmuch as ye do this, glory shall be added to the kingdom which ye have received. Inasmuch as ye do it not, it shall be taken, even that which ye have received.

D&C 43:8–10

Balance program content with the Spirit in meetings . . . not meetings for meetings' sake, but meetings with purpose and meetings with dedication. The things of the Spirit must radiate from us in our relations with each other in the way we lead and serve. We need to balance more carefully our emphasis on program content and how to get things done with the needs we all have to feel the spirit and power of the gospel in our lives.

(Harold B. Lee, *The Teachings of Harold B. Lee*, ed. Clyde J. Williams [Salt Lake City: Bookcraft, 1996], 467)

Daily Living

MEETINGS ARE TO INSPIRE AND UPLIFT US BY THE SPIRIT.

ꝏ A difference can be made through meetings when one acts upon the feelings of the Spirit and makes commitments to change and improve their behavior—D&C 20:77, 79

ELDERS TO TEACH

Again I say, hearken ye elders of my church, whom I have appointed: Ye are not sent forth to be taught, but to teach the children of men the things which I have put into your hands by the power of my Spirit; And ye are to be taught from on high. Sanctify yourselves and ye shall be endowed with power, that ye may give even as I have spoken.

D&C 43:15–16

We have only one object in view in going out amongst the nations, and that is to follow the Master's instructions—to go out and teach men. That is our work. We do not go out to win battles as debators; but we go out to teach men that which we have received, which we know is true. If men are not willing to receive it, that is their own concern, not ours. . . . The Elders do their duty, and leave the result to the Lord. Those who seek to debate with our Elders and thirst for the honor of beating them in argument, do not want to be taught; they simply want contention.

(Anthon H. Lund, in Conference Report, October 1902, 80–81)

Daily Living

EVERYONE TEACHES BY PRECEPT AND EXAMPLE.

ꝏ Missionaries and members are to teach and testify, not bash or contend with others on points of doctrine. As you become sanctified through prayer and fasting and by yielding your heart to God, you will indeed teach with the power and authority of God— Alma 17:3; Helaman 3:35

THE LORD CALLS AFTER ALL HIS CHILDREN

How oft have I called upon you by the mouth of my servants, and by the ministering of angels, and by mine own voice, and by the voice of thunderings, and by the voice of lightnings, and by the voice of tempests, and by the voice of earthquakes, and great hailstorms, and by the voice of famines and pestilences of every kind, and by the great sound of a trump, and by the voice of judgment, and by the voice of mercy all the day long, and by the voice of glory and honor and the riches of eternal life, and would have saved you with an everlasting salvation, but ye would not!

D&C 43:25

According to the most reliable information available the loss of human life since the commencement of the World War reaches the following appalling figures: The World War 9,000,000, Civil wars 6,000,000, Famine 6,000,000, Epidemics 40,000,000, Earthquake and Flood 2,000,000. In all this we recognize the voice of the Lord, spoken through His servants the prophets, calling the people of the world to repentance, and warning us that the hour of His judgments and the time of His second coming is at hand.

(James R. Clark, comp., *Messages of the First Presidency*, 6 vols. [Salt Lake City: Bookcraft, 1965–75], 5:254)

Daily Living

THE LORD CALLS AFTER HIS CHILDREN . . . . WE MUST BE AWARE.

ꟸ Everything that happens is part of earth's experiences to bring us closer to God and help us recognize that we are totally dependent upon God for life and the blessings of eternal life—Mosiah 1:17; 2:20–21; Alma 5:59; Helaman 12:3

April 27

LABOR IN THE VINEYARD FOR THE LAST TIME

Wherefore, labor ye, labor ye in my vineyard for the last time—for the last time call upon the inhabitants of the earth.
D&C 43:28

Zenos' allegory of the olive tree, recorded in Jacob 5, speaks of the latter-day labors of the righteous to the nethermost parts of the vineyard (see Jacob 5:71–72). . . .

The Doctrine and Covenants confirms that with the restoration of the gospel in 1830 the Lord was directing his servants to labor in the vineyard for the last time (D&C 33:3; 39:17; 43:28).

(Monte S. Nyman and Charles D. Tate, Jr., eds., *Fourth Nephi through Moroni: From Zion to Destruction* [Provo: BYU Religious Studies Center, 1995], 332)

Daily Living

WE MUST LABOR WITH ALL OUR MIGHT, FOR THIS IS THE LAST TIME.

- Now is the time, and we are the ones that have the responsibility to declare to the world that the gospel of Jesus Christ has been restored though the prophet Joseph—Jacob 5:70–71
- We must labor with all our heart, might, mind, and strength and thus be blameless—D&C 4:2
- We must stand as witnesses at all times, in all things, and in all places—Mosiah 18:9
- We invite all to come unto Christ that they may be perfected in Him—Moroni 10:32

FAITHFUL TO RECEIVE THE SPIRIT

And it shall come to pass, that inasmuch as they are faithful, and exercise faith in me, I will pour out my Spirit upon them in the day that they assemble themselves together.
D&C 44:2

Because the Holy Spirit speaks peace to the hearts of weary and disconsolate mortals, he is called the Comforter. He brings peace and solace, love and quiet enjoyment, the joy of redemption and the hope of eternal life. These words of promise are given to all who receive the gift of the Holy Ghost: "Therefore it is given to abide in you; the record of heaven; the Comforter; the peaceable things of immortal glory; the truth of all things; that which quickeneth all things, which maketh alive all things; that which knoweth all things, and hath all power, according to wisdom, mercy, truth, justice, and judgment" (Moses 6:61). How glorious is the word we have received! How wondrous is the Spirit that dwells in faithful hearts!

(Bruce R. McConkie, *A New Witness for the Articles of Faith* [Salt Lake City: Deseret Book, 1985], 268)

Daily Living

RECEIVE THE SPIRIT WITH FAITH, LOVE, PURITY, AND OBEDIENCE.

- We can feel the Spirit as we prepare with faith, demonstrate love and purity, and are obedient to the commandments—1 Nephi 10:17; D&C 76:116; 20:77, 79
- Pray in faith that those you serve and teach might have a portion of His Spirit—Alma 17:9; 24:8

MINISTER TO THE POOR AND NEEDY

Behold, I say unto you, that ye must visit the poor and the needy and administer to their relief, that they may be kept until all things may be done according to my law which ye have received. Amen.
D&C 44:6

George Q. Cannon has said, "At no time during the Prophet's career did the care of the poor escape his attention or become a matter of indifference to him. He was a man of large benevolence, and his sympathies were quickly aroused by any tale of sorrow or appeal for relief. In the most busy and trying periods of his life those who went to him for counsel in their troubles, always found him willing to listen, and they were sure to receive encouragement and assistance. To extend comfort to the bruised spirit, and to help the needy and distressed appeared a constant pleasure to him. His hospitality, also, was a marked feature in his character. His house was always open to entertain the stranger.

(Roy W. Doxey, comp., *Latter-day Prophets and the Doctrine and Covenants* [Salt Lake City: Deseret Book, 1978], 2:72)

Daily Living

THE LORD CONTINUALLY REMINDS US TO CARE FOR THE POOR.

- The Lord's continued emphasis of caring for the poor and needy is repeated throughout the scriptures. It isn't enough to pray—Alma 34:28–29; Mosiah 4:26
- Blessed are ye when you care for the poor—Psalms 41:1
- Do you love your substance more than the poor?—Mormon 8:37

CHRIST IS OUR ADVOCATE

Listen to him who is the advocate with the Father, who is pleading your cause before him—Saying: Father, behold the sufferings and death of him who did no sin, in whom thou wast well pleased; behold the blood of thy Son which was shed, the blood of him whom thou gavest that thyself might be glorified; Wherefore, Father, spare these my brethren that believe on my name, that they may come unto me and have everlasting life.

D&C 45:3–5

We have a relationship with Elohim as the father of our spirits and with Christ as the father of our spiritual birth. . . . Christ is our advocate with the Father, suggesting that when the Father is our judge, Christ pleads our case before him . . . [thus] our relationship with Christ may somehow parallel his relationship with the Father. He teaches us that we "may understand and know how to worship, and know what you worship, that you may come unto the Father in my name, and in due time receive of his fulness."

(Bruce C. Hafen and Marie K. Hafen, *The Belonging Heart: The Atonement and Relationships with God and Family* [Salt Lake City: Deseret Book, 1994], 152)

Daily Living

OUR SAVIOR PLEADS OUR CASE FOR HE IS OUR ADVOCATE.

℘ The Lord pleads our case as our Savior, Redeemer, and Advocate with the Father. Gratitude should fill our hearts knowing of the goodness and mercy of our Savior which surely will motivate us to follow the commandments of the Lord—Hebrews 9:24; 2 Nephi 2:9; Moroni 7:28; D&C 29:5

MAY

ꕤ

And ye are to be taught from on high.
Sanctify yourselves and ye shall be
endowed with power, that ye may give
even as I have spoken.

—Doctrine & Covenants 43:16

HEARKEN, LISTEN, AND HARDEN NOT YOUR HEART

Hearken, O ye people of my church,
and ye elders listen together, and hear my voice while
it is called today, and harden not your hearts.
D&C 45:6

But the scriptures speak of other kinds of death, deaths *in* the body, living deaths. These are the worst kind, deadening and desolating. Thus, for example, we die by degrees intellectually as we suppress the light within us and close our minds to spiritual things. We die emotionally and lapse into deceitfulness and hard-heartedness when we sin or shun the Christlike life. . . . All living deaths require atonement and healing. The atonement of Christ, through the ordinances of the house of the Lord, "reverses the blows of death." Christ cannot reach us inwardly if the very core of us is willfully corroded and corrosive. As we persist in sin, the result is a dulled mentality, a seared conscience, a closed and hardened heart, and stifled creativity.

(Donald W. Parry, ed., *Temples of the Ancient World: Ritual and Symbolism* [Salt Lake City and Provo: Deseret Book, Foundation for Ancient Research and Mormon Studies, 1994], 67)

Daily Living

HEARKEN TO THE LORD AND HARDEN NOT YOUR HEART.

- A hardened heart is past feeling the Spirit—1 Nephi 17:45
- Humility and a broken heart precede repentance and spiritual growth—Alma 7:23
- For as he thinketh in his heart, so is he—Proverbs 23:7
- Remember that hearken means to listen and do.

THE EVERLASTING COVENANT

And even so I have sent mine everlasting covenant into the world, to be a light to the world, and to be a standard for my people, and for the Gentiles to seek to it, and to be a messenger before my face to prepare the way before me.
Wherefore, come ye unto it, and with him that cometh I will reason as with men in days of old,
and I will show unto you my strong reasoning.
D&C 45:9–10

On several occasions in the Doctrine and Covenants, the Lord speaks of his "everlasting covenant" (D&C 1:15; 45:9; 49:9; 66:2; 76:101). "The gospel is the everlasting covenant because it is ordained by Him who is Everlasting and also because it is everlastingly the same. In all past ages salvation was gained by adherence to its terms and conditions, and that same compliance will bring the same reward in all future ages. Each time this everlasting covenant is revealed it is new to those of that dispensation. Hence the gospel is the *new and everlasting covenant*" (MD, 529–30).

(Hoyt W. Brewster, Jr., *Doctrine and Covenants Encyclopedia* [Salt Lake City: Bookcraft, 1988], 164)

Daily Living

RECEIVE THE EVERLASTING COVENANT OF THE GOSPEL.

ზ The gospel covenants and commandments that we honor and keep will assure us the blessings of exaltation—D&C 84:38; D&C 76:69; 131:2; 82:10; 130:20–21; Moroni 7:48; 3 Nephi 27:9–10, 20–21

SIGNS OF HIS COMING

And I will show it plainly as I showed it unto my disciples as I stood before them in the flesh, and spake unto them, saying: As ye have asked of me concerning the signs of my coming, in the day when I shall come in my glory in the clouds of heaven, to fulfil the promises that I have made unto your fathers.

D&C 45:16

And in that day shall be heard of wars and rumors of wars, and the whole earth shall be in commotion, and men's hearts shall fail them, and they shall say that Christ delayeth his coming until the end of the earth. And the love of men shall wax cold, and iniquity shall abound. And when the times of the Gentiles is come in, a light shall break forth among them that sit in darkness, and it shall be the fulness of my gospel.

(D&C 45:26–28; see also D&C 45:33, 40, 42, 48 for additional signs)

Daily Living

WATCH FOR THE SIGNS AND BE READY FOR THE LORD.

- It is given to us to know the signs of His coming—D&C 68:11
- Be prepared with oil in our lamps—Matthew 25:3–9
- This is the time to prepare to meet God—Alma 34:32
- If we are full of charity when He appears we will be like Him—Moroni 7:48
- Remember, no man knoweth the day or hour therefore it behooves us to be ready, for we know not the hour or day we may be required to return home—Matthew 24:36

CONDUCT MEETINGS BY THE SPIRIT

But notwithstanding those things which are written, it always has been given to the elders of my church from the beginning, and ever shall be, to conduct all meetings as they are directed and guided by the Holy Spirit.

D&C 46:2

We cannot live by written scripture alone, nor can we endure to the end in a wicked world with even the added benefit of prophetic declarations, handbooks, or resource manuals. The strength of this Church is to be found in the hearts and lives of its individual members, in the manner in which they seek for and obtain the mind of God through the instrumentality of the Holy Ghost. Ours is the privilege of belonging to the only true and living church upon the face of the whole earth (D&C 1:30), and our opportunity and our duty is to partake of the fruit of a living tree of life, to be governed by a living constitution. . . . The Church seeks to teach us guiding principles, but quite often it is the Holy Ghost who will teach us specific practices.

(Robert L. Millet, *Alive in Christ: The Miracle of Spiritual Rebirth* [Salt Lake City: Deseret Book, 1997], 190)

Daily Living

MEETINGS SHOULD BE DIRECTED BY THE SPIRIT.

ꝏ The Spirit is the key. The Doctrine and Covenants, along with all scriptures, teach that all things must be done by the Spirit in order to do the will of God, thus edifying and blessing those we serve—Moroni 6:9; D&C 50:17–22

May 5

HOLINESS OF HEART AND THANKSGIVING

But ye are commanded in all things to ask of God, who giveth liberally; and that which the Spirit testifies unto you even so I would that ye should do in all holiness of heart, walking uprightly before me, considering the end of your salvation, doing all things with prayer and thanksgiving, that ye may not be seduced by evil spirits, or doctrines of devils, or the commandments of men; for some are of men, and others of devils.

D&C 46:7

The Lord gave careful instructions and counsel to the new leaders to "ask of God, who giveth liberally; and that which the Spirit testifies unto you even so I would that ye should do in all holiness of heart. . . . Seek ye earnestly the best gifts, always remembering for what they are given; . . . they are given for the benefit of those who love me and keep all my commandments."

(David B. Haight, *A Light unto the World* [Salt Lake City: Deseret Book, 1997], 34)

Daily Living

DO ALL THINGS IN ALL HOLINESS OF HEART.

- We do things with holiness of heart—Mosiah 18:12
- Do things to glorify your Father in Heaven—3 Nephi 12:16
- Do things with an eye single to the glory of God—D&C 88:67
- The quorums of the Church make all decisions in holiness of heart and with the virtues and attributes of charity—D&C 107:30

SEEK THE BEST GIFTS—BE NOT DECEIVED

Wherefore, beware lest ye are deceived; and that ye may not be deceived seek ye earnestly the best gifts, always remembering for what they are given.
D&C 46:8

All spiritual gifts are needed in the Church (1 Cor. 12), but that some are more to be desired than others is evident from Paul's writings: One is to seek the best gifts. Of special significance for all who desire "a more excellent way" (1 Cor. 12:31) is to receive and develop the gift of charity. This "pure love of Christ" is a fundamental mark of true discipleship, a prerequisite to eternal life, and a quality one is therefore to pray and work for with all energy of heart (Moroni 7:47–48; 10:21; Ether 12:34). Paul's masterful exposition on charity (1 Cor. 13) further defines this attribute and confirms love as the great commandment and the Christian's crucial need. Disciples are to manifest this gift and also desire others (1 Cor. 14:1), working by the power of God and by the gifts of the Spirit (Moro. 10:25).

(*Encyclopedia of Mormonism*, 1–4 vols., ed. Daniel H. Ludlow [New York: Macmillan, 1992], 546)

Daily Living

SEEK GIFTS TO LIFT AND BLESS OTHERS.

- Let your motives for doing good always dictate your desires for the gifts of the Spirit and for the welfare of others, persuade them to do good and that for the glory of God—Enos 1:9; Luke 6:45; 2 Nephi 33:4; D&C 88:67

GIFTS ARE GIVEN TO THOSE WHO LOVE THE LORD

For verily I say unto you, they are given for the benefit of those who love me and keep all my commandments, and him that seeketh so to do; that all may be benefited that seek or that ask of me, that ask and not for a sign that they may consume it upon their lusts.

D&C 46:9

Latter-day Saints are commanded, "Seek ye earnestly the best gifts" which are given for the benefit of those who love the Lord and keep his commandments. (See D&C 46:8–9; compare 1 Cor. 12:31.) Furthermore, this is another safeguard against being deceived. (See D&C 46:7–8.) It will be remembered that the Lord earlier exhorted the people to follow the Prophet as another key against deception. (See D&C 43:5–6.) If one is to seek these gifts, he has to know what they are. (See D&C 46:10.) Not all receive the same gifts, but "to some is given one, and to some is given another, that all may be profited thereby" (D&C 46:12).

(Richard O. Cowan, *The Doctrine and Covenants: Our Modern Scripture* [Salt Lake City: Bookcraft, 1984], 83)

Daily Living

GIFTS ARE GIVEN TO THOSE WHO LOVE THE LORD.

- You become highly favored of the Lord according to the desires of your heart and obedience to His commandments—1 Nephi 1:1; 3:6; Mosiah 10:13
- Love is manifest through obedience—John 14:15
- With love of God and purity of heart, you receive the power of the Holy Spirit in your lives—D&C 76:116

GIFTS OF THE SPIRIT—TO PROFIT ALL

For all have not every gift given unto them; for there are many gifts, and to every man is given a gift by the Spirit of God. To some is given one, and to some is given another, that all may be profited thereby.
D&C 46:11–12

Spiritual gifts properly sought, properly received, and properly shared will establish faith, profit those who love God, and edify the Church. Elder Bruce R. McConkie provides this statement of purpose: "Their purpose is to enlighten, encourage, and edify the faithful so that they will inherit peace in this life and be guided toward eternal life in the world to come . . . " (*Mormon Doctrine*, 314). I would stress that God's gifts are not dispersed or cast about freely into the wind. They are reserved for those who love him and keep his commandments. They are given to benefit the children of God—not the children of men.

(Carlos E. Asay, *In the Lord's Service: A Guide to Spiritual Development* [Salt Lake City: Deseret Book, 1990], 125)

Daily Living

GIFTS OF THE SPIRIT ARE TO PROFIT ALL.

- The blessing of being an instrument in the hands of the Lord brings one joy—Alma 29:9–10
- Those receiving the blessings are filled with joy, thus all are blessed and edified by the Spirit—Alma 36:24; D&C 18:15–16; 50:21–22
- Ponder the multiplicity of blessings from the Spirit.

A GIFT—TO KNOW THAT JESUS IS THE CHRIST

To some it is given by the Holy Ghost to know that Jesus Christ is the Son of God, and that he was crucified for the sins of the world.
D&C 46:13

Let us keep in mind, also, that in mortality men are living under the powerful effects of a spiritual fall. Hence, many good and dedicated people may not have the quality of faith necessary to realize the manifestations of the Spirit in their lives in a phenomenal way. The Lord says, for example, "To some it is given by the Holy Ghost to know that Jesus is the Son of God, and that he was crucified for the sins of the world" (D&C 46:13). Here is a superior gift, to know independently, by revelation to yourself, that Jesus is the Christ. But, continued the Lord, "To others it is given to believe on their words, that they also might have eternal life if they continue faithful" (D&C 46:14).

(Hyrum L. Andrus, *The Glory of God and Man's Relation to Deity* [Provo: BYU Extension Publications, 1964], 40)

Daily Living

TO KNOW THAT JESUS IS THE CHRIST IS A GIFT OF THE SPIRIT.

- All should seek this gift, for knowing God and Jesus Christ, whom He has sent, is life eternal—John 17:3
- When we know that Jesus is the Christ, we accept His atoning sacrifice—1 Corinthians 2:2
- Remember that the knowledge of Christ is what draws us to Him. It is by the grace of God we are saved after all we can do—2 Nephi 25:23

A GIFT—TO BELIEVE ON THEIR WORDS

To others it is given to believe on their words, that they also might have eternal life if they continue faithful.
D&C 46:14

In connection with that gift it is said, "To others it is given *to believe on their words*,"—"their" meaning those who have great faith—"that they also might have eternal life if they continue faithful." Some people are gifted to know, and others are gifted to believe on what those people know. Or, to put it differently, some people have secondhand testimonies. My own conviction is that this is a preparatory gift. It is not sufficient unto itself. You cannot live and endure and overcome simply on the basis of believing the word of another. Sooner or later, and preferably sooner, you too will come to firsthand and direct knowledge for yourself.

(Truman G. Madsen, *Joseph Smith the Prophet* [Salt Lake City: Bookcraft, 1989], 37)

Daily Living

THE SPIRIT BEARS WITNESS TO BELIEVE IN OTHERS.

- Whatever it takes to progress line upon line and precept upon precept is good. We are all strengthened by one another—D&C 108:7; 81:5
- We teach one another the doctrines of the kingdom—D&C 38:23; 88:77–78; 109:7
- We are edified by the Spirit of truth, both the teacher and the learner—D&C 50:22

A GIFT—THE WORD OF WISDOM

And again, verily I say unto you, to some is given, by the Spirit of God, the Word of Wisdom.
D&C 46:17

"The . . . gift of the gospel which I present is that of wisdom. Wisdom cannot be disassociated from discernment, but it involves some other factors, and its applications are rather more specific. Wisdom is sometimes defined as sound judgment and a high degree of knowledge. I define wisdom as being the beneficent application of knowledge in decision. I think of wisdom not in the abstract but as functional. Life is largely made up of choices and determinations, and I can think of no wisdom that does not contemplate the good of man and society. Wisdom is true understanding. . . . I do not believe that true wisdom can be acquired or exercised in living without a sound fundamental knowledge of the truth about life and living. The cry of the world is for wisdom and wise men. . . . The fundamental knowledge which the Church brings you will bring you understanding. Your testimony, your spirit, and your service will direct the application of your knowledge; that is wisdom."

(Stephen L Richards, *Where is Wisdom?* [Salt Lake City: Deseret Book, 1955], 200–201)

Daily Living

SEEK WISDOM BY THE SPIRIT.

- Learn wisdom in your youth—Alma 37:35
- Happy is the man that findeth wisdom—Proverbs 3:13
- Seek the wisdom of God diligently—D&C 136:32
- Humble yourselves and call upon the Lord—D&C 97:1

A GIFT—THE WORD OF KNOWLEDGE

To another is given the word of knowledge, that all may be taught to be wise and to have knowledge.
D&C 46:18

Many years ago I read this scripture [D&C 46:18] and pondered it. I thought that among the gifts one might have in order to make himself useful to the Lord, the gift to teach by the Spirit would be supreme. The gift to teach the Word of Wisdom and to teach the word of knowledge by the Spirit is much to be desired. Why should such a gift not come to us if we desire it? If we desire to succeed as a teacher and we're willing to earn that ability, why should it not come to us? If we're willing to ask for it and pray for it, and we believe with sufficient faith that we can possess it, why should it be withheld from us?

(Boyd K. Packer, *Teach Ye Diligently*, [Salt Lake City: Deseret Book], 20)

Daily Living

SEEK KNOWLEDGE BY THE SPIRIT.

- Gospel knowledge deals with eternal truths given by God to man, and this kind of knowledge can save us, for man cannot be saved in ignorance—D&C 131:6
- Seek learning by study and faith. The faith that brings the Spirit—D&C 88:118; 1 Nephi 10:17
- Remember, knowledge brings understanding—Proverbs 9:10
- Knowledge is key to obtaining charity—2 Peter 1:5
- True knowledge is the knowledge of Christ—Helaman 15:13
- Remember, to be learned is good if we hearken to the counsels of God—2 Nephi 9:28–29

A GIFT—FAITH TO HEAL AND BE HEALED

And again, to some it is given to have faith to be healed; And to others it is given to have faith to heal.
D&C 46:19–20

Faith to heal the sick is one of the most desirable gifts of the gospel and should be sought after by all Melchizedek Priesthood holders. They should always be ready to exercise this power in behalf of those who need a blessing. They should seek to have and develop the gift of faith, faith to heal and faith to be healed. And whoso shall ask it in my name in faith, the Lord has said, they shall cast out devils; they shall heal the sick; they shall cause the blind to receive their sight, and the deaf to hear, and the dumb to speak, and the lame to walk (D&C 35:9).

(James A. Cullimore, "Gifts of the Spirit," *Ensign*, November 1974, 27)

Daily Living

EXERCISE FAITH TO HEAL AND TO BE HEALED.

- All blessings come by virtue of the power of faith. God works among the children of men according to their faith—2 Nephi 26:13; Moroni 7:33
- We are healed by virtue of faith—Alma 15:10; 3 Nephi 17:8
- All miracles are a result of the exercising of faith in the Lord Jesus Christ—Ether 12:12

A GIFT—THE WORKING OF MIRACLES

And again, to some is given the working of miracles.
D&C 46:21

If there is one thing that always attends and identifies those who believe in Christ it is this: they work miracles. Signs and gifts always attend their ministry. However much it may run counter to the course of Christendom, however severe the indictment may seem, speaking of the gifts of the Spirit, the word of the Lord is: "These signs shall follow them that believe" (Mark 16:17). "And if it so be that the church is built upon my gospel then will the Father show forth his own works in it" (3 Ne. 27:10).

Anyone who believes what the apostles believed will receive the same gifts they enjoyed, will perform the same miracles, and will do the same works. "He that believeth on me, the works that I do shall he do also" (John 14:12).

(Bruce R. McConkie, *The Promised Messiah* [Salt Lake City: Deseret Book, 1978, 298)

Daily Living

OBSERVE THE MIRACLES OF GOD IN ALL THINGS.

- Miracles are always wrought by and in the name of the Lord Jesus Christ—4 Nephi 1:5
- Miracles are done by the power of faith—Ether 12:16
- Miracles are performed by those cleansed from iniquity—3 Nephi 8:1
- Miracles have not ceased, neither have angels ceased to minister to the children of men—Moroni 7:29

A GIFT—TO PROPHESY

And to others it is given to prophesy.
D&C 46:22

That is, to speak in the name of the Lord, whether of things present, past, or future. This is a special gift. The Prophet Joseph had it in the highest degree. Heber C. Kimball also had the gift highly developed. At times he could see into the future as if it were an open book. During the time of famine in Salt Lake valley in 1847, when many subsisted on roots and hides of animals, and knew not where to obtain bread or clothing necessary, owing to the devastation by crickets, President Kimball declared in a public meeting that, within a short time, "state goods" would be sold in the streets of Salt Lake City cheaper than in New York, and that the people should be abundantly supplied with food and clothing. . . . The prophecy came true. . . . The California gold-hunters came through the Valley. Salt Lake City became their resting-place, and they were glad to exchange their goods for whatever they could get.

(*Whitney's Life of Heber C. Kimball*, 401–2; quoted in Smith and Sjodahl, *Doctrine and Covenants Commentary* [Salt Lake City: Deseret Book, 1978], 275)

Daily Living

PROPHECY IS FOR THE GOOD OF ALL MANKIND.

- The prophet Joel has said, "I will pour out my spirit upon all flesh; and your sons and your daughters shall prophesy, your old men shall dream dreams, your young men shall see visions." —Joel 2:28; Acts 2:17
- The spirit of prophesy is to know that Jesus is the Christ—Revelation 19:10

A GIFT—THE DISCERNING OF SPIRITS

And to others the discerning of spirits.
D&C 46:23

To all men in some degree and to the faithful saints in particular is given the spirit, gift, and power of discernment. This ability is conferred upon people generally by the operations of the light of Christ (Moro. 7:12–18), but in addition the faithful saints receive discerning power through revelation from the Holy Ghost. (D&C 63:41)

In its most important aspect, discernment is used to distinguish between good and evil (Moro. 7:12–18), between the righteous and the wicked (D&C 101:95; Mal. 3:18; 3 Ne. 24:18), between the false or evil spirits and those spirits who truly manifest the things of God. (D&C 46:23; 1 Cor. 12:10) . . . There is no perfect operation of the power of discernment without revelation.

(Bruce R. McConkie, *Mormon Doctrine*, 2d ed. [Salt Lake City: Bookcraft, 1966], 197)

Daily Living

THE BLESSING OF THE POWER OF DISCERNMENT.

- The gift and power of discernment is empowering. It is a source of protection. The things of God are spiritually discerned—1 Corinthians 2:14
- By the power of the Holy Ghost we are shown all things to do including the blessing of discernment to help us avoid and overcome the temptations and snares of the adversary—2 Nephi 32:5

A GIFT—SPEAKING IN OR INTERPRETATION OF TONGUES

And again, it is given to some to speak with tongues; And to another is given the interpretation of tongues.
D&C 46:24–25

Two of the gifts of the Spirit are speaking in tongues and interpretation of tongues (Moro. 10:15–16; D. & C. 46:24–25; 1 Cor. 12:10, 28, 30; 14). These gifts have been manifest among the saints in every age (Omni 25; Alma 9:21; 3 Ne. 29:6; Morm. 9:7), and they are desirable and useful in the Lord's work. "Let the gift of tongues be poured out upon thy people, even cloven tongues as of fire, and the interpretation thereof," the Prophet prayed at the dedication of the Kirtland Temple (D. & C. 109:36). . . . An ideal and proper use of tongues was shown forth on the day of Pentecost. By using this gift the apostles were enabled to speak in their own tongue and be understood by persons of many different tongues (Acts 2:1–18). Indeed, "the gift of tongues by the power of the Holy Ghost in the Church," as the Prophet said, "is for the benefit of the servants of God to preach to unbelievers, as on the day of Pentecost" (*Teachings,* 195).

(Bruce R. McConkie, *Mormon Doctrine,* 2d ed. [Salt Lake City: Bookcraft, 1966], 799–800)

Daily Living

THE BLESSING OF THE GIFT OF TONGUES.

ꟸ The essence of the gift of tongues is understanding. The use of the gift of tongues is so that all might hear the gospel in their own tongue—D&C 90:11

ASK IN THE SPIRIT AND RECEIVE IN THE SPIRIT

And it shall come to pass that he that asketh
in Spirit shall receive in Spirit.
D&C 46:28

The Spirit is the Lord's agent in bringing many blessings into our lives. The more the Holy Ghost can be with us, the more powerful our prayers will be. "The Spirit shall be given unto you," the Lord said, "by the prayer of faith" (D&C 42:14). The Holy Ghost can even help us to know what to pray for. "He that asketh in the Spirit asketh according to the will of God; wherefore it is done even as he asketh" (D&C 46:30). If we can receive the Spirit through a prayer of faith, we can then ask "in the Spirit," which will help us to ask "according to the will of God." Such prayers are always answered.

(Gene R. Cook, *Receiving Answers to Our Prayers* [Salt Lake City: Deseret Book, 1996], 69–70)

Daily Living

Ask in the Spirit and receive in the Spirit.

- As we pray as inspired by the Holy Spirit, we receive answers according to our faith. Remember the price to receive answers—D&C 9:7–9
- The fruits of the Spirit—Galatians 5:22–23
- Trust in the Spirit—D&C 11:12–13
- Don't expect grandiose or spectacular answers but the sweet whisperings of the Spirit, especially that of peace to your mind—D&C 6:23

ALL THINGS DONE IN THE NAME OF JESUS CHRIST

And again, I say unto you, all things must be done in the name of Christ, whatsoever you do in the Spirit.
D&C 46:31

Jesus Christ is the name given of the Father whereby salvation and all things incident thereto may be attained (Acts 4:12; Mosiah 3:17). It is the name the saints take upon them in the waters of baptism (D&C 18:21–25; 20:37); the name by which they are called (Alma 5:37–38; 3 Ne. 27:3–10), in which they worship (D&C 20:29), and which they use to seal their prayers (D&C 50:31); it is the name in which the saints serve God (D&C 59:5), work miracles (D&C 84:66–73), speak prophecies (D&C 130:12), and do all things (D&C 46:31). Use of the name of Christ centers one's faith in him and constitutes a solemn affirmation as to where all power and authority lies.

(Bruce R. McConkie, *Mormon Doctrine*, 2d ed. [Salt Lake City: Bookcraft, 1966], 525)

Daily Living

DO ALL THINGS OF THE SPIRIT IN THE NAME OF JESUS CHRIST.

- All things are done in the name of and through the Lord Jesus Christ—Colossians 3:17; Alma 19:4; D&C 84:66–68
- We pray only in the name of Jesus Christ—3 Nephi 18:19–23
- All miracles are in the name of Jesus Christ—3 Nephi 8:1
- We have faith in Jesus Christ. We repent through Jesus Christ. We take His name upon us as we are baptized. We receive the Holy Ghost from the Father because of Jesus Christ—3 Nephi 18:11; Moroni 2:2

GIVE THANKS IN THE SPIRIT

And ye must give thanks unto God in the Spirit for whatsoever blessing ye are blessed with.
D&C 46:32

President Hugh B. Brown has said, "How rich and radiant is the soul of a man who has a thankful heart. His gratitude increases with his unfolding awareness of himself, the universe and his Creator. Appreciation, like love, enriches both giver and receiver, and, when spontaneously expressed in word or deed, reveals a depth and delicacy of fine-grain character. True gratitude is motivated by a recognition of favors received. . . . They who have eyes to see, ears to hear, understanding hearts, will see the bounteous love of God everywhere manifest and will be inclined to reverently remove their shoes and exclaim: 'For the rock and for the river, The valley's fertile sod, For the strength of the hills we bless thee, Our God, our fathers' God.'" ["For the Strength of the Hills," Hymns:35] ("Gratitude Is a Spiritual Attribute," Instructor, Nov. 1957, 332) TLDP:269–70.

(quoted in Rulon T. Burton, *We Believe* [Salt Lake City: Tabernacle Books, 2004], 388)

Daily Living

GIVE THANKS FOR ALL YOUR BLESSINGS.

ꕤ Gratitude, one of the cardinal virtues of a righteous life, needs to be constantly on our minds. We should express it willingly and regularly to our Heavenly Father for His goodness and mercy as evidenced through His Beloved Son, our Savior Jesus Christ—Alma 34:38; D&C 59:15, 21

May 21

PRACTICE VIRTUE AND HOLINESS

And ye must practise virtue and holiness before me continually. Even so. Amen.
D&C 46:33

Virtue is akin to holiness, an attribute of godliness. A priesthood holder should actively seek for things that are virtuous and lovely and not that which is debasing or sordid. Virtue will "garnish [his] thoughts unceasingly" (D&C 121:45). Whenever a priesthood holder departs from the path of virtue in any form or expression, he loses the Spirit and comes under Satan's power. He then receives the wages of him whom he has chosen to serve. As a result, sometimes the Church must take disciplinary action, for we cannot condone nor pardon unvirtuous and unrepented actions.

All priesthood holders must be morally clean to be worthy to bear the authority of Jesus Christ.

(Ezra Taft Benson, *Come unto Christ* [Salt Lake City: Deseret Book, 1983], 49)

Daily Living

SEEK VIRTUE AND HOLINESS IN ALL THINGS.

ꝏ Virtue is expressed through righteousness by keeping the commandments of God. Holiness comes from purity, morality, and integrity. We are cleansed of sin and literally sanctified by the power of the Holy Ghost. Is it any wonder the Lord admonishes us to practice virtue and holiness? Remember that in virtue is power. Power comes from righteousness. Faith is the foundation of all righteousness. With faith we have power to do all things.

WO UNTO THE HYPOCRITE

But wo unto them that are deceivers and hypocrites, for, thus saith the Lord, I will bring them to judgment.
Behold, verily I say unto you, there are hypocrites among you, who have deceived some, which has given the adversary power; but behold such shall be reclaimed.

D&C 50:6–7

Let us live as we profess to believe. . . . In all sincerity I ask all of you who profess to be Christians if you do the works of the Master? . . . You are only a true Latter-day Saint when the conduct of your life has not prevented others from coming into the Church or being active in the Church. Let us not come under that condemnation of the Master when he said, "Ye hypocrites." Let us be true. Let us not just serve with our lips, but also with our hearts, minds, might, and strength.

(Harold B. Lee, *The Teachings of Harold B. Lee*, ed. Clyde J. Williams [Salt Lake City: Bookcraft, 1996], 617)

Daily Living

AVOID HYPOCRISY IN ALL THINGS.

ℵ We have all been hypocritical at one time or another. Hypocrisy is pretending to be something that you are not. It is being sanctimonious in judgment of others when you are guilty yourself. It is insincere and beguiling. It is a form of self-deception that undermines and destroys one's progress in becoming Christlike. Beware of hypocrisy for the Lord condemns hypocrites—Matthew 6:2–5, 16; 23:13–15, 23–25, 27; 3 Nephi 13:2–5, 16

May 23

REASON AND COUNSEL TOGETHER

And now come, saith the Lord, by the Spirit, unto the elders of his church, and let us reason together, that ye may understand; Let us reason even as a man reasoneth one with another face to face. Now, when a man reasoneth he is understood of man, because he reasoneth as a man; even so will I, the Lord, reason with you that you may understand.

D&C 50:10–12

The truth will never divide councils of the priesthood. . . . The truth will unite us and cement us together. It will make us strong, for it is a foundation that cannot be destroyed . . . when presidents and their counselors have any difference whatever in their sentiments or in their policy, it is their duty to get together . . . to pray together, to counsel together, to learn each other's spirit, to understand each other, and unite together, that there may be no dissension nor division among them.

(Joseph F. Smith, *Gospel Doctrine: Selections from the Sermons and Writings of Joseph F. Smith*, compiled by John A. Widtsoe [Salt Lake City: Deseret Book, 1939], 156)

Daily Living

REASON AND COUNSEL TOGETHER THAT YE MIGHT UNDERSTAND.

- Ponder the following: The purpose of reasoning is to come to a knowledge of the truth, thus we are of a sound understanding—Alma 17:2
- When we understand, then we can appreciate and have empathy and love for those in the discussion, for our wisdom has increased—Proverbs 10:23

PREACH THE WORD IN AND BY THE SPIRIT OF TRUTH

Verily I say unto you, he that is ordained of me and sent forth to preach the word of truth by the Comforter, in the Spirit of truth, doth he preach it by the Spirit of truth or some other way? And if it be by some other way it is not of God.
D&C 50:17–18

Here we learn that even though what is being taught is the truth, it is not of God unless it is being taught in the Lord's way. The great truths of the gospel must not be presented in the wrong setting, given voice by unworthy persons, accompanied by the wrong kind of music, or in other ways cheapened by association with what is not conducive to the spirit by which gospel truths must be taught. Only when "the word of truth" is taught and received "by the Spirit of truth" do we qualify for the promise that "he that preacheth and he that receiveth, understand one another, and both are edified and rejoice together" (D&C 50:19, 22). This is the Lord's prescribed way of gospel teaching and learning.

Modern revelation promises that the Holy Ghost will manifest "all things which are expedient" (D&C 18:18).

(Dallin H. Oaks, *The Lord's Way* [Salt Lake City: Deseret Book, 1991], 40)

Daily Living

PREACH THE WORD IN AND BY THE SPIRIT OF TRUTH.

ꕤ Remember, we can only teach and learn by the Spirit, for the Spirit is the key in teaching, preaching, learning, and understanding—D&C 42:14

RECEIVE THE WORD BY THE SPIRIT OF TRUTH

And again, he that receiveth the word of truth, doth he receive it by the Spirit of truth or some other way? If it be some other way it is not of God.
D&C 50:19–20

How may the rank and file of the Church recognize the prophetic voice, whether official or unofficial, when it speaks? The answer is simple enough. A person who is in harmony in his life, in thought and practice, with the gospel and its requirements, who loves truth so well that he is willing to surrender to it, will recognize a message from the Lord. My sheep know my voice, said the Savior in the Meridian of Time. In this day, the Lord has given the key for our guidance. . . . Thus the burden of proof is upon the hearer, not alone upon the speaker. Whoever quibbles about the validity of a message of the prophet would do well to engage in a serious self-examination. . . . Perhaps he is not "in tune" with truth. Perhaps he does not live the law of the gospel in such manner as to respond to the message of truth. . . . That doctrine may be applied when the prophet speaks to the Church or to the world.

(John A. Widtsoe, *Evidences and Reconciliations* [Salt Lake City: Bookcraft], 238)

Daily Living

RECEIVE THE WORD BY THE SPIRIT OF TRUTH.

- When one teaches by the Spirit, the Spirit carries it unto the hearts of the learner—2 Nephi 33:1
- Yield your heart unto God and thus be sanctified by the Spirit—Helaman 3:35

THE SPIRIT OF TRUTH EDIFIES

Therefore, why is it that ye cannot understand and know, that he that receiveth the word by the Spirit of truth receiveth it as it is preached by the Spirit of truth? Wherefore, he that preacheth and he that receiveth, understand one another, and both are edified and rejoice together. And that which doth not edify is not of God, and is darkness.

D&C 50:21–23

Experience also suggests the importance not only of meekness but also of the presence of the Spirit. Neither advice-giver nor circumstances can be perfect. Only the Spirit can leap across such deficiencies and convey the message lovingly and yet forcefully. . . . Absent mutual meekness, the counsel given may not only go unheeded, but, in fact, may even be resented.

(Neal A. Maxwell, *Meek and Lowly* [Salt Lake City: Deseret Book, 1987], 57–58)

Daily Living

BY THE SPIRIT OF TRUTH, BOTH ARE EDIFIED TOGETHER.

ஜ We teach by the Spirit and we learn by the Spirit—there is no other way. Edification, the process of being uplifted and nurtured spiritually, is accomplished through and by the Spirit of truth, one of the functions of the Holy Ghost. We are edified by the Spirit as we receive charity (see 1 Corinthians 8:10), through enlightenment (see Alma 32:28; D&C 11:13), by instruction of the word of God (see D&C 43:8; 136:24), and as we strengthen and nurture each other (see D&C 84:110; 88:122).

THOSE WHO ARE SENT FORTH ARE THE SERVANTS OF ALL

He that is ordained of God and sent forth, the same is appointed to be the greatest, notwithstanding he is the least and the servant of all. Wherefore, he is possessor of all things; for all things are subject unto him, both in heaven and on the earth, the life and the light, the Spirit and the power, sent forth by the will of the Father through Jesus Christ, his Son.

D&C 50:26–27

I am called of God. My authority is above that of the kings of the earth. By revelation I have been selected as a personal representative of the Lord Jesus Christ. He is my Master and He has chosen me to represent Him. To stand in His place, to say and do what He himself would say and do if He personally were ministering to the very people to whom He has sent me. My voice is His voice, and my acts are His acts; my words are His words and my doctrine is His doctrine. My commission is to do what He wants done. To say what He wants said. To be a living modern witness in word and deed of the divinity of His great and marvelous latter-day work.

(Bruce R. McConkie, *How Great Is My Calling* [address delivered while serving as president of the Australian Mission, 1961–64])

Daily Living

THOSE WHO ARE SENT FORTH ARE THE SERVANTS OF ALL.

- Christ loved, served, and gave Himself for us—Ephesians 5:25
- True service would encourage one to seek to be like Christ, serving as He would have us serve, for we live His doctrine and know it is true—John 7:17

BE PURIFIED AND CLEANSED

But no man is possessor of all things except he be purified and cleansed from all sin. And if ye are purified and cleansed from all sin, ye shall ask whatsoever you will in the name of Jesus and it shall be done.
D&C 50:28–29

The time will come when we shall know the will of God before we ask. Then everything for which we pray will be "expedient." Everything for which we ask will be "right." That will be when, as a result of righteous living, we shall so enjoy the companionship of the Spirit that he will dictate what we ask. . . . Nephi, the son of Helaman, so lived. He with unweariness declared the word of God. He sought not his own life but the will of God and to keep his commandments continually, and to him the Lord said, "All things shall be done unto thee according to thy word, for thou shalt not ask that which is contrary to my will" (Hel. 10:5).
(Marion G. Romney, *Look to God and Live* [Salt Lake City: Deseret Book, 1973], 203–204)

SEEK THE BLESSINGS OF BEING PURIFIED AND CLEANSED.

- Purity of heart is reflected in our behavior, in our thoughts, in our intentions, and through our affections toward God. When we have a change of heart, we must follow through with a change in the way we comport ourselves—cultivating a "godly walk and conversation"—D&C 20:69; Matthew 5:8; 3 Nephi 12:8
- As we become loving and pure we receive the blessings of the Spirit—D&C 76:116

POWER OVER SPIRITS NOT OF GOD

Wherefore, it shall come to pass, that if you behold a spirit manifested that you cannot understand, and you receive not that spirit, ye shall ask of the Father in the name of Jesus; and if he give not unto you that spirit, then you may know that it is not of God. And it shall be given unto you, power over that spirit; and you shall proclaim against that spirit with a loud voice that it is not of God.

D&C 50:31–32

Two important priesthood powers for missionary work are also identified in the Pearl of Great Price. The Lord promised Enoch that in the last days, "righteousness will I send down out of heaven" (Moses 7:62), in part a reference to the restoration of priesthood keys and powers restored in this dispensation. And to Moses, the Lord provided the use of priesthood powers to resist and overcome evil [see Moses 1:21]. . . . The power to cast out evil spirits and Lucifer himself is thus given as another important use of priesthood powers in missionary work.

(H. Donl Peterson and Charles D. Tate, Jr., eds., *The Pearl of Great Price: Revelations from God* [Provo: BYU Religious Studies Center, 1987], 54)

Daily Living

WE CAN HAVE POWER OVER THE ADVERSARY.

- We can have power over the adversary through the priesthood of God and in righteousness—1 Nephi 11:32; 22:26; Mosiah 3:6; 3 Nephi 7:19; Matthew 10:8; Mark 3:19

GROW IN GRACE AND THE KNOWLEDGE OF THE TRUTH

Behold, ye are little children and ye cannot bear all things now; ye must grow in grace and in the knowledge of the truth.
D&C 50:40

I see that it is impossible for humanity to come directly and without proper training into the presence of God. It is a long, hard labor that we shall have to perform to prepare ourselves for His presence. We need cultivation. It is like the farmer cultivating the soil, or like cultivating the mind in an educational way, only this is the greatest system of education that I have ever heard of. It is a gradual raising of the people. The mind is clearer each day in the man who studies and who understands the ways of God. In this way we draw nearer to God; and by and by, when Jesus appears, we shall know Him; for we shall be like Him. Without this training we would be as ignorant as the world at large; but with the system of education and cultivation which God has instituted [See D&C 88:77–80], we may rise to the dignity of being heirs of God and joint heirs with Jesus Christ.

(Brigham Young, in Conference Report, November 1901, 76)

Daily Living

GROW IN GRACE AND THE KNOWLEDGE OF THE TRUTH.

- Line upon line is part of the growth process here upon the earth—2 Nephi 28:30
- Taking upon oneself the divine nature of Christ requires patience. Within patience is a quality of "constancy" which helps us grow in grace and truth—2 Peter 1:3–12; D&C 4:6

UNIFIED WITH GOD

And the Father and I are one. I am in the Father and the Father in me; and inasmuch as ye have received me, ye are in me and I in you.

D&C 50:43

A Christian recognizes and accepts Christ's central role in the atonement. I like the literal meaning of the word "atonement," namely "at/one/ment." Man's goal is to become one with the Father and the Son, to bring his life in agreement with that of Deity. It begins with knowledge: "And this is life eternal, that they might know thee the only true God, and Jesus Christ, whom thou hast sent" (John 17:3). To become one with the Father and the Son, we must overcome three things: mortality, sin, and ignorance, because the Father and Son are immortal, sinless, and intelligent. Christ is the great mediator lifting us toward the Father. He died to bring to pass the resurrection.

(Lowell L. Bennion, *The Best of Lowell L. Bennion: Selected Writings 1928–1988*, ed. Eugene England [Salt Lake City: Deseret Book, 1988], 270)

Daily Living

WE CAN BE ONE WITH THE FATHER AND THE SON.

ஐ Unity and oneness with God the Father and our Savior Jesus Christ is a supernal doctrine that empowers the children of God with faith, hope, and charity and in this unity always having an eye single to the glory of God. This unity, or at-one-ment, comes through the infinite and atoning sacrifice of our Savior Jesus Christ—John 17:11, 21–22; Acts 4:32; Romans 12:5; D&C 35:2; 38:27

JUNE

ꟸ

For after much tribulation come the blessings. Wherefore the day cometh that ye shall be crowned with much glory; the hour is not yet, but is nigh at hand.

—Doctrine & Covenants 58:4

BUILD UPON THE SAVIOR

Wherefore, I am in your midst, and I am the good shepherd,
and the stone of Israel. He that buildeth upon
this rock shall never fall.
D&C 50:44

"My grace is sufficient . . . if they humble themselves before me, and have faith in me, then will I make weak things become strong unto them" (Ether 12:27). . . . You are painfully aware of your mortal weaknesses. . . . *Can the Savior really make those weak things become strong?* This is a doctrine more profound than any behavior-modification course, more penetrating than any resurgent attempts at willpower. Helaman added the promise that if we will build upon the rock of Christ, the devil will have no power over us (see Hel. 5:12).

(Dawn Anderson, Dlora Dalton, and Susette Green, eds., *Every Good Thing: Talks from the 1997 BYU Women's Conference* [Salt Lake City: Deseret Book, 1998], 77)

Daily Living

BUILD UPON THE SAVIOR, FOR HE IS IN OUR MIDST.

- Ponder and meditate on the mighty prayer and psalm of Nephi—2 Nephi 4:17–35
- We should put our trust in Christ—2 Nephi 4:34
- Our Savior is always there to support us through our afflictions—2 Nephi 4:20; Alma 7:11–12
- Remember that our Savior is our rock of salvation—2 Nephi 4:30; Helaman 5:12
- The Savior is in our midst and will bless us—D&C 85:88
- Remember that the Lord is our strength—Alma 26:11–12

FAITHFUL AND WISE STEWARD

And whoso is found a faithful, a just, and a wise steward shall enter into the joy of his Lord, and shall inherit eternal life.
D&C 51:19

Those words intrigue me. "A faithful, a just, and a wise steward." Every man here has a stewardship for others—faithful, just, and wise. Faithful in all he is asked to do. Just, even-handed, considerate of all for whom he has responsibility. Wise, with that wisdom which comes from the Lord. I would like to suggest that one verse to you as something you could write out and put on the mirror so that every morning you will see it and think of it and ponder it in terms of your responsibility.

(Gordon B. Hinckley, *Teachings of Gordon B. Hinckley* [Salt Lake City: Deseret Book, 1997], 613)

Daily Living

YOU ARE ACCOUNTABLE FOR YOUR STEWARDSHIPS.

- Everyone is accountable in all things—D&C 134:1
- When we are faithful, we are not only full of faith but we become just. "Just" in the scriptures refers to our honest and upright behavior and a state of righteousness which was used to describe those who will be made perfect—D&C 76:69
- We are continually counseled to gain wisdom—Alma 37:35
- Wisdom brings happiness—Proverbs 3:13
- Jacob said it best: "O be wise; what can I say more?"—Jacob 6:12

PRAYER—HUMILITY—OBEDIENCE

And again, I will give unto you a pattern in all things, that ye may not be deceived; for Satan is abroad in the land, and he goeth forth deceiving the nations—Wherefore he that prayeth, whose spirit is contrite, the same is accepted of me if he obey mine ordinances. He that speaketh, whose spirit is contrite, whose language is meek and edifieth, the same is of God if he obey mine ordinances.

D&C 52:14–15

The gift of the Holy Ghost . . . [comes] through humble, faithful obedience. There are those who have had this gift bestowed upon them but who have never received the guidance because they have not conformed their lives to the faithful performance of duty. We have no claim upon the companionship of this Spirit unless we are humbly and prayerfully obedient to all our covenants and responsibilities.

(Joseph Fielding Smith, *Church History and Modern Revelation*, 4 vols. [Salt Lake City: The Church of Jesus Christ of Latter-day Saints, 1946–1949], 4:30)

Daily Living

BE HUMBLE, PRAYERFUL, AND OBEDIENT.

- When we are obedient, we will always have His Spirit to be with us—2 Nephi 32:5; D&C 20:77, 79
- When we are humble, we will be submissive to the will of God—James 4:6–7; Mosiah 3:19
- Through prayer we are given knowledge and are strengthened—James 1:5–6; 3 Nephi 3:12; Ether 12:27

FORSAKE THE WORLD

Behold, I, the Lord, who was crucified for the sins of the world, give unto you a commandment that you shall forsake the world.
D&C 53:2

As we hear the Lord's answers, they are not always easy to bear. For example, Jesus' discourse on the dangers of wealth produced anxiety and inquiry among His followers: "When his disciples heard it, they were exceedingly amazed, saying, Who then can be saved?" (Matthew 19:25). Note the Savior's response as rendered by the Joseph Smith Translation: "But Jesus beheld their thoughts, and said unto them, With men this is impossible; but if they will forsake all things for my sake, with God whatsoever things I speak are possible" (JST, Matthew 19:26). We can succeed, if we will forsake the world. Otherwise the soul-stretching, mind-expanding demands of the gospel would be impossible to meet. To have one's soul "greatly enlarge[d] without hypocrisy" (D&C 121:42) is part of the journey of discipleship.

(Neal A. Maxwell, *Men and Women of Christ* [Salt Lake City: Bookcraft, 1991], 124)

Daily Living

SEEK THE LORD RATHER THAN THE WORLD AND ITS ENTICINGS.

- When we forsake the world we become free from the "things" which keep us from the Lord, His Spirit, and the blessings that the gospel brings—JST—Matthew 16:29
- The devil will lead us carefully down to hell, where he will bind us his—2 Nephi 26:22, 28:21

TAKE UP YOUR CROSS

And he that will not take up his cross and follow me, and keep my commandments, the same shall not be saved.
D&C 56:2

Take up your cross . . . lift yourself in the direction of the better. Regardless of where you have been, what you have done, or what you haven't done, trust God, believe on Him, relate to Him, worship Him as you carry your cross with dignity and determination. We save our lives by losing them for His sake. As you find yourself, you will find God. This is true. I declare that to you. It is His promise. Take up the real cross of Jesus Christ. What kind of cross do you bear? . . . the cross of loneliness; the cross of physical limitations—the loss of a leg, an arm, hearing, seeing, mobility—obvious crosses (we see people with these crosses and admire their strength in carrying them with dignity); the cross of poor health; the cross of transgression; the cross of success; the cross of temptation; the cross of beauty, fame, or wealth; the cross of financial burdens; the cross of criticism; the cross of peer rejection.

(Marvin J. Ashton, *Be of Good Cheer* [Salt Lake City: Deseret Book, 1987], 31–32)

Daily Living

YOUR CROSS CAN BE YOUR RESPONSIBILITIES OR AFFLICTIONS.

- The Savior will help us bear our burdens and nurture us through our afflictions—Alma 7:11–12
- The Savior will give us strength—Alma 26:11–12
- The Savior will give us peace—John 14:27

THE LORD COMMANDS AND REVOKES

Wherefore I, the Lord, command and revoke,
as it seemeth me good; and all this to be answered upon the
heads of the rebellious, saith the Lord.
D&C 56:4

If God is unchanging, why would he ever revoke his commandments? Even though God does not change, our circumstances do. His purposes and gospel principles are unchanging, but the means of carrying out those purposes and principles may vary from one circumstance to another. For example, the principle of taking care of our physical bodies is unchanging, but specific dietary laws essential in ancient Israel are not necessary now and are not applicable today. That the Lord made the seemingly routine matter of the reassignment of missionary companions a subject of revelation should remind us to keep ourselves receptive to his guidance even in what we may regard as the ordinary aspects of our lives.

(Richard O. Cowan, *Answers to Your Questions About the Doctrine and Covenants* [Salt Lake City: Deseret Book, 1996], 69)

Daily Living

THE LORD MAKES CHANGES ACCORDING TO OUR NEEDS.

- God is all powerful and all wise, yet works with His children according to their moral agency—D&C 101:78
- The gift of agency allows us to choose and also causes our Heavenly Father to alter and change things that will be for our betterment . . . what could show greater love for His children than this?—Helaman 11:3–5; Gen. 18

SEEK COUNSEL FROM THE LORD

Behold, thus saith the Lord unto my people—you have many things to do and to repent of; for behold, your sins have come up unto me, and are not pardoned, because you seek to counsel in your own ways.

D&C 56:14

When they speak of faith, they speak of faith in the Lord Jesus Christ, and when we seek to "counsel with the Lord in all [our] doings" we counsel in wisdom, and our decisions will be grounded in faith in Christ rather than in unrealistic speculation.

(Spencer J. Condie, *Your Agency: Handle with Care* [Salt Lake City: Bookcraft, 1996], 82)

Daily Living

SEEK COUNSEL FROM THE LORD AND NOT IN YOUR OWN WAYS.

- We are in jeopardy whenever we think we know of ourselves—2 Nephi 9:28–29
- As we seek guidance and direction from the Lord, we will be blessed in all things . . . even to be led by the Holy Spirit—1 Nephi 4:6
- We counsel with the Lord in all our doings—Jacob 4:10
- Remember, the Lord will direct thy path—Alma 37:37
- Hearken to the counsel of the Lord eagerly and immediately and receive the blessing—D&C 103:5

SEEK RIGHTEOUSNESS

And your hearts are not satisfied. And ye obey not the truth, but have pleasure in unrighteousness.
D&C 56:15

Men are taught to be meek, merciful, peacemaking, pure in heart, to suffer persecution for the sake of righteousness, to cast those things out of their lives which are offensive, not to swear, and to love their enemies. Also, the Lord said: do good to them that hate you, pray for them which despitefully use you and persecute you, be perfect, do almsgiving privately, pray sincerely avoiding show and vain repetitions, forgive your fellow men, fast without show, seek righteousness first, judge not, give not that which is holy to the dogs, ask, seek, and knock.

(David H. Yarn, *The Gospel: God, Man, and Truth* [Salt Lake City: Deseret Book, 1979], 70)

Daily Living

SEEK THE RIGHTEOUSNESS OF THE LORD.

- We should seek the righteousness of the Lord—Matthew 6:33
- To be accepted of the Lord we must do works of righteousness—Acts 10:35
- Righteousness comes of faith—Romans 9:30
- Wear the breastplate of righteousness—Ephesians 6:14
- If we are righteous, we are born of God—1 John 2:29
- If we are righteous, Satan has no power over us—1 Nephi 22:26
- The righteous shall inherit the kingdom of God—2 Nephi 9:18
- The righteous are honored by God—D&C 76:5

WO TO THE RICH—USE RICHES WISELY

Wo unto you rich men, that will not give your substance to the poor, for your riches will canker your souls; and this shall be your lamentation in the day of visitation, and of judgment, and of indignation: The harvest is past, the summer is ended, and my soul is not saved!

D&C 56:16

Elder Daniel H. Wells gives vital counsel to those who are blessed with the riches of the world, "I would say to you rich men, bring in your treasures to assist in building up God's kingdom. . . . I suppose the reason why so few of the wealthy embrace the Truth is, because they are too much choked up with pride, prejudice and the things of this life, so that there is scarcely room for anything else. 'The earth is the Lord's and the fulness thereof' [1 Cor. 10:26], and if the Lord gives a man means, he gives him an increase of power to do good, and he will consequently have more to account for. 'What shall it profit a man, if he should gain the whole world, and lose his own soul?' [Mark 8:36.]" (MS, October 23, 1864, 26:787).

(Roy W. Doxey, comp., *Latter-day Prophets and the Doctrine and Covenants* [Salt Lake City: Deseret Book, 1978], 2:214)

Daily Living

USE RICHES WISELY, ESPECIALLY TO BLESS THE POOR.

ᘓ How much is enough, how much should we save, how much do we give and to whom, what is best in the long run, when is spending unnecessary, when is giving of things hurtful rather than helpful? Remember the poor and needy—Alma 34:28; D&C 42:30

BEWARE OF GREED AND IDLENESS

Wo unto you poor men, whose hearts are not broken, whose spirits are not contrite, and whose bellies are not satisfied, and whose hands are not stayed from laying hold upon other men's goods, whose eyes are full of greediness, and who will not labor with your own hands!

D&C 56:17

President Marion G. Romney of the First Presidency explains, "I suppose the best way to live the principles of the law of consecration is to abide by the principles and practices of the welfare program. These principles and practices include avoiding idleness and greed, contributing liberal fast offerings and other welfare donations, paying a full tithing."

(Rulon T. Burton, *We Believe* [Salt Lake City: Bookcraft, 1994], 118)

Daily Living

BE GIVING AND WORK DILIGENTLY.

ꟸ In Paul's epistle to Timothy he cautions us to not be guilty in regard to being "not greedy of filthy lucre" (1 Timothy 3:3). The Lord reminds us, "Now, I, the Lord, am not well pleased with the inhabitants of Zion, for there are idlers among them; and their children are also growing up in wickedness; they also seek not earnestly the riches of eternity, but their eyes are full of greediness" (D&C 68:31). Greed is of pride and the devil, while charity comes from the pure love of Christ. Diligence and work are of the Lord, while idleness is of the devil—all good comes from God—Alma 5:40

PURITY OF HEART

But blessed are the poor who are pure in heart, whose hearts are broken, and whose spirits are contrite, for they shall see the kingdom of God coming in power and great glory unto their deliverance; for the fatness of the earth shall be theirs.
D&C 56:18

The pure-in-heart person will become Christ-like. . . . How can we think an unkind thought? How can we gossip or be critical if we have the pure love of Christ? How could we dare to be immodest in dress or thought? How would we dare to do less than our prophet has done? We must love and forgive every soul that walks the earth. . . . As you follow the Master you will find the fruit of your labors to be delicious unto your soul. You will find that all the world has to offer is sham compared to the gospel truths. Strive with all your . . . soul to be pure in heart that you may be worthy to see God and to live with him and with your family eternally.

(Vaughn J. Featherstone, "Purity of Heart," *New Era*, Aug 1973, 5)

Daily Living

BLESSED ARE THE PURE IN HEART.

ꟸ Seek with your whole soul to be pure in heart, for as you think in your heart so shall you be—Proverbs 23:7

CITY OF ZION

Wherefore, this is the land of promise, and the place for the city of Zion. And thus saith the Lord your God, if you will receive wisdom here is wisdom. Behold, the place which is now called Independence is the center place; and a spot for the temple is lying westward, upon a lot which is not far from the courthouse.
D&C 57:2–3

In 1830, the Lord indicated that the location for the city of Zion was not yet revealed (D&C 28:9). One year later, the Lord made known that this holy city was to be located at the place known as Independence, Jackson County, Missouri (D&C 57:1–4). Although the Saints failed in their initial attempts to establish this special city, it will be built and become known as the New Jerusalem. It will be the "sanctified place from whence shall go forth the law" of the Lord during the Millennium (DS 3:67). This city is not to be confused with the ancient city of Zion, established by Enoch (Moses 7:18–19, 68–69).

(Hoyt W. Brewster, Jr., *Doctrine and Covenants Encyclopedia* [Salt Lake City: Bookcraft, 1988], 87)

Daily Living

SEEK TO BUILD UP ZION BY BEING PURE IN HEART.

ஐ Remember that Zion is wherever the pure in heart dwell. Let us become a Zion-type people with a purity in our hearts that governs all our motives with righteousness, a Zion family, a Zion ward, a Zion Stake, even to a point that we are collectively a Zion Church, full of love and righteousness—D&C 97:21

BE SUBMISSIVE TO THE LORD

Let no man think he is ruler; but let God rule him that judgeth, according to the counsel of his own will, or, in other words, him that counseleth or sitteth upon the judgment seat.
D&C 58:20

This experience taught me firsthand that a testimony is not enough. I had just finished thirteen volumes about the life of Joseph Smith and I knew he was a prophet, but I wasn't doing much about it. Therefore, I realized, the gospel was not changing my life. I decided right then that I was going to be more submissive to what the Lord would have me do now, in this period of time, inasmuch as this is when He chose to have me come to the earth. In effect, I laid everything on the altar. The gospel is true. What would the Lord have me do about it?

(Glenn L. Pace, *Spiritual Plateaus* [Salt Lake City: Deseret Book, 1991], 48)

Daily Living

BE SUBMISSIVE WITH HUMILITY AND LOVE.

- Submissiveness is all about humility and love. It is a result of one who "yields to the enticings of the Holy Spirit, and putteth off the natural man and becometh a saint through the atonement of Christ the Lord, and becometh as a child, submissive, meek, humble, patient, full of love, willing to submit to all things which the Lord seeth fit to inflict upon him, even as a child doth submit to his father"—Mosiah 3:19
- We yield our hearts to God—Helaman 3:35

OBEY THE LAWS OF THE LAND

Let no man break the laws of the land, for he that keepeth the laws of God hath no need to break the laws of the land.
D&C 58:21

Just suppose that everyone in the world enthusiastically believed in and lived each one of the Ten Commandments, the Sermon on the Mount, the Word of Wisdom, and all of the other great laws of God. Then almost all of our problems would almost immediately disappear. If we followed the morality, the fairness, the honesty, the industry taught in the holy scriptures, the great divorce carnage that now desolates our land could be immediately wiped out. To follow the scriptures, obey the laws of the land, and utilize the other important principles of success would prosper us in our occupations, make us happy in our families, and give effectiveness to our social relationships. Following these great Christian principles would make us good citizens and pleasant neighbors, and would also lead us along that straight and narrow path to the celestial kingdom.

(Sterling W. Sill, *Principles, Promises, and Powers* [Salt Lake City: Deseret Book, 1973], 11)

Daily Living

OBEY THE LAWS OF THE LAND.

- The basic moral laws of good governments are rooted in the teachings of the Lord Jesus Christ. Therefore when we obey the laws of the land, we are obeying the laws of God—Article of Faith 1:12

ANXIOUSLY ENGAGED IN A GOOD CAUSE

For behold, it is not meet that I should command in all things; for he that is compelled in all things, the same is a slothful and not a wise servant; wherefore he receiveth no reward. Verily I say, men should be anxiously engaged in a good cause, and do many things of their own free will, and bring to pass much righteousness.

D&C 58:26–27

President Spencer W. Kimball . . . said, "I believe in goals, but I believe that the individual should set his own. Goals should always be made to a point that will make us reach and strain. Success should not necessarily be gauged by always reaching the goal set, but by progress and attainment." In setting our own goals we need to examine our own needs and abilities. The direction in which we are moving is more important than where we are at the moment. Goal-setting should cause us to stretch as we make our way.

(Marvin J. Ashton, *Be of Good Cheer* [Salt Lake City: Deseret Book, 1987], 49)

Daily Living

BE ANXIOUSLY ENGAGED IN A GOOD CAUSE.

❧ Our true self is expressed by what we do when we have free time, are alone, and have no external pressure to perform or obey. We could ask ourselves questions like, "What is the most enjoyable thing I have done lately?" "What goals am I setting?" "Who can I help today?" This little evaluation will bring in focus that which matters most to us—to be good and do good—2 Nephi 33:4; Moroni 7:16

YOU HAVE THE POWER TO DO GOOD

For the power is in them, wherein they are agents unto themselves. And inasmuch as men do good they shall in nowise lose their reward.
D&C 58:28

I want your prayers—your continued confidence, and your good wishes and fellowship. I want the Spirit of God and His angels to be with me; and I fear not earth, nor hell, nor men, nor devils, nor death. I desire power to do good continually, and to bring about the restoration of His people. I glory in my calling. I would not exchange it for any other position or calling on this earth.
(Parley P. Pratt, *Autobiography of Parley Pratt*, ed. Parley Pratt [Salt Lake City: Deseret Book, 1985], 357)

Daily Living

YOU HAVE THE POWER TO DO GOOD.

- We were created to do good works—Ephesians 2:10
- Use riches for the intent of doing good—Jacob 2:19
- Always abound in good works—Mosiah 5:15; Alma 7:24
- We show our faith by our good works—James 2:18
- Remember, it is by grace we are saved after all we can do—2 Nephi 25:23
- Good works are part of our gaining exaltation and eternal life, for we are judged by our works—Alma 5:15
- Remember, now is the time to perform our labors—Alma 34:32

DOUBT NOT—BE DILIGENT

But he that doeth not anything until he is commanded, and receiveth a commandment with doubtful heart, and keepeth it with slothfulness, the same is damned.
D&C 58:29

We should labor with fidelity and diligence to accomplish what God has designed to do through us. We should be men and women of faith and power as well as good works; and when we discover ourselves careless or indifferent in the least, it should be sufficient for us to know it in order to mend our ways and return to the path of duty.
(Lorenzo Snow, *The Teachings of Lorenzo Snow*, ed. Clyde J. Williams [Salt Lake City: Bookcraft, 1984], 48)

Daily Living

BE DILIGENT AND DEVOTED IN ALL THINGS.

ꝏ We can do all things by faith. Doubt and fear can destroy your faith. The seeds of doubt are sown with unbelief, lack of trust, uncertainty, and suspicion. To overcome doubt we strengthen our faith and drive doubt and fear out of our very being. We strengthen our faith with the word of God and fervent prayer. This takes effort, and the word the Lord uses over and over in His scriptures is *diligence.* To be diligent means to be conscientious, constant, hard-working, indefatigable, persistent, tireless, unflagging, unrelenting, and with all unwearyingness . . . in other words, work hard. May we be diligent in doing our duty in the work of the Lord—D&C 107:99–100

REPENT AND BE FORGIVEN

Behold, he who has repented of his sins, the same is forgiven, and I, the Lord, remember them no more. By this ye may know if a man repenteth of his sins—behold, he will confess them and forsake them.

D&C 58:42–43

Don't ever feel that you can't be forgiven. Our Father in Heaven loves you. . . . He has great concern for you. He reaches out to you in love and in forgiveness. . . . Our Father in Heaven will take care of the forgiveness. You put it behind you. You talk with your bishop. You live in righteousness. You do what is right and things will work out for you. I don't want to see you going around brooding forever about something. . . . There is hope. There is forgiveness. There is peace for those who follow the right path.

(Gordon B. Hinckley, *Teachings of Gordon B. Hinckley* [Salt Lake City: Deseret Book, 1997], 231)

Daily Living

SEEK FORGIVENESS THROUGH REPENTANCE AND RIGHTEOUSNESS.

ꙮ Forgiveness of sins and knowing our standing before our Savior and Heavenly Father is of great import to our minds and to our very souls. Our responsibility is to confess and forsake our sins. When we truly repent, we have an overwhelming desire to do good (see Enos 1; Helaman 12:24; Alma 36:24). Repentance and forgiveness are personified by good works and often require time to heal the soul. Repentance and forgiveness are processes, not events—Topical Guide, see "Repentance," "Forgiveness," and "Righteousness."

June 19

LOVE AND SERVE GOD

Wherefore, I give unto them a commandment, saying thus: Thou shalt love the Lord thy God with all thy heart, with all thy might, mind, and strength; and in the name of Jesus Christ thou shalt serve him.

D&C 59:5

If you would find yourself, learn to deny yourself for the blessing of others. Forget yourself and find someone who needs your service, and you will discover the secret to the happy, fulfilled life. You can get an individual to do selfless service. Such service is its own reward. Help him to have that experience, then he will know the joy that comes from serving the Lord. . . . To lose yourself in righteous service to others can lift your sights and get your mind off personal problems, or at least put them in proper focus.

(Ezra Taft Benson, *The Teachings of Ezra Taft Benson* [Salt Lake City: Bookcraft, 1988], 449)

Daily Living

LOVE AND SERVE GOD IN ALL THINGS.

- When we love the Lord we will always want to keep the commandments—John 14:15
- When we serve others we are in the service of God—Mosiah 2:17
- What we do for others is doing it to the Lord—Matt 25:40
- Yes, the love of God and your fellow men does fulfill all the law and the prophets—Matthew 22:36–40

LOVE THY NEIGHBOR

Thou shalt love thy neighbor as thyself. Thou shalt not steal; neither commit adultery, nor kill, nor do anything like unto it.
D&C 59:6

The Master said, "Love thy neighbor as thyself" (Matthew 22:39)—[love] is the key word to the Latter-day Saints, if I may use that term, to bring us near to the Lord, loving his children as we love ourselves and . . . bringing to them the knowledge of the truth. . . . The gospel teaches us to love our neighbor as ourselves, and if we will do that, we will not be distressed, we will not have our feelings wounded, part of us will not be well-to-do while others are living in poverty. If we love our neighbor as ourselves, we will all do our full part, and our Heavenly Father has promised us his blessings in return.

(George Albert Smith, *The Teachings of George Albert Smith*, ed. Robert McIntosh and Susan McIntosh [Salt Lake City: Bookcraft, 1996], 135)

Daily Living

LOVE YOUR NEIGHBOR, AND YOU WILL NOT SIN AGAINST HIM.

- When we truly love our neighbor we will not sin against them by committing sins like lying, stealing, coveting, and adultery or in any way bring harm to them. We do unto others as we would have them do unto us—Matthew 7:12
- When we love our neighbor, we care for the welfare of his soul—Mosiah 28:3

THANK THE LORD THY GOD

Thou shalt thank the Lord thy God in all things.
D&C 59:7

We pay our debt of gratitude by living in such a way as to bring credit to our parents and the name we bear, by doing good to others, by being of service, by being willing to share the light and knowledge we have received so that others will also have joy and happiness, by living the principles of the gospel in their fulness. Paul told us we should be filled with the Spirit, "giving thanks always for all things unto God and the Father in the name of our Lord Jesus Christ" (Ephesians 5:20).

(Howard W. Hunter, *The Teachings of Howard W. Hunter*, ed. Clyde J. Williams [Salt Lake City: Bookcraft, 1997], 93)

Daily Living

THANK THE LORD THY GOD IN ALL THINGS.

- There can never be enough said concerning the value and blessing of expressing thanksgiving. Expressing gratitude and thanksgiving is indeed a commandment, and it is offensive to God when we fail to give thanks—D&C 59:21
- Abound with thanksgiving—Colossians 2:7
- Prayer of praise and thanksgiving—D&C 136:28
- Start a gratitude journal. Make a list of all those you could call, e-mail, write, or visit to express your gratitude. You will feel terrific, and you will brighten their day.

OFFER A BROKEN HEART AND CONTRITE SPIRIT

Thou shalt offer a sacrifice unto the Lord thy God in righteousness, even that of a broken heart and a contrite spirit.
D&C 59:8

The "broken heart and contrite spirit" are reflected in one's attitudes and desires. This emphasis on the heart and the spirit demonstrates that training the inner man—inward spirituality—is also requisite for baptism by water and by fire. (See 2 Nephi 2:7; 3 Nephi 9:19–20; 3 Nephi 12:19; Ether 4:15.) . . . This kind of humility is not just sorrow for sin but is also an attitude of gratitude for the Savior's sacrifice and a recognition of one's total and complete dependence upon his merits and mercy.

(Joseph Fielding McConkie and Robert L. Millet, *Doctrinal Commentary on the Book of Mormon*, 4 vols. [Salt Lake City: Bookcraft, 1992], 4:329)

Daily Living

Offer a sacrifice of a broken heart and contrite spirit.

- From the beginning of time the Lord has required sacrifice to remind us of the Atonement—Moses 5:7
- A broken heart and contrite spirit reflect one's humility, sorrow for sin, and willingness to lay all upon the altar of the Lord, thus qualifying for baptism, partaking of the sacrament, and receiving the blessings of the Lord, and are required by the Lord today—3 Nephi 9:20
- The Lord is with those with a contrite spirit—Isaiah 57:15
- The Spirit enlightens the humble and contrite—D&C 136:33

THE SABBATH—A HOLY DAY

And that thou mayest more fully keep thyself unspotted from the world, thou shalt go to the house of prayer and offer up thy sacraments upon my holy day; For verily this is a day appointed unto you to rest from your labors, and to pay thy devotions unto the Most High.

D&C 59:9–10

It is a day of worship, a day in which the spiritual life of man may be enriched. . . . My belief is that it is the duty of Latter-day Saints to honor the Sabbath day and keep it holy, just as the Lord has commanded us to do. Go to the house of prayer. Listen to instructions. Bear your testimony to the truth. Drink at the fountain of knowledge and of instruction, as it may be opened for us from those who are inspired to give us instruction.

(Joseph F. Smith, *Gospel Doctrine: Selections from the Sermons and Writings of Joseph F. Smith*, compiled by John A. Widtsoe [Salt Lake City: Deseret Book, 1939], 242)

Daily Living

KEEP THE SABBATH DAY SACRED AND HOLY.

- The purpose of the Sabbath day is to worship God, rest from our daily labors, renew our covenants, receive gospel instruction, and receive edification to our spirits. The Sabbath is a day to magnify our callings, caring for those who need help or, in other words, practicing pure religion—James 1:27
- Sabbath observance "is a sign between me and you throughout your generations; that ye may know that I am the Lord that doth sanctify you"—Exodus 31:13

FAST AND PRAY WITH A CHEERFUL HEART

Verily, this is fasting and prayer, or in other words, rejoicing and prayer. And inasmuch as ye do these things with thanksgiving, with cheerful hearts and countenances, not with much laughter, for this is sin, but with a glad heart and a cheerful countenance.
D&C 59:14–15

An affair of the heart. Fasting is intended to be an affair of the heart rather than an outward manifestation, just as secret prayer is recommended by the Master in preference to the display of the Pharisees. One who fasts need not by a long face, or by a pained expression of countenance, or making a virtue of abstaining from his customary work, give public notice in this manner of his observance of the fast. The main thing is to bring the heart and being into a condition receptive to the influences of the good Spirit and to approach in prayer the throne of the Father with a soul filled with praise, humility and faith.

(George Q. Cannon, *Gospel Truth: Discourses and Writings of President George Q. Cannon*, selected, arranged, and ed. Jerreld L. Newquist [Salt Lake City: Deseret Book, 1987], 406)

Daily Living

LET US FAST AND PRAY WITH HUMILITY AND PURPOSE.

ꝏ We are counseled always to fast with a purpose: for the welfare of others, to know truth, or in improving ourselves in righteousness, seeking a worthy blessing, expressing our love and gratitude, or serving our God and our fellow man—Alma 5:46; 6:6; 17:3; Helaman 3:35; Mark 17:21

GRATITUDE TO GOD

And in nothing doth man offend God, or against none is his wrath kindled, save those who confess not his hand in all things, and obey not his commandments.

D&C 59:21

How magnificently we are blessed! . . . Let us cultivate a spirit of thanksgiving for the blessing of life and for the marvelous gifts and privileges each of us enjoys. The Lord has said that the meek shall inherit the earth (Matthew 5:5). I cannot escape the interpretation that meekness implies a spirit of gratitude as opposed to an attitude of self-sufficiency, an acknowledgment of a greater power beyond oneself, a recognition of God, and an acceptance of his commandments. This is the beginning of wisdom. Walk with gratitude before him who is the giver of life and every good gift.

(Gordon B. Hinckley, *Faith: The Essence of True Religion* [Salt Lake City: Deseret Book, 1989], 82)

Daily Living

GIVE THANKS UNTO GOD FOR ALL THINGS.

- In giving thanks unto God for all things, we are still indebted to Him—Mosiah 2:21
- When we live in thanksgiving daily, our minds are filled with gratitude for all things—Alma 34:38
- Every part of our life is a blessing from God. With a grateful heart we will recognize more and more of what God has given us. Remember, gratitude is a catalyst that moves us to action in everything—1 Thessalonians 5:18

BLESSINGS IN RIGHTEOUSNESS

But learn that he who doeth the works of righteousness shall receive his reward, even peace in this world and eternal life in the world to come.
D&C 59:23

The scriptures teach that righteousness is obedience to law. The scriptures also teach that every blessing is predicated upon obedience to law. Thus, righteousness results in blessings. However, righteousness (obedience to law) would not be possible unless unrighteousness (disobedience to law) were also a possibility. Our Heavenly Father gave to man the opportunity of choice by giving him law. He also gave the freedom of choice to man from the very beginning in the days of Adam. Agency *on this earth* is a gift from God and, when used in righteousness, can help man achieve blessings, including eternal life, which is the greatest blessing of all.

(Daniel H. Ludlow, *A Companion to Your Study of Doctrine and Covenants* [Salt Lake City: Deseret Book, 1978], 103)

Daily Living

EXALTATION IS CONDITIONAL UPON YOUR RIGHTEOUSNESS.

- Righteousness entails believing God, obeying Him, and enduring all the trials, tribulations, and persecutions of this life. We must hunger and thirst after righteousness, thus being filled with the Holy Ghost—3 Nephi 12:6
- Our obedience, which leads to righteousness, will prepare us to receive all the Lord's blessings—Mosiah 2:41

OPEN YOUR MOUTH

But with some I am not well pleased, for they will not open their mouths, but they hide the talent which I have given unto them, because of the fear of man. Wo unto such, for mine anger is kindled against them. And it shall come to pass, if they are not more faithful unto me, it shall be taken away, even that which they have.

D&C 60:2–3

This ought to be an ensample unto all those who are ordained to the holy Priesthood and moved upon by the Holy Ghost, and more especially to those whose mission is appointed unto them to preach the Gospel. Because the instruction is that "they shall speak as they are moved upon by the Holy Ghost."

(J. Golden Kimball, in Conference Report, April 1934, 33)

Daily Living

TO PLEASE THE LORD WE MUST OPEN OUR MOUTHS.

- We are to stand as witnesses at all times and places and in all things—Mosiah 18:9
- As we bear testimony, our sins are forgiven—D&C 62:3
- The Lord will give to us the things we need to say, provided we treasure up the word of God—D&C 84:85
- The Lord will go before our face so we have no need to fear—D&C 84:88
- Let us follow the Lord's counsel and open our mouths—D&C 33:8–11
- The Lord will put in our hearts what we should say—Helaman 13:5

BEAR YOUR TESTIMONY

Nevertheless, ye are blessed, for the testimony which ye have borne is recorded in heaven for the angels to look upon; and they rejoice over you, and your sins are forgiven you.
D&C 62:3

There are two dimensions to testimony. The one, a *testimony we bear to them*, has power to lift and bless them. The other, infinitely more important, *the testimony they bear themselves*, has the power to redeem and exalt them. You might say they can get a testimony from what we say. *The* testimony comes when they themselves bear a witness of the truth and the Holy Ghost confirms it to them.

(Boyd K. Packer, *Let Not Your Heart Be Troubled* [Salt Lake City: Bookcraft, 1991], 15)

Daily Living

BEAR YOUR TESTIMONY AND YOUR SINS ARE FORGIVEN.

ꟸ A testimony is the priceless knowledge of eternal truths received by the power of the Holy Ghost. You should: Desire to know the truth. 2. Study the word of God from the scriptures and living prophets. The word of God has power to change you (see Alma 13:5), and it will tell you all things to do (see 2 Ne. 32:3) 3. Fast and pray to know the truth. Heavenly Father will give you answers to your prayers (see James 1:5–6). 4. Live your testimony. When you live the things you believe, this practice becomes part of your nature. 5. Bear your testimony. The more you bear your testimony by the Spirit, the stronger it will become.

SIGNS

And he that seeketh signs shall see signs, but not unto salvation. Verily, I say unto you, there are those among you who seek signs, and there have been such even from the beginning; But, behold, faith cometh not by signs, but signs follow those that believe. Yea, signs come by faith, not by the will of men, nor as they please, but by the will of God. Yea, signs come by faith, unto mighty works, for without faith no man pleaseth God; and with whom God is angry he is not well pleased; wherefore, unto such he showeth no signs, only in wrath unto their condemnation.

D&C 63:7–11

It is a wicked and adulterous generation that seeketh after a sign. Show me Latter-day Saints who have to feed upon miracles, signs and visions in order to keep them steadfast in the Church, and I will show you members of the Church who are not in good standing before God. . . . By the whisperings of the still small voice of the Spirit of the living God, he gave to me the testimony I possess. . . . And no amount of marvelous manifestations will ever accomplish this.

(Joseph F. Smith, *Gospel Doctrine: Selections from the Sermons and Writings of Joseph F. Smith*, compiled by John A. Widtsoe [Salt Lake City: Deseret Book, 1939], 7)

Daily Living

UNDERSTAND THE SIGNS OF THE COMING OF THE LORD.

- Seek light and truth. Be wise to the signs given as to the coming of the Lord—Matthew 16:3; 24:3, 30

LUST

And verily I say unto you, as I have said before, he that looketh on a woman to lust after her, or if any shall commit adultery in their hearts, they shall not have the Spirit, but shall deny the faith and shall fear.

D&C 63:16

I postulated firmly, "No, my beloved young people, you did not love each other. Rather, you lusted for each other." . . . The beautiful and holy word of love they had defiled until it had degenerated to become a bed fellow with lust, its antithesis. . . . If one really loves another, one would rather die for that person than to injure him. At the hour of sin, pure love is pushed out of one door while lust sneaks in the other. . . . When the unmarried yield to lust, that is called fornication. When married fall into this same sin, that is called adultery.

(Spencer W. Kimball, *The Teachings of Spencer W. Kimball*, ed. Edward L. Kimball [Salt Lake City: Bookcraft, 1982], 279)

Daily Living

LUST NOT AT ALL ELSE YOU LOSE THE SPIRIT.

- Lusting often precedes the consummation of the act. Remember, as you think in your heart so are you—Proverbs 23:7
- When we think or desire these things which are unholy and sinful, we lose the Spirit—Mormon 1:13–14
- The Lord cannot reside in unclean and unholy temples but only in the hearts of the righteous—Alma 34:36

JULY

Verily, verily, I say unto you, ye are little children, and ye have not as yet understood how great blessings the Father hath in his own hands and prepared for you;

And ye cannot bear all things now; nevertheless, be of good cheer, for I will lead you along. The kingdom is yours and the blessings thereof are yours, and the riches of eternity are yours.

—Doctrine & Covenants 78:17–18

ENDURING FAITH AND OBEDIENCE

Nevertheless, he that endureth in faith and doeth my will, the same shall overcome, and shall receive an inheritance upon the earth when the day of transfiguration shall come.
D&C 63:20

We have taken upon ourselves the name of Jesus and the way of the disciple. Our way will also lead to gardens of anguished prayer, to crosses, to tombs. At those times, we, like the apostles, must endure in faith and love. We must endure despite our pain, *with* our pain, in the depths of our pain, until the moment of the resurrection in us when we understand the greater purpose in the cross and the tomb. I testify to you that those moments of understanding and acceptance will come.

(Chieko N. Okazaki, *Aloha!* [Salt Lake City: Deseret Book, 1995], 101)

Daily Living

ENDURE CHEERFULLY—ENDURE WITH FAITH—ENDURE TO THE END.

- One who endures is always doing the will of the Lord and is empowered by the Lord to overcome all trials and tribulations. He will give you support and strength—2 Nephi 4:20–35
- Press forward feasting upon the word of God and endure to the end, and ye shall have eternal life—2 Nephi 31:20

FORGIVE ONE ANOTHER

My disciples, in days of old, sought occasion against one another and forgave not one another in their hearts; and for this evil they were afflicted and sorely chastened. Wherefore, I say unto you, that ye ought to forgive one another; for he that forgiveth not his brother his trespasses standeth condemned before the Lord; for there remaineth in him the greater sin. I, the Lord, will forgive whom I will forgive, but of you it is required to forgive all men. And ye ought to say in your hearts—let God judge between me and thee, and reward thee according to thy deeds.

D&C 64:8–11

We should be patient and forgiving of ourselves as well as others. . . . But God is usually more willing to forgive us than we are willing to forgive ourselves. . . . We ought never to be destructive in our criticism of others, but perhaps our greatest caution needs to be regarding the tendency to be destructive in the criticism we apply to ourselves.

(Howard W. Hunter, *The Teachings of Howard W. Hunter*, ed. Clyde J. Williams [Salt Lake City: Bookcraft, 1997], 34–35)

Daily Living

BE FORGIVING AND OBTAIN FORGIVENESS.

- Lest we forget, our greatest need is to be forgiven of our sins, for all who seek righteousness seek forgiveness. Remember you are forgiven as you likewise are merciful and forgiving—3 Nephi 13:13–14
- In our own repentance we must be forgiving—Mosiah 26:31

CHURCH DISCIPLINE

And him that repenteth not of his sins, and confesseth them not, ye shall bring before the church, and do with him as the scripture saith unto you, either by commandment or by revelation. And this ye shall do that God may be glorified—not because ye forgive not, having not compassion, but that ye may be justified in the eyes of the law, that ye may not offend him who is your lawgiver—Verily I say, for this cause ye shall do these things.

D&C 64:12–14

Church discipline is founded upon gospel doctrines and principles, including the fact that repentance is necessary to qualify for the mercy made possible through the Atonement. Church discipline aids repentance and the change of life that is essential for salvation.

(Dallin H. Oaks, *The Lord's Way* [Salt Lake City: Deseret Book, 1991], 13)

Daily Living

CHURCH DISCIPLINE IS DESIGNED TO HELP PEOPLE REPENT.

- Church disciplinary action provides a way for people to repent. It is based on love just as the Lord's chastening is based upon His love for us—D&C 95:1–2
- Those who will not endure chastening through Church discipline are not worthy of the kingdom—D&C 136:31

BE NOT WEARY IN WELL-DOING

Wherefore, be not weary in well-doing, for ye are laying the foundation of a great work. And out of small things proceedeth that which is great.

D&C 64:33

All have the duty to share the gospel with others and to serve formally and informally as missionaries. All have a duty to identify their deceased ancestors and to help bring to them the blessings of the temple. All should diligently strive to be temporally prepared and to care for the poor and the needy. All should seek to strengthen those who are less active in the Church and to magnify their callings in their wards and stakes by giving faithful and devoted service. . . . Being true to one's duty is the mark of a true disciple of the Lord and a child of God. May we be valiant in our duty, stay in step, and not fail in our most important task: keeping our second estate. Being true to our duty will bring us to God.

(Joseph B. Wirthlin, *Finding Peace in Our Lives* [Salt Lake City: Deseret Book, 1995], 94–95)

Daily Living

OUR ATTITUDE TOWARD OUR EFFORTS DETERMINES OUR BLESSINGS.

- The motive for which an act is performed determines to a large extent the reward given by the Lord—Moroni 7:5–7
- The desires of our hearts will bring us joy in doing the work of the Lord—Alma 26:11, 35; 27:17; D&C 18:16
- When we become swallowed up in the service of our Savior and our fellow man we will never weary of good works—Alma 37:34

WHAT DOTH THE LORD REQUIRE?

Behold, the Lord requireth the heart and a willing mind; and the willing and obedient shall eat the good of the land of Zion in these last days.
D&C 64:34

A wise man of experience observed: Men will work hard for money. They will work harder for other men. But men will work hardest of all when they are dedicated to a cause. Until willingness overflows obligation, men fight as conscripts rather than following the flag as patriots. Duty is never worthily performed until it is performed by one who would gladly do more if only he could.

Man does not by himself run the race of life. When we help another in his race of life, we really serve our God. King Benjamin stated the principle so beautifully, ". . . when ye are in the service of your fellow beings ye are only in the service of your God" (Mosiah 2:17).

(Thomas S. Monson, *Pathways to Perfection* [Salt Lake City: Deseret Book, 1984], 278)

Daily Living

THE LORD REQUIRES THE HEART AND A WILLING MIND.

℘ All we can truly give is our heart and willing mind, a gift of self. The Lord said of Nephi, the son of Helaman, "I have beheld how thou hast with unwearyingness declared the word . . . hast sought my will . . . I will bless thee forever; and I will make thee mighty in word and in deed . . . even that all things shall be done unto thee according to thy word"—Helaman 10:4–5

PRAY FOR THE KINGDOM OF GOD

Call upon the Lord, that his kingdom may go forth upon the earth, that the inhabitants thereof may receive it, and be prepared for the days to come, in the which the Son of Man shall come down in heaven, clothed in the brightness of his glory, to meet the kingdom of God which is set up on the earth. Wherefore, may the kingdom of God go forth, that the kingdom of heaven may come, that thou, O God, mayest be glorified in heaven so on earth, that thine enemies may be subdued; for thine is the honor, power and glory, forever and ever. Amen.

D&C 65:5–6

The work of The Church of Jesus Christ of Latter-day Saints may be summed up as the preparation of the earth for the coming of its Lord and King . . . and the proclamation is made now, "The kingdom of heaven is at hand." [D&C 33:10; 42:7.] That proclamation is authoritatively sounded throughout the world, and the work of the Church, which is veritably the kingdom of God, is to prepare the earth for the coming of the King of earth and heaven, and for the establishment of the kingdom of heaven upon the earth.

(James E. Talmage, in Conference Report, April 1917, 66)

Daily Living

PRAY FOR THE KINGDOM OF GOD.

- Seek first to build up the kingdom of God and His righteousness—JST—Matthew 6:38
- Our prayers should seek blessings for the kingdom of God and His children—Matthew 6:10; Alma 6:6

SEEK AND KNOW GOD

And again, verily I say unto you that it is your privilege, and a promise I give unto you that have been ordained unto this ministry, that inasmuch as you strip yourselves from jealousies and fears, and humble yourselves before me, for ye are not sufficiently humble, the veil shall be rent and you shall see me and know that I am—not with the carnal neither natural mind, but with the spiritual.

D&C 67:10

I know, as well as I know that I live and look into your faces, that Jesus Christ lives, and he is the Redeemer of the world, that he arose from the dead with a tangible body. . . . For in the visions of the Lord to my soul, I have seen Christ's face, I have heard his voice. I know that he lives, that he is the Redeemer of the World.

(Melvin J. Ballard, in Conference Report, April 1920, 40–41)

Daily Living

SEEK AND PREPARE TO KNOW GOD.

℘ Put away your jealousies as you pray with all the energy of your heart for charity. Overcome fear with increased faith, perfect love, knowledge, preparation, and experience. You gain humility as you remember your total dependence upon Heavenly Father and understand and appreciate your relationship with Him. The fruits of humility are being teachable, easily entreated, submissive, and coming forth with a broken heart and contrite spirit—Moroni 7:48; 1 John 4:18; D&C 38:30; Helaman 3:35; Alma 7:23

SPEAK BY THE HOLY GHOST

And this is the ensample unto them, that they shall speak as they are moved upon by the Holy Ghost. And whatsoever they shall speak when moved upon by the Holy Ghost shall be scripture, shall be the will of the Lord, shall be the mind of the Lord, shall be the word of the Lord, shall be the voice of the Lord, and the power of God unto salvation.

D&C 68:3–4

Harold B. Lee said, "If you want to know what the Lord would have the Saints know and to have his guidance and direction for the next six months, get a copy of the proceedings of this conference. . . . And [also] all others who are not of us, but who believe what has been said has been 'the mind of the Lord, the will of the Lord, and the voice of the Lord, and the power of God unto salvation.'" (See D&C 68:4.)

(quoted in Daniel H. Ludlow, *A Companion to Your Study of the Doctrine and Covenants* [Salt Lake City: Deseret Book, 1978], 2:253)

Daily Living

SPEAK AS MOVED UPON BY THE HOLY GHOST.

- To speak by the Spirit, we must be a of a sound understanding, wax strong in the knowledge of the truth, search the scriptures, fast, and pray—Alma 17:2–3
- Pray with faith, else you cannot teach—D&C 42:14
- The Lord will provide what we should say—D&C 84:85
- The Lord will put it into our hearts—D&C 100:5–6

REQUIREMENTS TO BE SAVED

And he that believeth and is baptized shall be saved, and he that believeth not shall be damned.
D&C 68:9

All who believe on him and are baptized and endure to the end, shall be saved, no matter when they lived on the earth. Men everywhere must repent and believe in Christ, worshipping the Father in the name of the Son and enduring in faith, or they cannot be saved. Justification through grace is true, as also is sanctification, to all who love the Father with all their might, mind and strength. The dangers of falling away from grace are pointed out, with a warning to the members of the Church to "take heed and pray lest they fall into temptation."

(Joseph Fielding Smith, *Essentials in Church History* [Salt Lake City: Deseret Book, 1950], 74–75)

Daily Living

BELIEVE, BE BAPTIZED, AND BE SAVED.

- Remember that belief connotes the act of faith. Faith is necessary to please God—Hebrews 11:6
- Faith provides the power to repent—Enos 1:8
- Faith is exhibited and shown by your works—James 2:18
- Faith is necessary to do all things—Moroni 7:33
- We often take for granted our baptism, failing to remember the sacred covenant of taking the name of Jesus Christ upon us and remembering all of the associated commandments and qualifications to be baptized. It is well to review them and evaluate our life—D&C 20:37: Moroni 6:1–4; Mosiah 18:8

TEACH YOUR CHILDREN

And again, inasmuch as parents have children in Zion, or in any of her stakes which are organized, that teach them not to understand the doctrine of repentance, faith in Christ the Son of the living God, and of baptism and the gift of the Holy Ghost by the laying on of the hands, when eight years old, the sin be upon the heads of the parents. And they shall also teach their children to pray, and to walk uprightly before the Lord.

D&C 68:25, 28

David O. McKay said, "Let us begin at once as parents to maintain the kind of influence or home atmosphere that will contribute to the normal development of the children and eliminate from the home those elements which cause discord and strife. . . .

"The most effective way to teach religion in the home is not by preaching, but by living. If you would teach faith in God, show faith in him yourself; if you would teach prayer, pray yourself. Would you have them temperate? Then you yourself refrain from intemperance. If you would have your child live a life of virtue, of self-control, of good report, then set him a worthy example in all these things."

(Roy W. Doxey, comp., *Latter-day Prophets and the Doctrine and Covenants* [Salt Lake City: Deseret Book, 1978], 2:377–379)

Daily Living

PARENTS ARE TO TEACH THEIR CHILDREN.

১০ Teach your children by precept and example as directed by the Spirit. It is your greatest duty and joy as a parent.

IDLENESS, WICKEDNESS, AND GREED

Now, I, the Lord, am not well pleased with the inhabitants of Zion, for there are idlers among them; and their children are also growing up in wickedness; they also seek not earnestly the riches of eternity, but their eyes are full of greediness.
D&C 68:31

Greediness—the avaricious grasping for an unreasonable amount of this world's goods—is a sin (Prov. 1:19; 15:27; 21:26; Ezek. 22:12; Eph. 4: 19; 1 Tim. 3:3, 8; Judges 11). The idle poor who lay hold on other men's goods because their "eyes are full of greediness" are condemned by the Lord (D&C 56:17). Similar condemnation rests upon the saints who "seek not earnestly the riches of eternity but their eyes are full of greediness" (D&C 68:31).

(Bruce R. McConkie, *Mormon Doctrine*, 2d ed. [Salt Lake City: Bookcraft, 1966], 340)

Daily Living

DEVASTATION—THE RESULTS OF IDLENESS AND GREED.

- Again the Lord reminds of us of the devastating effects of idleness and greed. Nephi taught that pride and greed are part of the great and abominable church—1 Nephi 13:8
- Whether rich or poor, the Lord condemns those who will not give of their substance, who seek other men's goods and substance with greed, and yet are unwilling to labor with their own hands—D&C 56:16–17
- Remember, idleness is precursor to sin—1 Nephi 12:23; 2 Nephi 5:24

STEWARDSHIP AND ACCOUNTABILITY

Behold, this is what the Lord requires of every man in his stewardship, even as I, the Lord, have appointed or shall hereafter appoint unto any man. And behold, none are exempt from this law who belong to the church of the living God.
D&C 70:9–10

I have no doubt but that you will agree with me that men will be held accountable for the things which they have and not for the things they have not, or that all the light and intelligence communicated to them from their beneficent creator, whether it is much or little, by the same they in justice will be judged, and that they are required to yield obedience and improve upon that and that only which is given, for man is not to live by bread alone but by every word that proceeds out of the mouth of God.

(Joseph Smith, *Encyclopedia of Joseph Smith's Teachings*, ed. Larry E. Dahl and Donald Q. Cannon [Salt Lake City: Bookcraft, 1997], 448)

Daily Living

THE LORD REQUIRES OF EVERY MAN HIS STEWARDSHIP.

- We stand accountable before the Lord. We are accountable for our gifts and talents from God, our callings and eternal roles, our desires, thoughts, and actions. We will stand before the Lord to be judged according to our works—Alma 41:3
- Every stewardship we have been given will require an accounting before the Lord—Luke 16:2
- Be a diligent and wise steward—D&C 136:27

STEWARDSHIP AND ACCOUNTABILITY

And verily in this thing ye have done wisely, for it is required of the Lord, at the hand of every steward, to render an account of his stewardship, both in time and in eternity. For he who is faithful and wise in time is accounted worthy to inherit the mansions prepared for him of my Father. Verily I say unto you, the elders of the church in this part of my vineyard shall render an account of their stewardship unto the bishop, who shall be appointed of me in this part of my vineyard.

D&C 72:3–5

The stewardship principle *does* require us to make clear to those we supervise what their tasks, roles, and duties and our expectations of them are, so that they can know what is expected of them. The stewardship principle *does* place a premium on the leader's being a helping resource to the person who is being led or supervised. The leader should be seen as a friend and resource, rather than as a "threat" or someone who is always checking up. The stewardship principle *does* involve accountability at all levels for the tasks assigned.

(Neal A. Maxwell, *The Smallest Part* [Salt Lake City: Deseret Book, 1973], 57)

Daily Living

THE LORD CONTINUALLY EMPHASIZES ACCOUNTABILITY.

ꝏ The Lord uses repetition in teaching and continually reminds us of the things expected of us. Evaluate your stewardships and make your very best effort to magnify your callings—D&C 107:99–100

LITTLE CHILDREN ARE HOLY

But little children are holy, being sanctified through the atonement of Jesus Christ; and this is what the scriptures mean.
D&C 74:7

We are instructed to become as little children—dependent, submissive, trusting, humble, patient and persistent, delighted by simple pleasures, alive to life, carefree, and quick to forgive. And, above all, we are instructed to become pure through the atoning blood of our blessed Redeemer, even as children are. Mormon counseled his son Moroni: "This thing shall ye teach—repentance and baptism unto those who are accountable and capable of committing sin; yea, teach parents that they must repent and be baptized, and humble themselves as their little children, and they shall all be saved with their little children" (Moroni 8:10).

(Robert L. Millet, *Alive in Christ: The Miracle of Spiritual Rebirth* [Salt Lake City: Deseret Book, 1997], 71–72)

Daily Living

WE ARE TO BECOME AS LITTLE CHILDREN.

- We are to become as a child, "submissive, meek, humble, patient, full of love, willing to submit to all things which the Lord seeth fit to inflict upon him"—Mosiah 3:19)
- We are to be holy like unto the temple—1 Corinthians 3:17
- Walk in holiness before the Lord—D&C 20:69
- Remember, holiness refers to purity, sanctification, being morally complete, and free from sin.

FAITHFUL LADEN WITH SHEAVES

And thus, if ye are faithful ye shall be laden with many sheaves, and crowned with honor, and glory, and immortality, and eternal life.
D&C 75:5

The term *sheaves* is used four times in the Doctrine and Covenants, each time relating to missionary labors (D&C 31:5; 33:9; 75:5; 79:3). Those who go forth in the ministry, faithfully proclaiming the gospel with all their souls, shall be "laden with sheaves," or, in other words, reap a harvest of souls. "He that goeth . . . bearing precious seed, shall doubtless come again with rejoicing, bringing his sheaves with him," declared the Psalmist (Ps. 126:6). The great missionary Ammon reminded his fellow laborers that their faithful efforts had produced a number of sheaves (Alma 26:5).

(Hoyt W. Brewster, Jr., *Doctrine and Covenants Encyclopedia* [Salt Lake City: Bookcraft, 1988], 515)

Daily Living

FAITHFUL MISSIONARIES BRING MANY SOULS TO CHRIST.

- Missionaries (members, too) who faithfully and diligently open their mouths (see D&C 33:8–11), and thrust in their sickles with all their might, shall not only bring souls to Christ but shall be forgiven of sins—D&C 31:5
- Missionary work truly personifies our charity and caring for our fellow men—Mosiah 28:3
- We will find joy in the work—Alma 29:9–10; 36:24; D&C 18:10–16

BE DILIGENT IN ALL THINGS

Let every man be diligent in all things. And the idler shall not have place in the church, except he repent and mend his ways.
D&C 75:29

We must progress or lose what we have. . . . There is no man or woman who can stand still any great length of time. . . . Latter-day Saints should not permit themselves to stand still. It is a privilege we have to serve the Lord and enjoy His spirit in our labors, but many of the people lose that portion of happiness that they might enjoy because of not reflecting seriously upon their duties and acting wisely and prudently.

(Lorenzo Snow, *The Teachings of Lorenzo Snow*, ed. Clyde J. Williams [Salt Lake City: Bookcraft, 1984], 95)

Daily Living

BE DILIGENT IN ALL THINGS.

- Diligence encompasses applying all your skills with utmost care, with patience and constancy, exerting all your heart with unwearyingness and with vigor.
- We hearken diligently—Isaiah 55:2
- We search the scriptures diligently—Alma 17:2
- Give heed and diligence to the word of God—Alma 49:30
- We labor diligently—Moroni 9:6
- We serve with all diligence—Mosiah 7:33
- Be diligent in keeping the commandments—D&C 6:20
- Be diligent in pursuing charity, the divine nature of Christ—2 Peter 1:5; D&C 4:6

THE LORD HONORS THOSE WHO SERVE HIM

For thus saith the Lord—I, the Lord, am merciful and gracious unto those who fear me, and delight to honor those who serve me in righteousness and in truth unto the end. Great shall be their reward and eternal shall be their glory.

D&C 76:5–6

By putting everything we have on the altar of the Lord and not waiting for Him to give us a receipt, we show our submissiveness. Otherwise our giving may become linked with expecting recognition or with soliciting proof of the Lord's appreciation. After all, one day He will give everything to the faithful (D&C 84:38). God, who is perfect in His gratitude, "delights to honor those who serve" Him (D&C 76:5). Mortal recognition is so fleeting, but God remembers always those who remember Him.

(Neal A. Maxwell, *Not My Will, But Thine* [Salt Lake City: Bookcraft, 1988], 96)

Daily Living

THE LORD DELIGHTS TO HONOR THOSE WHO SERVE HIM.

- We are loved. All that our Heavenly Father and Savior do for us is motivated by love—John 3:16; 2 Nephi 26:24. This knowledge should fill our soul with gratitude and love for our Heavenly Father and Savior to the point that our desires are to love, serve, and keep the commandments of God, thus bringing joy to our Heavenly Father and our Savior. Their work and glory is found in blessing their children that they might partake of immortality and eternal life—Moses 1:39

THE POWER OF THE SPIRIT

By the power of the Spirit our eyes were opened and our understandings were enlightened, so as to see and understand the things of God.
D&C 76:12

It will come by the Holy Spirit, not by scholarly study or by mortal reasoning. When it comes, it will reveal to those who fear God and serve him "all mysteries, yea, all the hidden mysteries of [God's] kingdom from days of old, and for ages to come" (D&C 76:7). "Yea, verily I say unto you, in that day when the Lord shall come, he shall reveal all things" (D&C 101:32). In that day, as foreseen by Isaiah, "the earth shall be full of the knowledge of the Lord" (Isa. 11:9; 2 Ne. 21:9; also see D&C 84:98).

(Dallin H. Oaks, *The Lord's Way* [Salt Lake City: Deseret Book, 1991], 73)

Daily Living

THE POWER OF THE SPIRIT—TO UNDERSTAND AND ENLIGHTEN.

- We can only understand truth and the things of God by the power of the Holy Ghost—Moroni 10:5
- When we trust in the Spirit we will have a desire to do good, and our minds will be enlightened—D&C 11:12–13
- And thus we see that the Spirit is the key to all knowledge, learning, and the edifying of our souls—D&C 50:21–22
- We must live worthy of the Spirit and pray for its companionship and thus be shown all things what we should do—2 Nephi 32:5

THE RESURRECTION OF THE JUST

Speaking of the resurrection of the dead, concerning those who shall hear the voice of the Son of Man: And shall come forth; they who have done good in the resurrection of the just; and they who have done evil, in the resurrection of the unjust.
D&C 76:16–17

The term *resurrection of the just* appears in the Doctrine and Covenants only in the revelation known as "a vision" (D&C 76:17, 50, 65), although it is also found in the New Testament (Luke 14:14; Acts 24:15; JST, John 5:29). This phrase has been defined by Smith and Sjodahl as follows: "This is also called the *first resurrection*, but the truth is here taught that only those who are just will have part in it. To be *just* is to be upright and sincere in one's actions and dealings with others. It is to be like Christ, who suffered, the just for the unjust (1 Peter 3:18). To be just is also to be justified. That is to say, *one who is just is, by God Himself, declared to be as he ought to be.* Such are they who have part in the first resurrection" (SS, 459; italics added). The resurrection of the just includes both celestial and terrestrial beings, the latter being the "honorable men of the earth" (D&C 76:75).

(Hoyt W. Brewster, Jr., *Doctrine and Covenants Encyclopedia* [Salt Lake City: Bookcraft, 1996], 466)

Daily Living

COME FORTH IN THE MORNING OF THE FIRST RESURRECTION.

ఐ Prepare to meet God—Alma 34:32

TESTIMONY OF JESUS CHRIST

And now, after the many testimonies which have been given of him, this is the testimony, last of all, which we give of him: That he lives! For we saw him, even on the right hand of God; and we heard the voice bearing record that he is the Only Begotten of the Father—That by him, and through him, and of him, the worlds are and were created, and the inhabitants thereof are begotten sons and daughters unto God.

D&C 76:22–24

Joseph Smith and Sidney Rigdon also saw him, and bore testimony that they saw Him, even as Stephen saw Him [Acts 7:54–56], clothed in glory, surrounded by those inhabiting the celestial kingdom of God. They also saw God seated on His throne and Jesus Christ at His right hand, "And they heard the voice bearing record that He is the only begotten of the Father" [D&C 76:23]. So far as the Latter-day Saints are concerned, we know these things are true.

(Hyrum M. Smith, in Conference Report, October 1907, 34–35)

Daily Living

GAIN AND BEAR A PURE TESTIMONY OF JESUS CHRIST.

- We must never waver in bearing or living pure testimony. God is our Father, Jesus is the Christ, and the gospel has been restored through the Book of Mormon, which was translated by Joseph Smith through the gift and power of God and is the foundation of The Church of Jesus Christ of Latter-day Saints. That revelation by the power of the Holy Ghost is operating today and reveals to us all truth, and we are led by living prophets today—Alma 4:19

THE DEVIL AND HIS PURPOSES

And while we were yet in the Spirit, the Lord commanded us that we should write the vision; for we beheld Satan, that old serpent, even the devil, who rebelled against God, and sought to take the kingdom of our God and his Christ—Wherefore, he maketh war with the saints of God, and encompasseth them round about.

D&C 76:28–29

There are three things that Satan sets out to do. First, he plans to destroy the agency of man. . . . Satan's second purpose is to possess the bodies of Adam and his posterity. . . . John Taylor has taught, "[Satan] exerts an invisible agency over the spirits of men, darkens their minds. . . . He uses his influence over the spirits of those who have bodies, to resist goodness, virtue, purity, intelligence, and the fear of God." . . . The third purpose of Satan, which is described carefully and accurately in the scriptures, was to make captive the souls of men (see Alma 34:35; 2 Nephi 26:22).

(Harold B. Lee, *The Teachings of Harold B. Lee*, ed. Clyde J. Williams [Salt Lake City: Bookcraft, 1996], 37–38)

Daily Living

THE DEVIL IS REAL AND SEEKS YOUR DESTRUCTION.

- The devil is at war with you to make you miserable like unto himself—2 Nephi 2:27
- We must be prepare to overcome temptation by putting on the armor of God—Ephesians 6:11–17; D&C 27:15–18
- We must hold fast to the word of God—1 Nephi 15:24
- We must fast and pray—3 Nephi 18:18

SONS OF PERDITION

Thus saith the Lord concerning all those who know my power, and have been made partakers thereof, and suffered themselves through the power of the devil to be overcome, and to deny the truth and defy my power—They are they who are the sons of perdition, of whom I say that it had been better for them never to have been born; For they are vessels of wrath, doomed to suffer the wrath of God, with the devil and his angels in eternity; Concerning whom I have said there is no forgiveness in this world nor in the world to come—Having denied the Holy Spirit after having received it, and having denied the Only Begotten Son of the Father, having crucified him unto themselves and put him to an open shame.

D&C 76:31–35

Those in this life who gain a perfect knowledge of the divinity of the gospel cause, a knowledge that comes only by revelation from the Holy Ghost, and who then link themselves with Lucifer and come out in open rebellion, also become sons of perdition. . . . Joseph Smith said: "All sins shall be forgiven, except the sin against the Holy Ghost; for Jesus will save all except the sons of perdition (*Teachings,* 358).

(Bruce R. McConkie, *Mormon Doctrine*, 2d ed. [Salt Lake City: Bookcraft, 1966], 746)

Daily Living

SEEK NEVER TO BECOME A SON OF PERDITION.

ຍ Yield to the Holy Spirit and put off the natural man, and never deny the Holy Ghost—Mosiah 3:19; Alma 39:6

THE GOSPEL OF JESUS CHRIST

And this is the gospel, the glad tidings, which the voice out of the heavens bore record unto us—That he came into the world, even Jesus, to be crucified for the world, and to bear the sins of the world, and to sanctify the world, and to cleanse it from all unrighteousness; That through him all might be saved whom the Father had put into his power and made by him.

D&C 76:40–42

Behold I have given unto you my gospel, and this is the gospel which I have given unto you—that I came into the world to do the will of my Father, because my Father sent me. And my Father sent me that I might be lifted up upon the cross; and after that I had been lifted up upon the cross, that I might draw all men unto me, that as I have been lifted up by men even so should men be lifted up by the Father, to stand before me, to be judged of their works. . . . Now this is the commandment: Repent, all ye ends of the earth, and come unto me and be baptized in my name, that ye may be sanctified by the reception of the Holy Ghost, that ye may stand spotless before me at the last day. Verily, verily, I say unto you, this is my gospel.

(3 Nephi 27:13–14, 20–21)

Daily Living

CENTRAL TO THE GOSPEL IS THE SAVIOR'S ATONEMENT.

- It is this power which draws us to Him. We can partake of His Atonement, His goodness, and mercy in our lives through faith unto repentance—Alma 34:15–17

THE CELESTIAL GLORY

They are they who received the testimony of Jesus, and believed on his name and were baptized after the manner of his burial, being buried in the water in his name, and this according to the commandment which he has given—That by keeping the commandments they might be washed and cleansed from all their sins, and receive the Holy Spirit by the laying on of the hands of him who is ordained and sealed unto this power; And who overcome by faith, and are sealed by the Holy Spirit of promise, which the Father sheds forth upon all those who are just and true. . . . They are they into whose hands the Father has given all things.

D&C 76:51–55; SEE ALSO VERSES 56–70

By devotion and faithfulness, by enduring to the end in righteousness and obedience, it is then possible to merit a celestial reward (2 Ne. 31:17–21). . . . "The sanctified" are "them of the celestial world" (D. & C. 88:2). "In the celestial glory there are three heavens or degrees," [D&C 131:1] and in the same sense that baptism starts a person out toward an entrance into the celestial world, so celestial marriage puts a couple on the path leading to an exaltation in the highest heaven of that world (D&C 131:1–4; 132).

(Bruce R. McConkie, *Mormon Doctrine*, 2d ed. [Salt Lake City: Bookcraft, 1966], 116)

Daily Living

SEEK THE GLORY OF GOD AND THE CELESTIAL KINGDOM.

ꝏ Seek the celestial glory and presence of God.

THE TERRESTRIAL GLORY

And again, we saw the terrestrial world, and behold and lo, these are they who are of the terrestrial, whose glory differs from that of the church of the Firstborn who have received the fulness of the Father, even as that of the moon differs from the sun in the firmament. These are they who are honorable men of the earth, who were blinded by the craftiness of men.

D&C 76:71, 75; SEE ALL VERSES 71–80

To the terrestrial kingdom will go: 1. Accountable persons who die without law (and who, of course, do not accept the gospel in the spirit world under those particular circumstances which would make them heirs of the celestial kingdom); 2. Those who reject the gospel in this life and who reverse their course and accept it in the spirit world; 3. Honorable men of the earth who are blinded by the craftiness of men and who therefore do not accept and live the gospel law; and 4. Members of The Church of Jesus Christ of Latter-day Saints who have testimonies of Christ and the divinity of the great latter-day work and who are not valiant, but who are instead lukewarm in their devotion to the Church and to righteousness (D&C 76:71–80).

(Bruce R. McConkie, *Mormon Doctrine*, 2d ed. [Salt Lake City: Bookcraft, 1966], 784)

Daily Living

SEEK THE GLORY OF GOD AND THE CELESTIAL KINGDOM.

- Always seek the glory of God with all your heart that you might be worthy of the celestial kingdom.

THE TELESTIAL GLORY

And again, we saw the glory of the telestial, which glory is that of the lesser, even as the glory of the stars differs from that of the glory of the moon in the firmament. These are they who received not the gospel of Christ, neither the testimony of Jesus.

D&C 76:81–82; SEE ALL VERSES 81–89, 98–106, 109–112

The inhabitants of this lowest kingdom of glory will be "as innumerable as the stars in the firmament of heaven, or as the sand upon the seashore." They will be the endless hosts of people of all ages who have lived after the manner of the world; who have been carnal, sensual, and devilish; who have chosen the vain philosophies of the world rather than accept the testimony of Jesus; who have been liars and thieves, sorcerers and adulterers, blasphemers and murderers (D. & C. 76:81–112; Rev. 22:15). Their number will include "all the proud, yea, and all that do wickedly" (Mal. 4:1), for all such have lived a telestial law. "And they shall be servants of the Most High; but where God and Christ dwell they cannot come, worlds without end" (D. & C. 76:112).

(Bruce R. McConkie, *Mormon Doctrine*, 2d ed. [Salt Lake City: Bookcraft, 1966], 778)

Daily Living

SEEK THE GLORY OF GOD AND THE CELESTIAL KINGDOM.

- Always seek the glory of God and serve Him with all your heart that you might be worthy of the celestial kingdom.

ADMINISTER TO THE POOR

For verily I say unto you, the time has come, and is now at hand; and behold, and lo, it must needs be that there be an organization of my people, in regulating and establishing the affairs of the storehouse for the poor of my people, both in this place and in the land of Zion.

D&C 78:3

The Lord, by revelation, has commanded that storehouses be established. The surpluses, or "residue," from the consecrated properties under the united order were to be kept in the storehouses "to administer to the poor and the needy" (D&C 42:34). . . . Today . . . bishops storehouses . . . are used for almost the identical purpose they were used for under the united order. Members consecrate their time and talents and means to produce, process, package, manufacture, and purchase commodities to care for those in need. . . . Storehouses are only established to care for the poor and the needy.

(Ezra Taft Benson, *Ensign,* May 1977, 82)

Daily Living

THE LORD CONTINUALLY REMINDS US TO CARE FOR THE POOR.

ᘓ The Lord is ever concerned with those who have not, and it is our duty to be generous with our donations, monies, and time that the poor are cared for in every facet of life—temporal, social, emotional, intellectual, and spiritual—D&C 42:30

BE THANKFUL IN ALL THINGS

And he who receiveth all things with thankfulness shall be made glorious; and the things of this earth shall be added unto him, even an hundred fold, yea, more.
D&C 78:19

The Prophet Joseph is reported to have said at one time that one of the greatest sins for which the Latter-day Saints would be guilty would be the sin of ingratitude. I presume most of us have not thought of that as a serious sin. There is a great tendency for us in our prayers—in our pleadings with the Lord—to ask for additional blessings. Sometimes I feel we need to devote more of our prayers to expressions of gratitude and thanksgiving for blessings already received. Of course we need the daily blessings of the Lord. But if we sin in the matter of prayer, I think it is in our lack of the expressions of thanksgiving for daily blessings.

(Ezra Taft Benson, *The Teachings of Ezra Taft Benson* [Salt Lake City: Bookcraft, 1988], 363)

Daily Living

RECEIVE ALL THINGS WITH THANKSGIVING.

ᢀ An attitude of gratitude and thanksgiving brings with it many blessings that enliven the soul. When expressed, others are uplifted and enjoy a feeling of appreciation and self-worth. Surely gratitude and thanksgiving should become some of our cardinal virtues by which we should live because there are so many trailing blessings that accompany these marvelous and empowering traits.

THE SPIRIT AND MISSIONARY WORK

And I will send upon him the Comforter, which shall teach him the truth and the way whither he shall go.
D&C 79:2

I pray God that those who have entered into covenant with the Lord and with one another will not forget their position; that they will not forget why they are here and where they came from, nor forget their duty to God and to one another. I pray God to bless us all, and to give us His spirit to guide and direct us through our mission and probation here in the flesh.

(Brian H. Stuy, ed., *Wilford Woodruff, Collected Discourses*, 5 vols. [Burbank, Calif., and Woodland Hills, UT: B.H.S. Publishing, 1987], 1:313–314)

Daily Living

THE SPIRIT WILL DIRECT YOUR MISSIONARY EFFORTS.

- The Spirit will direct you, even though you may not know beforehand what you should do—1 Nephi 4:6
- You will teach by the Spirit—D&C 42:14; Alma 17:3
- You bear your testimony of the word according to the spirit of revelation—Alma 4:20
- The Lord will pour His Spirit upon you that the work will go forward—Mosiah 18:10, 12; 25:24
- The Spirit is the key in missionary work. It is the key to testifying and conversion.

PREACH THE GOSPEL

Wherefore, go ye and preach my gospel, whether to the north or to the south, to the east or to the west, it mattereth not, for ye cannot go amiss.
D&C 80:3

In a later revelation, two missionaries were told that they could set forth to preach the gospel "whether to the north or to the south, to the east or to the west, it mattereth not, for ye cannot go amiss" (D&C 80:3). Opportunities and options abound all about us to "bring to pass much righteousness." We would be staggered and ashamed if we saw fully the unused and unexplored possibilities for service that surround each of us all of the time. He is a loving, encouraging, and emancipating Lord who urges us to use our minds and talents in good causes. He who has arranged this planet for us with adequate natural resources ("enough and to spare") has also supplied a surplus of opportunities for the stretching of our souls, if we but desire to do so.

(Neal A. Maxwell, *Wherefore, Ye Must Press Forward* [Salt Lake City: Deseret Book, 1977], 34)

Daily Living

PREACH AND SPREAD THE GOSPEL AT ALL TIMES AND PLACES.

℘ We, as members of the Church, should always be looking for opportunities to share the gospel by example and precept, by opening our mouths to start gospel conversations, and using pass-along cards to encourage interest that we might invite all to come unto Christ and be witnesses at all times—Mosiah 18:9

BE FAITHFUL IN YOUR CALLING

Therefore, verily I acknowledge him and will bless him, and also thee, inasmuch as thou art faithful in counsel, in the office which I have appointed unto you, in prayer always, vocally and in thy heart, in public and in private, also in thy ministry in proclaiming the gospel in the land of the living, and among thy brethren. And in doing these things thou wilt do the greatest good unto thy fellow beings, and wilt promote the glory of him who is your Lord.

D&C 81:3–4

Every calling in the Lord's church includes the responsibility to teach the gospel. The calling of a counselor is not administrative only. He should use the opportunities afforded in his calling to share the principles and teachings of the gospel in order to assist in the ministry of saving the souls of men.

(L. G. Otten and C. M. Caldwell, *Sacred Truths of the Doctrine and Covenants* [Salt Lake City: Deseret Book, 1983], 2:56)

Daily Living

BE FAITHFUL IN YOUR CALLING AND ALWAYS SHARE THE GOSPEL.

- As disciples of Jesus Christ, we are always seeking to magnify our callings by being faithful and true to our duty and responsibilities. We are disciples of Jesus Christ, thus declaring His gospel of everlasting life—3 Nephi 5:13
- Show love to your fellow men—John 13:34–35
- Strengthen others (D&C 108:7) and open your mouth to invite others to come unto Christ—D&C 33:8–11

AUGUST

Leave judgment alone with me, for it is mine and I will repay. Peace be with you; my blessings continue with you.

—Doctrine & Covenants 82:83

NURTURE AND LIFT OTHERS

Wherefore, be faithful; stand in the office which I have appointed unto you; succor the weak, lift up the hands which hang down, and strengthen the feeble knees.
D&C 81:5

As latter-day Christians, we know that the "royal law" (James 2:8) of love in action is to "succor the weak, lift up the hands which hang down, and strengthen the feeble knees"(D&C 81:5). Do we catch the significance of this thought? We demonstrate the depth of our love for the Savior when we care enough to seek out the suffering among us and attend to their needs.

(J. Richards Clarke, *Love* [Salt Lake City: Deseret Book, 1986], 56)

Daily Living

SEEK TO NURTURE AND LIFT EVERY SOUL YOU SEE.

- The essence of pure discipleship and "doing as Jesus would do" is in lifting, nurturing, and strengthening our fellow men—3 Nephi 27:27; Luke 22:32
- The gospel is not just in acknowledged beliefs of the doctrines but should cause change in our attitude and behavior . . . even a mighty change—Alma 5:14
- The test of pure saints is to seek after the one, be a good Samaritan, to visit the fatherless and widows, and indeed bless all those who have burdens to bear and stand in need of comfort—Ezekiel 34:16; Luke 10:30–37; James 1:27; Mosiah 18:8–9

FORGIVENESS

Verily, verily, I say unto you, my servants, that inasmuch as you have forgiven one another your trespasses, even so I, the Lord, forgive you.
D&C 82:1

Ever keep in exercise the principle of mercy, and be ready to forgive our brother on the first intimations of repentance, and asking forgiveness; and should we even forgive our brother, or even our enemy, before he repent or ask forgiveness, our Heavenly Father would be equally as merciful unto us.

(Joseph Smith, *History of The Church of Jesus Christ of Latter-day Saints*, 7 Vols. [Salt Lake City; Deseret Book, 1948], 3:383)

Daily Living

FORGIVE OTHERS AND BE FORGIVEN.

- It seems as though we, as mortals, need continual reminding and repetition of principles and doctrines so we can stay on the strait and narrow path. Weekly we partake of the sacrament to remember the covenants we have made. Is it any wonder the Lord repeats many doctrines again and again? Since forgiveness is so necessary for our exaltation, the Lord calls to our attention the fact that if we don't forgive, we simply cannot be forgiven of our sins. Mercy begets mercy as forgiveness engenders forgiveness. May we forgive readily, cheerfully, and sincerely, and thus partake of the goodness of God.
- Have an absolutely wonderful experience and read all the scriptures in the Topical Guide on forgiving and forgiveness—Topical Guide, 156–157.

WHERE MUCH IS GIVEN

For of him unto whom much is given much is required; and he who sins against the greater light shall receive the greater condemnation.
D&C 82:3

Jesus made it plain [see Matt. 25:14–39] that each will be required to give an accounting only for the talents or aids he has received: "for unto whomsoever much is given, of him shall be much required." (See Luke 12:48.) No man can say that he has received nothing. Even though it be but one talent, he will be expected to develop that talent so that when his Lord comes, he will be able to return it with profit. It will also be noted, that unto him that hath shall be given, and he shall have abundance: but from him that hath not shall be taken away even that which he has.

(LeGrand Richards, *A Marvelous Work and a Wonder* [Salt Lake City: Deseret Book, 1976], 298)

Daily Living

WHERE MUCH IS GIVEN, MUCH IS REQUIRED.

- The parable of the talents teaches us what the Lord expects of us in terms of how we use knowledge, gifts, and talents we receive from Him—Matthew 25:14–30
- We best be diligent in pursuing the things that are of most worth—bringing souls unto Christ—D&C 15:6
- Living the gospel and blessing others is truly magnifying our talents. What good would the talents of faith, knowledge, and works be if, in the end, they did not lift and bless others?—Matthew 25:40; Galatians 6:7; Mosiah 2:17; D&C 6:13; 18:38

FORMER SINS CAN RETURN

And now, verily I say unto you, I, the Lord, will not lay any sin to your charge; go your ways and sin no more; but unto that soul who sinneth shall the former sins return, saith the Lord your God.
D&C 82:7

It is present salvation and the present influence of the Holy Ghost that we need every day to keep us on saving ground. When an individual refuses to comply with the further requirements of heaven, then the sins he had formerly committed return upon his head [see Ezek. 3:20]; his former righteousness departs from him, and is not accounted to him for righteousness: but if he had continued in righteousness and obedience to the requirements of heaven, he is saved all the time through baptism, the laying on of hands, and obeying the commandments of the Lord and all that is required of him by the heavens—the living oracles. He is saved now, next year, and continually, and is prepared for the celestial kingdom of God whenever the time comes for him to inherit it.

(Brigham Young, *Journal of Discourses*, July 15, 1860, 8:124–125)

Daily Living

FORMER SINS CAN RETURN.

- True repentance and forgiveness involves forsaking one's sins—D&C 58:42–43
- Should we falter, we must not succumb to the devil's constant chanting, "See, you can't do it." Remember, as oft as we repent with real intent, the Lord is forgiving—Mosiah 26:29–30; Moroni 6:8

THE LORD KEEPS HIS PROMISES

I, the Lord, am bound when ye do what I say; but when ye do not what I say, ye have no promise.
D&C 82:10

"Mormonism" has taught me that God holds Himself accountable to law even as He expects us to do. He has set us the example in obedience to law. I know that to say this would have been heresy a few decades ago. But we have the divine word for it: [Sec. 82:10, quoted.] He operates by law and not by arbitrariness or caprice. He is no tyrant to be propitiated and placated by honeyed words. He cannot be moved by wordy oratory. He is not a judge sitting to be influenced by the specious pleas of crafty advocates; and yet there is an eloquence that moves Him; there is a plea that influences Him. The eloquence of prayer from a broken heart and a contrite spirit prevails with him. . . . He will take all circumstances into account and will give unto every man that which is his.

(James E. Talmage, in Conference Report, April 1930, 96–97)

Daily Living

THE LORD BLESSES HIS COVENANT-KEEPING PEOPLE.

- The Lord always keeps His promises. Be baptized and keep the commandments and be saved—3 Nephi 11:33–34
- Keep the commandments and always have His Spirit to be with you—D&C 20:77, 79
- Endure to the end and inherit eternal life—2 Nephi 31:20
- Enter into the everlasting covenant of marriage and keep your covenants and have eternal increase—D&C 131:2–4

ZION MUST INCREASE IN BEAUTY

For Zion must increase in beauty, and in holiness; her borders must be enlarged; her stakes must be strengthened; yea, verily I say unto you, Zion must arise and put on her beautiful garments.
D&C 82:14

Then again, did Enoch build up a Zion? So we are doing. What is it? The Zion of God. What does it mean? The pure in heart in the first place. In the second place those who are governed by the law of God—the pure in heart who are governed by the law of God. Shall we build up a Zion? We shall. . . . Now, this is what we are building up, and they built up a similar thing before the flood; and the elders went forth in those days as they now go forth; and they baptized people and laid hands upon them, and gathered them to Zion; and after a while that Zion was caught up from the earth. And we will build up a Zion: that is what we are aiming at. And that Zion also, when the time comes, will ascend to meet the Zion from above, which will descend, and both, we are told, will fall on each other's necks and kiss each other.

(John Taylor, *Journal of Discourses*, October 20, 1881, 26:109–110)

Daily Living

HELP BUILD UP ZION—ZION MUST INCREASE.

℘ Let us seek to build up the kingdom of God by inviting all mankind to come unto Christ and becoming pure in heart, thus establishing and building up Zion—JST—Matthew 6:38; D&C 97:16–21

SEEK THE INTEREST OF OTHERS

Every man seeking the interest of his neighbor, and doing all things with an eye single to the glory of God.
D&C 82:19

The test of putting others' interests ahead of self-interest is a rigorous one. It is inherent in the practice of consecration, which the Lord described as "every man seeking the interest of his neighbor, and doing all things with an eye single to the glory of God" (D&C 82:19). It is the essence of the example of our Lord and Savior, Jesus Christ, who gave himself as a sacrifice for all of us.

The test of putting others' interests ahead of our own is obviously a test grounded in the Lord's way, not the way of the world. It is required by principles of right rather than by rules of law.

(Dallin H. Oaks, *The Lord's Way* [Salt Lake City: Deseret Book, 1991], 184)

Daily Living

SEEK TO BLESS OTHERS WITH AN EYE SINGLE TO THE GLORY OF GOD.

- When does one seek the interest of his neighbor first? When one possesses the pure love of Christ and is in fact the Lord's disciple—Moroni 7:44–48; John 13:34–35
- When one seeks to love and glorify God, it is always in loving and blessing His children, which is part of the great commandment, even to love God and thy neighbor as thyself—Matthew 22:36–40; 25:40; D&C 88:67

LEAVE JUDGMENT TO THE LORD

Leave judgment alone with me, for it is mine and I will repay. Peace be with you; my blessings continue with you.
D&C 82:23

Yes, I remembered now, he was one of the "bad guys," at least in my former way of thinking. I was aware of some things he had done that were wrong by almost any definition, yet here he was giving his last precious can of jam to me, me who in some respects was his enemy—at least to his life-style.

I experienced an overwhelming feeling about the importance of not judging (see D&C 64:8–11). We must leave judgment to the Lord. He alone knows all the facts. We may have had some experiences with some people at some time, but only God comprehends all experiences with all people at all times. Only he can weigh everything in its proper context.

(John H. Groberg, *In the Eye of the Storm* [Salt Lake City: Bookcraft, 1993], 115)

Daily Living

NEVER JUDGE . . . LEAVE JUDGMENT TO THE LORD.

- Never judge another. Never judge another. Never judge another. Remember, as ye judge, so shall ye be judged—Matthew 7:2; Luke 6:37; 3 Nephi 14:2; Moroni 7:18
- There is wisdom in looking for the good in others and being merciful, for that mercy will come back to you from the Lord—3 Nephi 12:7

THE MELCHIZEDEK PRIESTHOOD

And this greater priesthood administereth the gospel and holdeth the key of the mysteries of the kingdom, even the key of the knowledge of God.
D&C 84:19

Concerning the primary purposes of the Melchizedek Priesthood, a revelation said: "And this greater priesthood administereth the gospel and holdeth the key of the mysteries of the kingdom, even the key of the knowledge of God." [D&C 84:19] Such knowledge was not that which was acquired by theological understanding alone, but by personal revelation, including as a major factor the knowledge acquired by the Second Comforter. In another revelation, the Prophet [Joseph Smith] wrote more pointedly: "The power and authority of the higher, or Melchizedek Priesthood, is to hold the keys of all the spiritual blessings of the church."

(Hyrum L. Andrus, *Doctrines of the Kingdom* [Salt Lake City: Bookcraft, 1998], 156–157)

Daily Living

THE MELCHIZEDEK PRIESTHOOD ADMINISTERETH IN ALL THINGS.

- May we ever be mindful of the great blessing of the restoration of the Melchizedek Priesthood in this, the dispensation of the fullness of times—D&C 27:12
- We receive the Lord as we receive the priesthood and exercise it in righteousness—D&C 84:35
- This is the Lord's earth, gospel, priesthood, Church, and kingdom, therefore it is His priesthood that administers all things—Jacob 4:9; 3 Nephi 27:7–14; D&C 107:3

POWER OF GODLINESS MANIFESTED

Therefore, in the ordinances thereof, the power of godliness is manifest. And without the ordinances thereof, and the authority of the priesthood, the power of godliness is not manifest unto men in the flesh.

D&C 84:20–21

That is what holds these people together—the power of the priesthood. And in the administration of it we have seen and do see the power of godliness; not a form of godliness, mind you, but the power of godliness. . . . Have you ever seen it manifested in your lives? We heard of it this morning from the leader of the Church as manifested in the healing of the sick. We see it in the temples of the Lord; we see it in the sick rooms; we see it manifested in presidencies of stakes, bishoprics of wards. In all the leadership of the priesthood you see that same power of godliness. . . . It is the power of godliness, of godly lives. It is the power of godly men and godly women, through the ordinances of the priesthood made manifest; and everyone shares in it.

(Charles W. Nibley, in Conference Report, April 1927, 26–27)

Daily Living

ALL BLESSINGS ARE RECEIVED THROUGH THE PRIESTHOOD.

ꕥ Godliness is manifested in our lives in all things as we receive lifesaving ordinances, keep our covenants, and live a life patterned after our Savior Jesus Christ. And thus He commands us to become perfect—3 Nephi 12:48

OATH AND COVENANT OF THE PRIESTHOOD

For whoso is faithful unto the obtaining these two priesthoods of which I have spoken, and the magnifying their calling, are sanctified by the Spirit unto the renewing of their bodies. They become the sons of Moses and of Aaron and the seed of Abraham, and the church and kingdom, and the elect of God.

D&C 84:33–34

And so Melchizedek is the prototype, the example, the scriptural illustration. He received the priesthood, magnified callings in the priesthood, and chose to work righteousness; he made it possible for himself and his people to enter into the rest of the Lord through applying the atoning blood of Christ and by virtue of the sealing powers of the priesthood. . . . Those who abide by the *covenant* of the priesthood, magnify their callings therein, and live by every word of God, eventually receive what Enoch and Melchizedek received: God swears unto them with an *oath*, by his own voice, that the fulness of eternal reward will be theirs (see D&C 84:33–40).

(Monte S. Nyman and Charles D. Tate, Jr., eds., *Alma, the Testimony of the Word* [Provo: BYU Religious Studies Center, 1992], 83–84)

Daily Living

BE FAITHFUL TO THE OATH AND COVENANT OF THE PRIESTHOOD.

ꟹ We can receive all that the Father has—D&C 84:38

BLESSINGS OF THE PRIESTHOOD

And also all they who receive this priesthood receive me, saith the Lord; For he that receiveth my servants receiveth me; And he that receiveth me receiveth my Father; And he that receiveth my Father receiveth my Father's kingdom; therefore all that my Father hath shall be given unto him.

D&C 84:35–38

The Father has promised his sons who receive the Holy Priesthood and faithfully abide by the conditions of its oath and covenant that they are to share in all that which the Father hath. The Father possesses kingdoms, thrones, principalities, powers, dominions, and exaltations. These the faithful will receive of him as heirs of God and joint-heirs with Jesus Christ. This promise—and the Lord will not fail—is a challenging encouragement for all to do his will. It is natural for a father to share his estate with his children. Our Heavenly Father is no exception. He does so with a binding covenant with his faithful sons: Listen to the words of this promise.

(Delbert L. Stapley, in Conference Report, April 1961, 67)

Daily Living

RECEIVE THE BLESSINGS OF THE PRIESTHOOD.

ꟸ Our blessings are dependent upon being true and faithful by keeping and honoring the oath and covenant of the priesthood. As with all blessings they depend upon our obedience to that law upon which it is predicated—D&C 130:20–21

BREAKING THE COVENANT

And this is according to the oath and covenant which belongeth to the priesthood. Therefore, all those who receive the priesthood, receive this oath and covenant of my Father, which he cannot break, neither can it be moved. But whoso breaketh this covenant after he hath received it, and altogether turneth therefrom, shall not have forgiveness of sins in this world nor in the world to come.

D&C 84:39–41

This [Sec. 84:33–41] makes a very serious matter of receiving this covenant and this Priesthood; for those who receive it must, like God Himself, abide in it, and must not fail, and must not be moved out of the way; for those who receive this oath and covenant and turn away from it, and cease to do righteously and to honor this covenant, and will to abide in sin, and repent not, there is no forgiveness for them either in this life or in the world to come.

(Joseph F. Smith, in Conference Report, April 1898, 65)

Daily Living

DON'T BREAK THE OATH AND COVENANT OF THE PRIESTHOOD.

Recognizing that God our Father has given us the right to act for Him in and through the name of the Lord Jesus Christ is no trivial matter. It is with reverence that we look upon the sacred responsibility of bearing the Lord's Priesthood and serving others. Words cannot express the great joy of receiving and honoring the priesthood or the consequences and horror of failing to magnify and all together to turn away from the priesthood.

LIVE BY EVERY WORD OF GOD

And I now give unto you a commandment to beware concerning yourselves, to give diligent heed to the words of eternal life. For you shall live by every word that proceedeth forth from the mouth of God.

D&C 84:43–44

Scriptures contain the record of the self-revelation of God, and through them God speaks to man. Where could there be more profitable use of time than reading from the scriptural library, the literature that teaches us to know God and understand our relationship to him? Time is always precious; but study of the scriptures is absolutely essential.

(Howard W. Hunter, *The Teachings of Howard W. Hunter*, ed. Clyde J. Williams [Salt Lake City: Bookcraft, 1997], 50)

Daily Living

LIVE BY EVERY WORD THAT PROCEEDETH FORTH FROM GOD.

- We live by the Word of God, for the Word of God is indeed the Lord Jesus Christ—John 1; Revelation 19:13
- We feast upon the word of God—2 Nephi 32:3
- Hold to the iron rod, the word of God, and thus resist and overcome temptation—1 Nephi15:24
- The word has the greatest power to cause change in our lives—Alma 31:5
- The word gives direction like a Liahona—Alma 37:43–47
- The word empowers our very being as we liken it to our lives for our profit and learning—1 Nephi 19:23

THE WORD OF THE LORD IS TRUTH

For the word of the Lord is truth, and whatsoever is truth is light, and whatsoever is light is Spirit, even the Spirit of Jesus Christ. And the Spirit giveth light to every man that cometh into the world; and the Spirit enlighteneth every man through the world, that hearkeneth to the voice of the Spirit.

D&C 84:45–46

At the same time we have the sweet influence of the Spirit of God pleading with us to do that which is right, pleading with every human being that does not drive it from him; for every human being has a portion of the Spirit of God given unto him. We sometimes call it conscience; we call it by one name and we call it by another; but it is the Spirit of God that every man and woman possesses that is born on the earth. God has given unto all his children this Spirit. Of course it is not the gift of the Holy Ghost in its fulness; for that is only received by obedience to the commandments of God [Acts 5:32; John 14:16–17; D&C 35:5–6].

(George Q. Cannon, *Journal of Discourses,* September 28, 1884, 26:191)

Daily Living

THE WORD IS TRUTH, LIGHT, AND THE SPIRIT OF JESUS CHRIST.

- The truth will make us free—John 8:32
- Christ is the way, the truth, and the life, and the only way back to the Father—John 14:6
- This Spirit of Jesus Christ and light is given to every man that he may know good from evil and know the way to judge—Moroni 7:15–19

HEARKEN TO THE SPIRIT

And every one that hearkeneth to the voice of the Spirit cometh unto God, even the Father. And the Father teacheth him of the covenant which he has renewed and confirmed upon you, which is confirmed upon you for your sakes, and not for your sakes only, but for the sake of the whole world.

D&C 84:47–48

The members of the Church are entitled to receive revelation which is needful for their progress, and if they will hearken to the Spirit of truth and walk humbly before the Lord, they will not fall short of this spiritual guidance. Members of the Church, who neglect their duty and who are indifferent to the commandments, place themselves in danger of being deceived. Failing to obtain the guiding influence of the Holy Ghost, they become liable to the enticing influence of deceivers because they lack the ability to discern between truth and error.

(Daniel H. Ludlow, *A Companion to Your Study of Doctrine and Covenants* [Salt Lake City: Deseret Book, 1978], 274–275)

Daily Living

HEARKEN TO THE SPIRIT AND COME UNTO GOD.

- When we hearken to the Spirit we listen and do. We trust in the Spirit—D&C 11:12–13; Galatians 5:22–23
- We are sanctified by the Spirit when we yield our hearts to God—Helaman 3:35
- Remember that the priesthood operates as directed by the Spirit and is for the blessing of all of God's children.

August 17

THE THINGS OF GOD

And your minds in times past have been darkened because of unbelief, and because you have treated lightly the things you have received—Which vanity and unbelief have brought the whole church under condemnation. And this condemnation resteth upon the children of Zion, even all. And they shall remain under this condemnation until they repent and remember the new covenant, even the Book of Mormon and the former commandments which I have given them, not only to say, but to do according to that which I have written.

D&C 84:54–57

President Benson's emphasis on the Book of Mormon was nothing new. For years he had quoted the scripture teaching that the Church was under condemnation for taking that book of scripture lightly (See D&C 84:57). . . . Repeatedly he counseled the Saints to "make the study of the Book of Mormon a lifetime pursuit."

(Sheri L. Dew, *Ezra Taft Benson: A Biography* [Salt Lake City: Deseret Book, 1987], 491–492)

Daily Living

NEVER TREAT THE THINGS OF GOD LIGHTLY.

ꝏ This condemnation and rebuke of the Saints saddens the soul. Think of the effort of the early prophets and the Prophet Joseph and all they went through to make, record, and translate the Book of Mormon. We must never take lightly this sacred record which restored the fullness of the gospel. Feast upon the words of Christ, for they will tell you all things to do—2 Nephi 32:3

FORGIVENESS OF SINS

I will forgive you of your sins with this commandment—that you remain steadfast in your minds in solemnity and the spirit of prayer, in bearing testimony to all the world of those things which are communicated unto you. Therefore, go ye into all the world; and unto whatsoever place ye cannot go ye shall send, that the testimony may go from you into all the world unto every creature.
D&C 84:61–62

Isn't that glorious! The Savior promises us forgiveness of our sins and calls us his friends if we remain steadfast in prayer and testimony.
(Chieko N. Okazaki, *Aloha!* [Salt Lake City: Deseret Book, 1995], 142)

Daily Living

FORGIVENESS GRANTED TO THOSE WHO REMAIN STEADFAST.

- Forgiveness of sins is through the Atonement of Christ. We make the Atonement efficacious in our lives as we repent and seek to build up the kingdom of God, and by assisting others to come unto Christ. Repentance and forgiveness requires a manifestation of our works—D&C 20:37
- We can be forgiven as we bear our testimonies of the Savior Jesus Christ—D&C 62:3
- Assist in the conversion of others, thus covering a multitude of sins—James 5:20
- Thrust in your sickle to bring souls to Christ, and thus your sins are forgiven—D&C 31:5

SIGNS FOLLOW THOSE THAT BELIEVE

And these signs shall follow them that believe—In my name they shall do many wonderful works; In my name they shall cast out devils; In my name they shall heal the sick; In my name they shall open the eyes of the blind, and unstop the ears of the deaf; And the tongue of the dumb shall speak; And if any man shall administer poison unto them it shall not hurt them; And the poison of a serpent shall not have power to harm them. But a commandment I give unto them, that they shall not boast themselves of these things, neither speak them before the world; for these things are given unto you for your profit and for salvation.

D&C 84:65–73

When we believe and seek spiritual gifts to benefit others "and not for a sign" (D&C 46:9), we are told that signs will follow. "Behold, . . . signs follow those that believe. Yea, signs come by faith, not by the will of men, nor as they please, but by the will of God. Yea, signs come by faith, unto mighty works" (D&C 63:9–11). The Holy Ghost "maketh manifest unto the children of men, according to their faith" (Jarom 1:4).

(Dallin Oaks, "Spiritual Gifts," Mary E. Stovall and Carol Cornwall Madsen, eds., *A Heritage of Faith: Talks Selected from the BYU Women's Conferences* [Salt Lake City: Deseret Book, 1988], 31)

Daily Living

SIGNS FOLLOW THOSE THAT BELIEVE.

- Signs are given to man from God for his benefit and the blessing of their fellow men—Mormon 9:24; D&C 35:8

BAPTISM IS ESSENTIAL TO SALVATION

Verily, verily, I say unto you, they who believe not on your words, and are not baptized in water in my name, for the remission of their sins, that they may receive the Holy Ghost, shall be damned, and shall not come into my Father's kingdom where my Father and I am. And this revelation unto you, and commandment, is in force from this very hour upon all the world, and the gospel is unto all who have not received it.

D&C 84:74–75

The Gospel of Christ is the power of God unto salvation unto all those who believe it. . . . Notwithstanding He was crucified for the sins of the world and His blood was shed for the redemption of mankind; notwithstanding all this, no man on the earth will ever be saved by the Gospel unless he believes it. . . . The Gospel is not the power of God unto salvation to the unbeliever, but it is destined to save all who believe and obey it.

(Hyrum M. Smith, in Conference Report, April 1904, 51)

Daily Living

BAPTISM IS ESSENTIAL TO SALVATION.

so Baptism is the symbol that we are willing to take the name of Jesus Christ upon us, repent of our sins, keep our hearts broken and our spirits contrite, have a determination to serve our Savior to the end, and manifest by our works that we have received the Spirit of Christ unto the remission of sins that we might endure to the end and gain eternal life—D&C 20:37; 2 Nephi 31:19–20

August 21

SHARING THE GOSPEL

But, verily I say unto all those to whom the kingdom has been given—from you it must be preached unto them, that they shall repent of their former evil works; for they are to be upbraided for their evil hearts of unbelief, and your brethren in Zion for their rebellion against you at the time I sent you. And again I say unto you, my friends, for from henceforth I shall call you friends, it is expedient that I give unto you this commandment, that ye become even as my friends in days when I was with them, traveling to preach the gospel in my power.

D&C 84:76–77

The faithful elders who go forth . . . should have the guiding influence of his Spirit go before them. [Sec. 84:79, quoted.] What a wonderful blessing is promised them: [Sec. 84:80, quoted.] Thousands of missionaries have put this promise to the test, and the Lord has kept his promise to all those who have been faithful in their calling.

(Joseph Fielding Smith, *Church History and Modern Revelation*, 1948, 2:108–9)

Daily Living

LIVE AND SHARE THE GOSPEL EVERY MOMENT OF EVERY DAY.

- This is the duty of the dispensation of the fullness of times—Mormon 9:22; Jacob 5:71–72
- Warn our neighbors—D&C 88:81
- Pray for opportunities to share the gospel and for those who know not God—Alma 6:6
- Open our mouths—D&C 33:8–11
- Strengthen your brothers and sisters—D&C 108:7

FAITHFULNESS IN ALL THINGS

And any man that shall go and preach this gospel of the kingdom, and fail not to continue faithful in all things, shall not be weary in mind, neither darkened, neither in body, limb, nor joint; and a hair of his head shall not fall to the ground unnoticed. And they shall not go hungry, neither athirst.

D&C 84:80

The Lord has kept his promise to all those who have been faithful in their calling. Surely if the Father notices when a sparrow falls, he will not forsake any who in faithful obedience to his will seek his aid. That there have been those who have gone forth and have been weary in body and mind, and who have gone hungry, there is no doubt, for there are missionaries who have not given all their heart to the Lord and they have idled away valuable time when it was needful for them to proclaim the truth.

(Joseph Fielding Smith, *Church History and Modern Revelation*, 4 vols. [Salt Lake City: The Church of Jesus Christ of Latter-day Saints, 1946–1949], 2:108)

Daily Living

BE FAITHFUL DISCIPLES IN ALL THINGS.

- ☙ The Lord will make you equal to the task. He will give the words to say and be beside you—D&C 84:85; 100:5–6; D&C 84:88
- ☙ Remember, if we are humble in our weakness, He will strengthen our faith to make us strong, for in His strength we can do all things—Ether 12:27; Alma 26:11–12

TREASURE UP THE WORDS OF LIFE

Neither take ye thought beforehand what ye shall say; but treasure up in your minds continually the words of life, and it shall be given you in the very hour that portion that shall be meted unto every man.
D&C 84:85

The faithful servants of the Lord, in this dispensation, have the same promise extended to them which was given to the ancient Apostles and disciples—viz., that the Spirit shall bring to their remembrance all things that are necessary for them to utter when they stand up in advocacy and defence of the Gospel. But, if their minds are vacant and have never been stored with the principles of the Gospel and general, useful knowledge, there would be nothing for the Spirit of the Lord to operate upon; and, as it would be impossible for any being to bring to their remembrance that which they never knew, they would be very likely to be extremely disappointed in the aid which they expected to receive. It is the duty of the Elders to constantly study the revelations which the Lord has given to his children in all ages, and to make themselves thoroughly familiar with all the doctrines and principles of the Church.

(George Q. Cannon, *Gospel Truth: Discourses and Writings of George Q. Cannon*, ed. Jerreld L Newquist [Salt Lake City: Deseret Book, 1987], 466)

Daily Living

TREASURE UP THE WORD OF GOD IN YOUR VERY SOUL.

ꝏ The sons of Mosiah are perfect examples of preparation and being able to preach with the power and authority of God—Alma 17:2–3; D&C 11:21; 100:5–6

THE LORD WILL BE WITH YOU

And whoso receiveth you, there I will be also, for I will go before your face. I will be on your right hand and on your left, and my Spirit shall be in your hearts, and mine angels round about you, to bear you up.
D&C 84:88

There is not anything desirable that you will not be able to do with the aid and the help of the Lord, and every gift and power will be with you to accomplish his work if you will do your full part.

(Ezra Taft Benson, *A Labor of Love: The 1946 European Mission of Ezra Taft Benson* [Salt Lake City: Deseret Book, 1989], 238)

Daily Living

REMEMBER THAT THE LORD IS WITH YOU IN HIS WORK.

- What comfort and peace we have in knowing that or Savior is with us in all that we do as we seek to build up the kingdom of God. He is our strength—Psalms 27:1
- We go forward in His strength—Psalms 71:16
- Remember, in the strength of the Lord we can do all things—Alma 20:4; 26:12
- The Lord is with us in all things—1 Nephi 17:55; 2 Nephi 5:11; Alma 38:4; Helaman 16:2
- The Lord will always provide the way for us to accomplish His commandments—1 Nephi 3:7; 17:3
- The Lord will be your support, will lead you through your afflictions, and preserve you in difficulties—2 Nephi 4:20

August 25

THE CHURCH HATH NEED OF EVERY PERSON

Therefore, let every man stand in his own office, and labor in his own calling; and let not the head say unto the feet it hath no need of the feet; for without the feet how shall the body be able to stand? Also the body hath need of every member, that all may be edified together, that the system may be kept perfect.
D&C 84:109–110

God bless you, my beloved associates in this great work. We are all in this together. None of us can slip down without taking the whole Church down somewhat. None of us can do better without lifting the whole Church somewhat. You are important. Everyone is important. We are all a part of it. We can do a little better. I pray that we will work at it just a little harder, with a little more devotion, a little more love, a little more prayer, a little more enthusiasm. This is the Savior's work. This is not my church, it is the Savior's church. He stands at the head. We are merely here to do His bidding, to listen to His voice, and try to give expression to it the best way we know how.

(Gordon B. Hinckley, *Teachings of Gordon B. Hinckley* [Salt Lake City: Deseret Book, 1997], 137)

Daily Living

WE ALL NEED EACH OTHER TO BUILD UP THE KINGDOM OF GOD.

- We all teach one another—D&C 38:23; 88:77–78
- We are all to strengthen one another—D&C 108:7
- We are to serve, watch over, and care for one another—Mosiah 18:8–9
- We all should love one another—John 13:34–35

LIGHT OF THE LORD

And the light which shineth, which giveth you light, is through him who enlighteneth your eyes, which is the same light that quickeneth your understandings; Which light proceedeth forth from the presence of God to fill the immensity of space—The light which is in all things, which giveth life to all things, which is the law by which all things are governed, even the power of God who sitteth upon his throne, who is in the bosom of eternity, who is in the midst of all things.

D&C 88:11–13

By choosing the light of the Lord, knowledge and truth, and the light of love in our lives, we will be qualified to live by the light of the Spirit. If we cultivate a heart that is constantly in tune with the Spirit of the Lord, our lives will be enriched. We will be able to make good decisions, and we will be comforted in times of trial and adversity.

(Joseph B. Wirthlin, *Finding Peace in Our Lives* [Salt Lake City: Deseret Book, 1995], 75)

Daily Living

THE LORD IS THE LIGHT IN ALL THINGS.

- He is the light that we hold up—3 Nephi 18:24
- It is His light that shines forth from us that glorifies our Father in Heaven—3 Nephi 12:16
- When our eye is single to the glory of God, our whole bodies will be filled with light—D&C 88:67
- We, like Ammon, can boast of the goodness of our God and His matchless power—Alma 26:35–36

REDEMPTION OF THE SOUL

And the spirit and the body are the soul of man. And the resurrection from the dead is the redemption of the soul. And the redemption of the soul is through him that quickeneth all things, in whose bosom it is decreed that the poor and the meek of the earth shall inherit it. Therefore, it must needs be sanctified from all unrighteousness, that it may be prepared for the celestial glory.

D&C 88:15–18

As a universal gift flowing from the atonement of Christ, the Resurrection will clothe with a permanent, perfected, restored body every spirit ever born into mortality. Furthermore, for every person who accepts the principles and ordinances of the gospel, that person's body will be something of a robe of righteousness. Therein is the redemption of the soul, and therein is a fullness of joy throughout all eternity, including, in its highest order, "a fulness and a continuation of the seeds forever and ever."

(Jeffrey R. Holland, *Christ and the New Covenant: The Messianic Message of the Book of Mormon* [Salt Lake City: Deseret Book, 1997], 244)

Daily Living

THE REDEMPTION OF OUR SOULS IS THROUGH THE LORD.

- Christ has redeemed our souls. Our fate without the atoning sacrifice and Resurrection of our Savior would leave us subject to the devil—2 Nephi 9:7–9
- The goodness of God has provided a way for our escape for which we should be eternally grateful—2 Nephi 9:10

RIGHTEOUSNESS EMBRACES EVERY FORM OF RIGHTEOUSNESS

For intelligence cleaveth unto intelligence; wisdom receiveth wisdom; truth embraceth truth; virtue loveth virtue; light cleaveth unto light; mercy hath compassion on mercy and claimeth her own; justice continueth its course and claimeth its own; judgment goeth before the face of him who sitteth upon the throne and governeth and executeth all things.
D&C 88:40

If we do evil, evil impressions come naturally, and if we love to do good a good influence, a good spirit, is with us, and round about us, and in our being and we are sustained and supported thereby; and if we are corrupt and wicked and abominable and rebellious, the effects of our acts are right in our nature and these things will be disclosed just as naturally as the opening of books made of paper and written with ink.

(Charles W. Penrose, in Conference Report, April 1917, 18)

Daily Living

RIGHTEOUSNESS EMBRACES EVERY FORM OF RIGHTEOUSNESS.

- That which we seek becomes that which we receive and love. If our minds are on the things of God, we think of eternal and spiritual things—Article of Faith 1:13
- Remember, "Let thy bowels also be full of charity towards all men, and to the household of faith, and let virtue garnish thy thoughts unceasingly . . . and thy scepter an unchanging scepter of righteousness and truth; and thy dominion shall be an everlasting dominion"—D&C 121:45–46

DRAW NEAR UNTO THE LORD

Draw near unto me and I will draw near unto you; seek me diligently and ye shall find me; ask, and ye shall receive; knock, and it shall be opened unto you.
D&C 88:63

Mark, how clear-cut are these words [in D&C 88:63]. There is no doubt, no dubiety. It does not say if and peradventure you call upon the Lord, He may be gone on a long journey and you cannot reach Him; or He is very busy. . . . No. This revelation does not give forth any such ideas. . . . And yet—think of it! He says to you and to me: He says to this poor man and to this poor woman: He says to this rich man and to this rich woman. . . . "My ear will be opened to hear your prayer and to answer it."

(Rudger Clawson, in Conference Report, April 1904, 97)

Daily Living

DRAW NEAR UNTO ME, AND I WILL DRAW NEAR UNTO YOU.

- The Lord comes to us and knocks and stands waiting at the door; if we but open it He will come unto us—Revelation 3:20
- Asking with the promise of receiving is an eternal verity, as Nephi taught. "And I said unto them: Have ye inquired of the Lord? Then Laman and Lemuel responded by saying that the Lord has made no such thing known unto them. Why? Because they had not inquired of the Lord—1 Nephi 15:8
- We must ask in faith, even like the Prophet Joseph. Ask and it will be given—James 1:5–6; D&C 4:7

ASK FOR THOSE THINGS WHICH ARE EXPEDIENT

Whatsoever ye ask the Father in my name it shall be given unto you, that is expedient for you; And if ye ask anything that is not expedient for you, it shall turn unto your condemnation.
D&C 88:64–65

When we ask amiss, God, being perfect, must reject our petitions: "And whatsoever ye shall ask the Father in my name, *which is right*, believing that ye shall receive, behold it shall be given unto you" (3 Nephi 18:20; italics added). The task is to draw close enough to the Lord that we progress to the point where we petition Him according to His will, not ours. "And this is the confidence that we have in him, that, if we ask any thing according to his will, he heareth us" (1 John 5:14). . . . When we become sufficiently purified and cleansed from sin, we can ask what we will in the name of Jesus "and it shall be done" (D&C 50:29). The Lord even promises us that when one reaches a certain spiritual condition, "it shall be given you what you shall ask" (D&C 50:30).

(Neal A. Maxwell, *All These Things Shall Give Thee Experience* [Salt Lake City: Deseret Book, 1979], 94)

Daily Living

ASK FOR THOSE THINGS WHICH ARE EXPEDIENT.

ꟻ What is expedient? We must be concerned about what matters most—the welfare of our souls and the souls of our fellow men. We pray to become more Christlike and help others come unto Christ. Ask according to the will of God and our true needs—Helaman 10:5

EYE SINGLE TO THE GLORY OF GOD

And if your eye be single to my glory, your whole bodies shall be filled with light, and there shall be no darkness in you; and that body which is filled with light comprehendeth all things. Therefore, sanctify yourselves that your minds become single to God, and the days will come that you shall see him; for he will unveil his face unto you, and it shall be in his own time, and in his own way, and according to his own will.

D&C 88:67–68

To be faithful is to strive each day to keep the commandments, to hunger and thirst after righteousness, to plead for divine guidance, and to seek for and listen to the still, small voice. To be faithful . . . is active, joyful, anxious engagement in good causes, reverence for righteousness, an eye single to the glory of God.

(Alexander B. Morrison, *Feed My Sheep: Leadership Ideas for Latter-day Shepherds* [Salt Lake City: Deseret Book, 1992], 63)

Daily Living

HAVE AN EYE SINGLE TO THE GLORY OF GOD IN ALL THINGS.

- An eye single to the glory of God—Our will is the will of God. We are admonished several times to have an eye single to the glory of God—D&C 4:5; 27:2; 55:1; 59:1; 82:19
- As we seek to glorify our God through righteousness, He joys in our growth as we seek to become like Him. He is our Father whose work and glory is our immortality and eternal life—Moses 1:39

SEPTEMBER

And, inasmuch as they are faithful, I will multiply blessings upon them and their seed after them, even a multiplicity of blessings.

—Doctrine & Covenants 104:33

SANCTIFY YOURSELVES

And I give unto you, who are the first laborers in this last kingdom, a commandment that you assemble yourselves together, and organize yourselves, and prepare yourselves, and sanctify yourselves; yea, purify your hearts, and cleanse your hands and your feet before me, that I may make you clean; That I may testify unto your Father, and your God, and my God, that you are clean from the blood of this wicked generation; that I may fulfil this promise, this great and last promise, which I have made unto you, when I will.

D&C 88:74–75

One who is sanctified through the Spirit has "no more disposition to do evil, but to do good continually" (Mosiah 5:2).

(Hoyt W. Brewster, Jr., *Doctrine and Covenants Encyclopedia* [Salt Lake City: Bookcraft, 1996], 490)

Daily Living

SANCTIFY YOURSELVES AND PURIFY YOUR HEARTS.

- We must stand before the Lord clean, pure, and sanctified so He can be our Advocate with the Father to present us as worthy heirs with Him in the kingdom of our Father. It is made possible through the grace and goodness of the Lord Jesus Christ—Moroni 10:32–33
- We become sanctified as we yield our hearts to God—Helaman 3:35
- We become pure before God and look upon sin with abhorrence—Alma 13:11–12

CONTINUE IN PRAYER AND FASTING

Also, I give unto you a commandment that ye shall continue in prayer and fasting from this time forth.
D&C 88:76

I am confident that as leaders we do not do enough fasting and praying. If you want to get the spirit of your office and calling as a new president of a quorum, a new high councilman, a new bishop—try fasting for a period. I don't mean just missing one meal, then eating twice as much the next meal. I mean really fasting, and praying during that period. It will do more to give you the real spirit of your office and calling and permit the Spirit to operate through you than anything I know.

(Ezra Taft Benson, *The Teachings of Ezra Taft Benson* [Salt Lake City: Bookcraft, 1988], 331–332)

Daily Living

FAST AND PRAY THAT THE BLESSINGS OF THE LORD CAN BE YOURS.

- Alma fasted and prayed many days that he might gain knowledge—Alma 5:46
- Fast and pray for faith and humility—Helaman 3:35
- The sons of Mosiah fasted and prayed that they might teach with the power and authority of God—Alma 17:3
- Consider every fast Sunday how we can become more like our Savior by fasting and praying to take upon ourselves His divine nature—2 Peter 1:3–12; Moroni 7:48; D&C 4:6

TEACH ONE ANOTHER

And I give unto you a commandment that you shall teach one another the doctrine of the kingdom. Teach ye diligently and my grace shall attend you, that you may be instructed more perfectly in theory, in principle, in doctrine, in the law of the gospel, in all things that pertain unto the kingdom of God, that are expedient for you to understand.

D&C 88:77–78

Learning enjoined by the Lord has ever been concerned with eternity. For example: . . . "teach one another words of wisdom; yea, seek ye out of the best books words of wisdom" (D&C 88:118). "Of things both in heaven and in the earth, and under the earth; things which have been, things which are, things which must shortly come to pass; things which are at home, things which are abroad; the wars and the perplexities of the nations, and the judgments which are on the land; and a knowledge also of countries and of kingdoms" (D&C 88:77–79).

This familiar scripture is often cited to illustrate the wide scope of learning in which the Lord desires us to be interested.

(Marion G. Romney, *Learning for the Eternities* [Salt Lake City: Deseret Book, 1977], 50)

Daily Living

TEACH ONE ANOTHER THE DOCTRINE OF THE KINGDOM.

- As you seek to teach and to learn, remember that both are equal in role—Alma 1:26
- Edification comes to the teacher and the learner by the Spirit of Truth—D&C 50:17–22

WARN YOUR NEIGHBOR

Behold, I sent you out to testify and warn the people, and it becometh every man who hath been warned to warn his neighbor. Therefore, they are left without excuse, and their sins are upon their own heads.

D&C 88:81–82

Many of us take pride in referring to the growth of the Church or the success of the worldwide missionary effort but have never fellowshipped an acquaintance or a neighbor. When returning mission presidents are asked, "How could you have had more conversions in your mission," we hear the same reply: "If only we could get the members to assist the missionaries by preparing their friends and neighbors to receive the elders."

Have we forgotten our obligation? Have we forgotten what the Lord said? . . . "And let your preaching be the warning voice, every man to his neighbor." [D&C 38: 41].

(David B. Haight, in Conference Report, October 1976, 26)

Daily Living

TESTIFY AND WARN YOUR NEIGHBOR.

ꕥ Prayerfully consider your friends, neighbors, and acquaintances who might be interested in hearing the gospel. Then set a date to do those things that will show them the beauty and the happiness the gospel offers . . . thus preparing them to hear the gospel message from the full-time missionaries. Remember that the Lord will provide a way—1 Nephi 3:7; Alma 6:6; D&C 33:8–11; 62:3; 84:85–88; 100:5–6

September 5

LABOR DILIGENTLY

Therefore, tarry ye, and labor diligently, that you may be perfected in your ministry to go forth among the Gentiles for the last time, as many as the mouth of the Lord shall name, to bind up the law and seal up the testimony, and to prepare the saints for the hour of judgment which is to come.
D&C 88:84

I now called the people together and exhorted them to sell their property and prepare to accompany me to the land of Zion. I had labored hard for many days for the temporal and spiritual welfare of the inhabitants of those islands, and the Lord had blessed my labors and given me many souls as seals of my ministry, for which I felt to praise Him; and now I felt to labor quite as zealously to gather out those who had embraced the gospel, and lead them to Zion.

(Wilford Woodruff, *Leaves from My Journal* [Salt Lake City: Juvenile Instructor Office, 1881], 55)

Daily Living

LABOR DILIGENTLY THAT YOU MAY BE PERFECTED.

- Come unto Christ with charity and you can be perfected—Moroni 10:32
- You are perfected as you do temple work—D&C 128:15
- Diligently take upon yourself the divine nature of Christ and make your calling and election sure—2 Peter 1:3–12
- Oh, the joy and blessing of being a true disciple of the Lord Jesus Christ in sharing the gospel message—3 Nephi 5:13; Alma 29:9–10; 36:24; D&C 31:5; 62:3; James 5:20

SEEK LEARNING BY STUDY AND FAITH

And as all have not faith, seek ye diligently and teach one another words of wisdom; yea, seek ye out of the best books words of wisdom; seek learning, even by study and also by faith.
D&C 88:118

If mankind could know the object God has in their creation, and what they might obtain by doing right and by applying to the source and fountain of wisdom for information, how quickly they would turn away from every ungodly action and custom. . . . Instead of seeking unto the Lord for wisdom, they seek unto the vain philosophy and the deceit and traditions of men, which are after the rudiments of the world and not after Christ. They are led by their own imaginations and by the dictates of their selfish will, which will lead them in the end, to miss the object of their pursuit.
(Brigham Young, *Journal of Discourses*, June 14, 1863, 10:209)

Daily Living

SEEK LEARNING BY STUDY AND FAITH.

- Desire and effort are key ingredients. To study effectively and to increase in faith, we must have a desire to believe and work and even experiment upon the word—Alma 32:27
- Be wise in your study habits, pray, and exercise your mental exertion to increase your faith in the Lord Jesus Christ. He is the way, the truth, and the light of the world—Ether 4:12

ORGANIZE EVERY NEEDFUL THING

Organize yourselves; prepare every needful thing; and establish a house, even a house of prayer, a house of fasting, a house of faith, a house of learning, a house of glory, a house of order, a house of God.

D&C 88:119

Prepare well. Our noble thoughts must be part of a purposeful plan, if the dream castles we have envisioned are to become a reality. The Lord taught: "Organize yourselves; prepare every needful thing" (D&C 88:119). A reading of the book of Genesis gives one insight into the painstaking planning undertaken by God himself.

At times the preparation period may appear dull, uninteresting, and even unnecessary. But experience continues to demonstrate that the future belongs to those who prepare for it. And if we are to become leaders, we cannot skimp on our preparation. . . . Spiritual preparation is vital. Spirituality is not like a water faucet in that it can be turned off or turned on at will. . . . To be prepared spiritually for leadership overshadows all other types of preparation. I challenge each of us to prepare well.

(Thomas S. Monson, *Be Your Best Self* [Salt Lake City: Deseret Book, 1979], 121–122)

Daily Living

PREPARE AND ORGANIZE YOURSELF—SET GOALS—MAKE PLANS.

- The gospel itself is God's plan for us—the "great plan of happiness"—Alma 42:8; see also Alma 12:25, 30; 34:9; 42:15
- Plan well to achieve your goal of eternal life.

LOVE ONE ANOTHER

See that ye love one another; cease to be covetous; learn to impart one to another as the gospel requires.
D&C 88:123

True love is a process. True love requires personal action. Love must be continuing to be real. Love takes time . . . speak and reassure others of our love and the long time it takes to prove it by our actions. Real love does take time. The Great Shepherd had the same thoughts in mind when he taught, "If ye love me, keep my commandments" (John 14:15) and "If ye love me feed my sheep" (John 21:16). . . . Love is a process . . . [and] we can often best show our love through the processes of *feeding* and keeping.

(Marvin J. Ashton, *Ensign*, November 1975, 108)

Daily Living

LOVE ONE ANOTHER IN ALL THINGS AND IN ALL WAYS.

- The commandment to love is extolled time and time again throughout the scriptures as the great commandment that fulfills all the law and the prophets—Matthew 22:36–40
- Love is the motive for all that our Heavenly Father and Savior do for us—John 3:16; 2 Nephi 26:24
- We show our love of God when we love and serve our fellowmen—Mosiah 2:17
- Disciples of the Lord love everyone—John 13:34–35
- This is why we should pray with all the energy of our hearts that we might possess the pure love of Christ—Moroni 7:48

CEASE YOUR WRONG DOINGS

Cease to be idle; cease to be unclean; cease to find fault one with another; cease to sleep longer than is needful; retire to thy bed early, that ye may not be weary; arise early, that your bodies and your minds may be invigorated.

D&C 88:124

Now, my brethren, you who have sinned, repent of your sins. I can say to you in regard to Jesus and the atonement . . . that Christ has died for all. He has paid the full debt, whether you receive the gift or not. But if we continue to sin, to lie, steal, bear false witness, we must repent of and forsake that sin to have the full efficacy of the blood of Christ. Without this it will be of no effect; repentance must come, in order that the atonement may prove a benefit to us. Let all who are doing wrong cease doing wrong; live no longer in transgression, no matter of what kind; but live every day of your lives according to the revelations given, and so that your examples may be worthy of imitation.

(Brigham Young, *Discourses of Brigham Young*, selected and arranged by John A. Widtsoe [Salt Lake City: Deseret Book, 1954], 156)

Daily Living

CEASE YOUR WRONG DOINGS AND WORK RIGHTEOUSNESS.

℘ The Lord, in His ever tutoring and chastening of His children, reminds us and commands us to cease from our sins and to be wise in the use of time. Time, the precious commodity of life, cannot be stored or replenished. For now is the time to prepare to meet God—Alma 34:32

CLOTHE YOURSELF WITH CHARITY

And above all things, clothe yourselves with the bond of charity, as with a mantle, which is the bond of perfectness and peace.
D&C 88:125

"Charity is the pure love of Christ, and it endureth forever; and whoso is found possessed of it at the last day, it shall be well with him" (Moro. 7:47; Ether 12:34; 2 Ne. 26:30). As the love of Christ, charity is characterized as selfless and self-sacrificing (1 Cor. 13:5), emanating from a pure heart, a good conscience, and faith unfeigned (1 Tim. 1:5). Thus, more than an act, charity is an attitude, a state of heart and mind (1 Cor. 13:4–7) that accompanies one's works and is proffered unconditionally (D&C 121:45). It follows, but surpasses in importance, faith and hope (1 Cor. 13:13).

(Addie Fuhriman, *Encyclopedia of Mormonism*, 1–4 vols., ed. Daniel H. Ludlow [New York: Macmillan, 1992], 264)

Daily Living

CLOTHE YOURSELF IN CHARITY, THE PURE LOVE OF CHRIST.

ಬ Clothed with charity suggests an inner quality that is in our very being. It is who we are. It is what we do. It is in our countenance. Our feelings, attitudes, values, perceptions, and, above all, our actions are charitable like unto Christ. Charity will never fail. Oh, that we might be filled with this love, "which he hath bestowed upon all who are true followers of his Son, Jesus Christ; that ye may become the sons of God; that when he shall appear we shall be like him . . ." —Moroni 7:48; 2 Peter 1:3–10

THE WORD OF WISDOM

Given for a principle with promise, adapted to the capacity of the weak and the weakest of all saints, who are or can be called saints.
D&C 89:3

We encourage you to live the Word of Wisdom. The Apostle Peter challenged the Saints of his day to be "a peculiar people" (1 Peter 2:9). One of the unique characteristics of the Latter-day Saints is obedience to this law which encourages us to avoid that which is damaging to our body. . . . We should not partake of tea, coffee, tobacco, alcohol, or any substance that contains illegal drugs or harmful or habit-forming ingredients. . . . We encourage you to walk squarely on the Lord's side of the line. Do not tamper with any of these substances, nor similar products which give the "appearance of evil" (1 Thess. 5:22).

(Howard W. Hunter, *The Teachings of Howard W. Hunter*, ed. Clyde J. Williams [Salt Lake City: Bookcraft, 1997], 104)

Daily Living

THE WORD OF WISDOM IS A PRINCIPLE WITH A PROMISE.

ꕥ As with all the commandments of God there are blessings and consequences. There is nothing so apparent to the destruction of the body as is the violation of the Word of Wisdom in regard to our health and well being. The medical knowledge of today has proven the prophetic nature of the Prophet Joseph and that the revelations of God are true and withstand the test of time. Oh, be wise: keep the Word of Wisdom.

BLESSINGS FOR OBEDIENCE TO THE WORD OF WISDOM

And all saints who remember to keep and do these sayings, walking in obedience to the commandments, shall receive health in their navel and marrow to their bones; And shall find wisdom and great treasures of knowledge, even hidden treasures; And shall run and not be weary, and shall walk and not faint. And I, the Lord, give unto them a promise, that the destroying angel shall pass by them, as the children of Israel, and not slay them. Amen.

D&C 89:18–21

If we desire the blessings of life, of health, of vigor of body and mind; if we desire the destroying angel to pass us by . . . as he did in the days of the children of Israel, we must obey the Word of Wisdom. We then may rest assured that God is bound, for He has so declared, and the blessings shall come to us.

(Heber J. Grant, *Gospel Standards: Selections from the Sermons and Writings of Heber J. Grant*, compiled by G. Homer Durham [Salt Lake City: Deseret Book, 1981], 48)

Daily Living

BLESSINGS FOR OBEDIENCE TO THE WORD OF WISDOM.

ꝏ Blessings for keeping the Word of Wisdom are not just of a healthy body. Your mind and intellect will be clear. You will be in control of your emotions. Your social behavior will be appropriate. You will not put others in jeopardy by impaired faculties. Your spiritual blessings will abound, for the Spirit can dwell only in a clean and holy temple—1 Corinthians 6:19

RECEIVE THE ORACLES OF GOD

And all they who receive the oracles of God, let them beware how they hold them lest they are accounted as a light thing, and are brought under condemnation thereby, and stumble and fall when the storms descend, and the winds blow, and the rains descend, and beat upon their house.

D&C 90:5

His [The Lord's] children are on shaky ground when they take lightly the words of his prophet. In the midst of apostasy in the trying Kirtland years, the Lord reminded the Church of the importance of the First Presidency: "Whosoever receiveth me, receiveth the First Presidency" (D&C 112:20). President Marion G. Romney said, "What they say as a presidency is what the Lord would say if he were here in person." The Saints again in Nauvoo were told that they could not be blessed if they did not hearken unto the voice of his servants (D&C 124:45–46).

(Robert L. Millet and Kent Jackson, eds., *Studies in Scripture, Vol. 1: The Doctrine and Covenants* [Salt Lake City: Deseret Book, 1989], 156)

Daily Living

THE PROPHETS OF GOD ARE ORACLES.

- The Lord reminds us that whosoever receiveth my servants receiveth me—Matthew 10:40–41; John 13:20; 3 Nephi 12:1–2; 3 Nephi 28:34; D&C 1:38; 21:4–6; 84:36–37
- The Lord considers it a grievous sin when we set aside the word of God and the teachings of the prophets—2 Nephi 9:28–29; 3 Nephi 28:34–35

HEAR THE GOSPEL IN THEIR OWN TONGUE

For it shall come to pass in that day, that every man shall hear the fulness of the gospel in his own tongue, and in his own language, through those who are ordained unto this power, by the administration of the Comforter, shed forth upon them for the revelation of Jesus Christ.

D&C 90:11

At the time these revelations were received, it probably seemed almost impossible that all individuals could be taught in their own tongue or language. Now, however, we live in a day when modern transportation, satellite and television communication, and computer translation and printing capabilities make it possible for every individual in the world to hear the gospel in his own tongue. Today missionaries are trained in languages and sent to every part of the world in fulfillment of this command to spread the gospel "unto every nation, and kindred, and tongue, and people" (D&C 133:37).

(Byron R. Merrill et al., comps., *The Heavens Are Open: The 1992 Sperry Symposium on the Doctrine and Covenants and Church History* [Salt Lake City: Deseret Book, 1993], 131)

Daily Living

THE GOSPEL WILL BE PREACHED IN THEIR OWN LANGUAGE.

ᢀ The Lord requires His ministers to preach the gospel in the native tongue of each of His children. This ensures understanding and appreciation of the word of God. Seek to learn another language, thus being able to assist others in understanding the gospel of Jesus Christ.

SEARCH DILIGENTLY AND WALK UPRIGHTLY

Search diligently, pray always, and be believing, and all things shall work together for your good, if ye walk uprightly and remember the covenant wherewith ye have covenanted one with another.

D&C 90:24

If the Latter-day Saints will wake up to their privileges, and exercise faith in the name of Jesus Christ, and live in the enjoyment of the fulness of the Holy Ghost constantly day by day, there is nothing on the face of the earth that they could ask for, that would not be given to them. The Lord is waiting to be very gracious unto this people, and to pour out upon them riches, honor, glory, and power, even that they may possess all things according to the promises He has made through His apostles and prophets.

(Brigham Young, *Journal of Discourses*, July 1865, 11:114–115)

Daily Living

SEARCH DILIGENTLY, PRAY ALWAYS, AND BE BELIEVING.

- Blessings are predicated upon our obedience—D&C 130:20–21
- Search the scriptures—John 5:39; Alma 14:1; 33:2; 3 Nephi 10:14; 3 Nephi 23:5–6
- Pray always—2 Nephi 32:9; 3 Nephi 18:18–19; D&C 10:5
- Be believing—John 10:27; Mormon 9:27
- If we walk uprightly to the commandments and covenants that we have made and do our part, the Lord will keep His promises—D&C 82:10

KEEP THE COMMANDMENTS

Verily, thus saith the Lord: It shall come to pass that every soul who forsaketh his sins and cometh unto me, and calleth on my name, and obeyeth my voice, and keepeth my commandments, shall see my face and know that I am.

D&C 93:1

The Lord will bless us to the degree to which we keep His commandments. Nephi put this principle in a tremendous orbit when he said, "For we labor diligently to write, to persuade our children, and also our brethren, to believe in Christ, and to be reconciled to God; for we know that it is by grace that we are saved, after all we can do" (2 Nephi 25:23). The Savior's blood, His atonement, will save us, but only after we have done all we can to save ourselves by keeping His commandments.

(Harold B. Lee, *The Teachings of Harold B. Lee*, ed. Clyde J. Williams [Salt Lake City: Bookcraft, 1996], 186)

Daily Living

WHAT SHOULD WE DO?—KEEP THE COMMANDMENTS.

- Consider this the formula for a righteous life with promised blessings: Repent and come unto Christ with all your heart, calling upon the Father in the name of the Lord, and obey His words and keep the commandments, and you shall see the Lord as He is and know Him—Moroni 7:48; John 17:3; D&C 67:10
- The gospel requires faithful obedience—Moses 5:6

THE LIGHT AND REDEEMER OF THE WORLD

The light and the Redeemer of the world; the Spirit of truth, who came into the world, because the world was made by him, and in him was the life of men and the light of men.
D&C 93:9

Let members of the Church, and honest men in every clime accept, not as an abstract, inapplicable saying, but as an eternal and guiding truth, the declaration of the Redeemer: "I am the light of the world: he that followeth me shall not walk in darkness, but shall have the light of life" (John 8:12).

(David O. McKay, in Conference Report, October 1942, 70)

Daily Living

ACCEPT THE LIGHT AND REDEEMER OF THE WORLD.

ഗ Oh, the greatness and goodness of our Lord and Savior Jesus Christ. We are continually indebted to Him for all things. Take a moment and turn to King Benjamin's address (see Mosiah 2–5), of which part was given to him by an angel of God, and ponder all that Christ has done in our lives. You, like the people of King Benjamin, will feel differently. "And they all cried with one voice, saying: Yea, we believe all the words which thou hast spoken unto us; and also, we know of their surety and truth, because of the Spirit of the Lord Omnipotent, which has wrought a mighty change in us, or in our hearts, that we have no more disposition to do evil, but to do good continually"—Mosiah 5:2

THE TRUTH

And truth is knowledge of things as they are, and as they were, and as they are to come;
The Spirit of truth is of God. I am the Spirit of truth, and John bore record of me, saying: He received a fulness of truth, yea, even of all truth.
D&C 93:24, 26

How is such knowledge to be obtained? . . . How then, is the whole truth to be secured? The key is to be found in another revelation, "the Spirit of truth is of God." [D&C 93:26.] That being so, we must, of necessity have God's aid in the acquisition of truth. His aid comes through faith and prayer. . . . It postulates humility and dependence on divine power, the antipathies of egotism and self-sufficiency. A contrite heart is a fertile field for planting the seeds of truth. In such a field they come to fruition in a knowledge, understanding, and conviction of the great concepts of life which defy the reason and philosophy of the arrogant and self-sufficient who will not stoop to the methods of the humble.

(Stephen L Richards, in Conference Report, April 1939, 40–41)

Daily Living

THE SPIRIT OF TRUTH IS OF GOD.

- Truth is found in the Lord Jesus Christ. He is "the light, and the life, and the truth of the world"—Ether 4:12
- One of the main purposes of our Savior is to "bear witness unto the truth" (John 18:37). Truth is found in all the things of God: His word (see John 17:17), His law (see Psalms 119:142), and His works (see Daniel 4:37).

TRUTH AND LIGHT

He that keepeth his commandments receiveth truth and light, until he is glorified in truth and knoweth all things.
D&C 93:28

The word *intelligence* may have two distinct meanings: (1) academic ability or mental capacity, and (2) that part of our being that has existed from the beginning. . . . Notice how Doctrine and Covenants 93:36 equates God's glory with "light and truth," and verse 29 indicates that these were attributes of man "in the beginning." In other words, we had the same qualities that constitute God's glory, but we had them in only a small degree whereas he has them in full. The essential message of section 93 is that by keeping God's commandments we can receive "truth and light" until we have them in full and are glorified (vv. 20, 28). On the other hand, we are cautioned that Satan "taketh away light and truth through disobedience" (v. 39).

(Richard O. Cowan, *Answers to Your Questions About the Doctrine and Covenants* [Salt Lake City: Deseret Book, 1996], 116)

Daily Living

KEEP THE COMMANDMENTS—RECEIVE TRUTH AND LIGHT.

- If we keep the commandments, we will always have the Spirit with us. The Spirit testifies of all truth—Moroni 10:5
- When our bodies are filled with truth and light there is no darkness in us, and we will comprehend all things, and thus we become glorified in the Lord for receiving His light and His truth—D&C 88:67

THE GLORY OF GOD

The glory of God is intelligence, or, in other words, light and truth. Light and truth forsake that evil one.
D&C 93:36–37

Intelligence, as light and truth, is the glory of God (D&C 93:36). . . . "One is saved no faster than he gets knowledge" (*TPJS*, 217); and he gains knowledge of the truths of the gospel no faster than he is saved—that is, no faster than he receives Christ into his life. "Knowledge through our Lord and Savior Jesus Christ is the grand key that unlocks the glory and mysteries of the kingdom of heaven" (*TPJS,* 298).

(*Encyclopedia of Mormonism*, 1–4 vols., ed. Daniel H. Ludlow [New York: Macmillan, 1992], 1341)

Daily Living

THE GLORY OF GOD—LIGHT AND TRUTH.

ຮ Pure intelligence is the light and truth which comes from our Savior Jesus Christ and our Heavenly Father. The glory of our Father and Savior is made evident not only because of their omnipotence (all power), omnipresence (present in all things), and omniscience (all knowledge), but because of Their perfect state of holiness and righteousness through light and truth; this is part of Their glory—pure intelligence. When we begin to receive this light and truth, we become empowered to forsake sin and the devil. We, through the grace of God, can have immortality and eternal life—Moses 1:39

LOSING LIGHT AND TRUTH

And that wicked one cometh and taketh away light and truth, through disobedience, from the children of men, and because of the tradition of their fathers.
D&C 93:39

The Lord has said that the devil takes away light and truth from the children of men in two ways, generically speaking. First, by the disobedience of men they lose the truth, and secondly, through the traditions of their fathers (D&C 93:39). One is held accountable only for the light and truth he receives or has opportunity to receive. If he is born in an environment where he has access to the full light of the gospel, his responsibility will be different from that of the person who is born in an environment devoid of that light.

(David H. Yarn, *The Gospel: God, Man, and Truth* [Salt Lake City: Deseret Book, 1979], 108)

Daily Living

LIGHT AND TRUTH ARE LOST THROUGH DISOBEDIENCE.

- Disobedience comes with a terrible price. We lose the Spirit with all its attendant gifts and blessings—Mormon 1:13–14; 2 Nephi 32:5
- The power is within you to choose liberty and life eternal or captivity and death—2 Nephi 2:27
- You will choose eternal life if you are faithful to the word of God according to the will of the Holy Spirit—2 Nephi 2:28

TEACH YOUR CHILDREN

But I have commanded you to bring up your children in light and truth.
D&C 93:40

It is the power of the wicked one or Satan to deceive and lead children astray after they arrive at the years of accountability [Sec. 68:25], which parents must guard against, not only by teaching their children correct principles, doctrines, and life's true values, but also by setting the proper example before them; otherwise, false traditions will be built up in the home which children will absorb to their eternal harm.

As parents we should ask ourselves this question: What kind of traditions are we building up in our home for our children to absorb and accept into the pattern of their own lives? . . . To bring up children in light and truth is to bring them up in an understanding and acceptance of the true word of God. Do your children understand the doctrine of repentance, of faith in Christ the Son of the Living God, and the importance of baptism . . . the need of receiving the gift of the Holy Ghost?

(Delbert L. Stapley, in Conference Report, October 1960, 98)

Daily Living

BRING YOUR CHILDREN UP IN LIGHT AND TRUTH.

- Parents are to teach their children—D&C 68:25–28
- Loving and teaching your children is your highest priority. Your eternal joy is in a righteous posterity and to see your children walk in truth—3 John 1:4

PRAY ALWAYS

What I say unto one I say unto all; pray always lest that wicked one have power in you, and remove you out of your place.
D&C 93:49

We have this instruction from our risen Lord as He ministered among the Nephite people on this Western Hemisphere: "Ye must watch and pray always, lest ye be tempted by the devil, and ye are led away captive by him. (Book of Mormon, 3 Nephi 18:15)

Here are five ways to improve our communication with our Heavenly Father.

1. *We should pray frequently . . .*
2. *We should find an appropriate place where we can meditate and pray . . .*
3. *We should prepare ourselves for prayer . . .*
4. *Our prayers should be meaningful and pertinent . . .*
5. *After making a request through prayer, we have a responsibility to assist in its being granted . . .*

(Ezra Taft Benson, *Come unto Christ* [Salt Lake City: Deseret Book, 1983], 25)

Daily Living

PRAY ALWAYS LEST THE DEVIL HATH POWER OVER YOU.

ꝏ The power of prayer draws down the powers of heaven. We cannot make it through life without the constant help and support from our Heavenly Father, our Savior, and the blessings of the Holy Ghost. It is in the strength of the Lord that we are able to overcome all things including trials and temptations—3 Nephi 18:18; Alma 26:12; Ether 12:27

CHASTENING FROM THE LORD

Verily, thus saith the Lord unto you whom I love, and whom I love I also chasten that their sins may be forgiven, for with the chastisement I prepare a way for their deliverance in all things out of temptation, and I have loved you—Wherefore, ye must needs be chastened and stand rebuked before my face.

D&C 95:1–2

There is no more righteous motive for chastisement than a desire to help others obtain freedom from mistakes of the past and extend forgiveness to them in an act of brotherly love. Before acting in the role of a chastiser, a person should wisely inquire of himself: "What is my motive?" . . . Most people will have the responsibility of chastising or correcting others from time to time . . . [and in such cases] follow the Lord's pattern:

1. Love is expressed and extended to one being chastised.
2. The motive of the chastiser is that of correcting and forgiving.
3. The chastiser teaches how to improve and overcome mistakes.

(L. G. Otten and C. M. Caldwell, *Sacred Truths of the Doctrine and Covenants* [Salt Lake City: Deseret Book, 1983], 2:151–152)

Daily Living

THE LORD CHASTENS THOSE HE LOVES.

ꟷ Remember that chastening is sign of love. You must always chasten in love, as directed by the Spirit, and lives will be blessed—D&C 121:41–44

WALKING IN DARKNESS

If you keep not my commandments, the love of the Father shall not continue with you, therefore you shall walk in darkness.
D&C 95:12

Just as light is of God (1 John 1:5), darkness is of the devil, for he "is an enemy unto God, and fighteth against him continually" (Moro. 7:12). Darkness represents the evil influence of the devil's domain. It symbolizes that which does not edify (D&C 50:23). John declared that the devil's kingdom is full of darkness (Rev. 16:10). Those whose deeds are evil love darkness and reject light (D&C 10:21; 29:45; John 3: 19). An ancient prophet proclaimed the fate of those who yield to the enticings of the devil and "choose works of darkness rather than light": they "must go down to hell" (2 Ne. 26:10).

(Hoyt W. Brewster, Jr., *Doctrine and Covenants Encyclopedia* [Salt Lake City: Bookcraft, 1996], 120)

Daily Living

KEEP THE COMMANDMENTS—WALK IN THE LIGHT.

- In darkness we have no knowledge. We are left to the buffetings of Satan. In righteousness we are favored and will walk in the light of the Lord—1 Nephi 17:35
- If we fail to repent we will be without the light and will lose the Spirit, for it cannot always strive with man in sin (see D&C 1:31–33). The phrase "The love of the Father shall not continue with you" refers to the power of the Atonement in that it will not suffice for unrepented sins, hence we must suffer for our sins—D&C 19:15–19

THE TEMPLE

Behold, this is the tithing and the sacrifice which I, the Lord, require at their hands, that there may be a house built unto me for the salvation of Zion—For a place of thanksgiving for all saints, and for a place of instruction for all those who are called to the work of the ministry in all their several callings and offices.
D&C 97:12–16

Let us truly be a temple-attending and a temple-loving people. We should hasten to the temple as frequently . . . as our personal circumstances allow. We should go not only for our kindred dead but also for the personal blessing of temple worship, for the sanctity and safety that are within those hallowed and consecrated walls. As we attend the temple, we learn more richly and deeply the purpose of life and the significance of the atoning sacrifice of the Lord Jesus Christ. Let us make the temple, with temple worship and temple covenants and temple marriage, our ultimate earthly goal and the supreme mortal experience (95–01, 5).

(Howard W. Hunter, *The Teachings of Howard W. Hunter*, ed. Clyde J. Williams [Salt Lake City: Bookcraft, 1997], 236)

Daily Living

THE TEMPLE IS A PLACE OF INSTRUCTION AND THANKSGIVING.

℘ The temple is His Holy House, where we receive all the covenants and ordinances and crowning blessings relating to our exaltation. We must always be worthy and look to the temple that we might receive the covenants and ordinances of eternal life.

ZION—THE PURE IN HEART

Therefore, verily, thus saith the Lord, let Zion rejoice, for this is Zion—THE PURE IN HEART; therefore, let Zion rejoice, while all the wicked shall mourn.
D&C 97:21

For my purpose here today, I shall look upon Zion as being a condition and not a place, and the world likewise. " . . . verily, thus saith the Lord, let Zion rejoice, for this is Zion,—the pure in heart" (D&C 97:21).

There is no fence around Zion or the world, but to one of discernment, they are separated more completely than if each were surrounded with high unscalable walls. Their underlying concepts, philosophies, and purposes are at complete variance one with the other. The philosophy of the world is self-sufficient, egotistical, materialistic, and skeptical. The philosophy of Zion is humility, not servility, but a willing recognition of the sovereignty of God and dependence on his providence.

(Stephen L Richards, in Conference Report, October 1951, 110–17)

Daily Living

BECOME A ZION PEOPLE WITH PURE HEARTS.

- Purity of heart indicates that our intentions and behavior reflect an obedient and righteous spirit. When we have a change of heart and yield it to God, we become pure and receive the blessings and sanctification of the Spirit—Helaman 3:35; 2 Thessalonians 2:13
- Remember, the pure in heart will see God—3 Nephi 12:8
- A pure heart is broken and is accompanied by a contrite spirit—D&C 56:18
- A pure heart will hear the word of God—Jacob 3:1–3

YOU CAN BE FREE

I, the Lord God, make you free, therefore ye are free indeed; and the law also maketh you free.
D&C 98:8

We often speak of our freedoms. There is no freedom like the freedom of righteousness. The penalty of sin is slavery and death. He who is the victim of his own evil conduct is in reality much more a slave than the cowering subjects of the most dictatorial despot.

If America would remain mighty, she must have the strength of sobriety, of chastity, and virtue, of honesty and integrity, and power of true spirituality. If she would be strong, America must enjoy—in addition to her political freedoms . . . those other freedoms which are as essential to her welfare as any of the liberties listed in the Bill of Rights.

(Mark E. Peterson, in Conference Report, October 1947, 107–8)

Daily Living

THE LORD AND THE LAW CAN MAKE YOU FREE.

- Let us never forget it is the Lord and Savior Jesus Christ that gives us freedom from death and sin—2 Nephi 9:6–9; 2 Nephi 2:8; 9:5, 21; Alma 34:8–9
- Through obedience to the laws and ordinances of the gospel we can be forgiven, remembering, "to believe in Christ, and to be reconciled to God; for we know that it is by grace that we are saved, after all we can do"—2 Nephi 25:23

SEEK HONEST MEN TO GOVERN

Wherefore, honest men and wise men should be sought for diligently, and good men and wise men ye should observe to uphold; otherwise whatsoever is less than these cometh of evil.
D&C 98:10

"Is the 'Mormon' Church in politics?" I answered him: "Most assuredly it is in politics, and also in business, in statesmanship, in all the affairs of life, teaching the people to do what is right so far as it possibly can." "Well, has the Church any candidates in the pending election?" "Yes, indeed," said I, "the Church has a full ticket, and is counseling its members just how to vote."

Now, let me tell you just how you should vote, just as I told him. The Church is telling its members to look upon the franchise as a sacred gift, to exercise it according to their very best judgment before the Lord, and the Church's ticket is the ticket of the best men, according to the best judgment of the people, to whichever party they belong. Vote the party ticket if you honestly feel that to be best, or vote for the men you think will most effectively subserve the needs of country, state, and people.

(James E. Talmage, in Conference Report, October 1920, 66)

Daily Living

SEEK HONEST MEN WHO WILL UPHOLD THE LAW.

ℰ𝒪 Do your best to be involved in community and national affairs by seeking out the good and noble people with high moral values, that all might be blessed with just laws, with courage to uphold truth and righteousness.

FORSAKE EVIL AND CLEAVE TO THE GOOD

And I give unto you a commandment, that ye shall forsake all evil and cleave unto all good, that ye shall live by every word which proceedeth forth out of the mouth of God.
D&C 98:11

The seed is good and the soil is good, but they choose to let thorns and thistles continue to grow along with the seeds of righteousness. They seek to serve both God and mammon at one and the same time. . . . The good word of God calls for men to bridle their passions, forsake all that is evil, and cleave unto all that is good, but the lusts of the flesh remaining in the hearts of believing men cannot do other than lead them on a downward course. True saints seek, not the pleasures of this life—the things that money and power and learning confer—but the eternal joys born of the Spirit.

(Bruce R. McConkie, *The Mortal Messiah: From Bethlehem to Calvary*, 4 vols. [Salt Lake City: Deseret Book, 1980], 2:251)

Daily Living

FORSAKE EVIL AND CLEAVE UNTO ALL THAT IS GOOD.

- Forsake evil with the armor of God, fasting and prayer, and by holding fast to and feasting upon the word of God—D&C 27:15–18; 3 Nephi 18:18; 1 Nephi 15:24; 2 Nephi 32:3
- Desire the things of God, recognizing the blessings of happiness associated with keeping the commandments—Mosiah 2:41
- There is joy in righteous doing—1 Nephi 19:11; Alma 7:4; Helaman 7:8; Moses 7:67

OCTOBER

And this cannot be brought to pass until mine elders are endowed with power from on high.

For behold, I have prepared a great endowment and blessing to be poured out upon them, inasmuch as they are faithful and continue in humility before me.

—Doctrine & Covenants 105:11–12

October 1

LINE UPON LINE

For he will give unto the faithful line upon line, precept upon precept; and I will try you and prove you herewith.
D&C 98:12

Truth is revealed incrementally. The Lord has outlined the process by which he reveals truth and by which we learn wisdom: . . . It is a process that rewards patience and persistence. We learn wisdom by moving through levels of understanding. Advancing to a new level requires desire and effort, openness and receptivity. Learning is an experience more like climbing a mountain than jumping a ditch. It occurs step by step.

(Susan Easton Black, ed., *Expressions of Faith: Testimonies of Latter-day Saint Scholars* [Salt Lake City and Provo: Deseret Book, Foundation for Ancient Research and Mormon Studies, 1996], 27–28)

Daily Living

THE LORD WILL GIVE US LINE UPON LINE AND TEST US.

- The process of growing and becoming occurs one step at a time. The Lord will give us line upon line to see if we hearken to the precepts and learn wisdom, and if we do, He will give us more—2 Nephi 28:30
- Hopefully, the joy is in the process as well as the culmination, and then we come to realize that it is not an event but rather a lifelong pursuit of happiness: this is the test to prove ourselves worthy—Abraham 3:25

SACRIFICE ALL

And whoso layeth down his life in my cause, for my name's sake, shall find it again, even life eternal.
D&C 98:13

Sacrifice is the very essence of religion; it is the keystone of happy home life, the basis of true friendship, the foundation of peaceful community living, of sound relations among people and nations. . . . Without sacrifice there is no true worship of God. I become increasingly convinced of that every day. "The Father gave his Son, and the Son gave his life," and we do not worship unless we give—give of our substance, give of our time, give of our strength, give of our talent, give of our faith, give of our testimonies. A religion which requires devotion, which asks for sacrifice, which demands discipline, also enjoys the loyalty of its membership and the interest and respect of others.

(Gordon B. Hinckley, *Teachings of Gordon B. Hinckley* [Salt Lake City: Deseret Book, 1997], 565)

Daily Living

SACRIFICE—GIVE ALL FOR THE LORD AND GAIN ETERNAL LIFE.

- Through the spirit of sacrifice, we enter a condition of profound change: we are in a state of humility; we offer a broken heart and a contrite spirit—3 Nephi 9:20
- It is giving one's will and one's decisions to the will of God—John 5:30; 6:38
- If motivated by love, we too will give all for the benefit of mankind—John 3:16; 2 Nephi 26:24

PROCLAIM PEACE AND TURN HEARTS

Therefore, renounce war and proclaim peace, and seek diligently to turn the hearts of the children to their fathers, and the hearts of the fathers to the children.
D&C 98:16

The Lord instructed his Saints in D&C 98:16 to "renounce war and proclaim peace, and *seek diligently* to turn the hearts of the children to their fathers, and the hearts of the fathers to the children" (Emphasis added). As we come to understand the fifth commandment and the spirit of the work of Elijah, we will see the relationship between peace and the turning of parents' and children's hearts toward one another. The peace we proclaim and find in this way will bring peace to our minds, our homes, and our society.

(Bruce C. Hafen and Marie K. Hafen, *The Belonging Heart: The Atonement and Relationships with God and Family* [Salt Lake City: Deseret Book, 1994], 199)

Daily Living

PROCLAIM PEACE AND TURN THE HEARTS OF FATHERS AND CHILDREN.

- True peace can only come from living the gospel of Jesus Christ. You are at peace. War began premortally and continues today in all facets of life from the home and families in strife to nations at war over greed and ideologies. If our hearts were turned to one another with love and compassion, we would live in peace in our homes and then throughout the world—2 Corinthians 13:11
- Learn of the Lord, and ye shall have peace—D&C 19:23

TRUST IN THE LORD

Therefore, verily I say unto you, lift up your voices unto this people; speak the thoughts that I shall put into your hearts, and you shall not be confounded before men; For it shall be given you in the very hour, yea, in the very moment, what ye shall say.

D&C 100:5–6

Knowing just what to say, on any occasion, is very important. Knowing how to say it, or having the power to say it in a way that appeals, is equally so. A machine in a big plant broke down, and an expert was called in to fix it. He gave two taps with his hammer, and the machine started. The bill was $250. The superintendent as soon as he could get his breath, demanded an itemized statement. It came, and read as follows. "Tapping with hammer, $1.00; knowing where to tap, $249.00." It is just so with the speaker. He must know where to tap and even then must leave it to the Lord to do the tapping. Our Heavenly Father knows our needs, and He alone can supply them. He knows where to tap, and the speaker is the hammer that he taps with. The sledge-hammer blows struck during this Conference are samples of His handiwork. They ought to be sufficient to set any machine going—in the right direction.

(Orson F. Whitney, in Conference Report, October 1927, 144)

Daily Living

THE LORD WILL PUT INTO YOUR HEARTS WHAT TO SAY.

- We must trust in the Lord, and He will give us the words we need to say—D&C 84:85; Helaman 13:4–5

WALK UPRIGHTLY

Therefore, let your hearts be comforted; for all things shall work together for good to them that walk uprightly, and to the sanctification of the church.

D&C 100:15

The Lord promised Joseph Smith that "all things shall work together for your good, if ye walk uprightly" (D&C 90:24). To walk uprightly is to walk erect; to be morally correct, honest, and just; and to be "pointing upward," according to Webster. It is the opposite of being stooped in sin. One who has walked uprightly can enter the presence of the Lord with a humble head held erect.

Parents are specifically commanded to teach their children to "walk uprightly before the Lord" (D&C 68:28).

(Hoyt W. Brewster, Jr., *Doctrine and Covenants Encyclopedia* [Salt Lake City: Bookcraft, 1996], 623)

Daily Living

WALK UPRIGHTLY AND ALL THINGS SHALL WORK TOGETHER FOR GOOD.

- Walking in the ways of the Lord by keeping the commandments brings personal blessings—D&C 90:24
- The Lord is admonishing all of us to set an example, to be righteous, and walk uprightly in the ways of the Lord that blessings might come upon the Church as a whole, even to the sanctification and purifying of it—that Zion might be established. Seek to establish Zion—D&C 6:6; 14:6
- Let your light shine, thus glorifying your Father in Heaven. His glory is in building up His kingdom through the immortality and eternal life of His children—3 Nephi 12:16; Moses 1:39

ENDURE CHASTENING

Therefore, they must needs be chastened and tried, even as Abraham, who was commanded to offer up his only son. For all those who will not endure chastening, but deny me, cannot be sanctified.

D&C 101:4–5

Can we endure well corrective counsel. . . . The Prophet Joseph taught, "When a corrupt man is chastised he gets angry and will not endure it." Joseph and other valiants endured well having their occasional chastisements from the Lord, including having these set forth publicly for all to see. The world is often either too cruel in correction or abstains altogether therefrom. For us, "speaking the truth in love" (Ephesians 4:15) and showing forth "an increase of love" (D&C 121:43) make all the difference. Enduring involves coping successfully with customized chastening. "If ye endure chastening, God dealeth with you as with sons; for what son is he whom the father chasteneth not? . . . Now no chastening for the present seemeth to be joyous, but grievous: nevertheless afterward it yieldeth the peaceable fruit of righteousness unto them which are exercised thereby" (Hebrews 12:7, 11).

(Neal A. Maxwell, *If Thou Endure It Well* [Salt Lake City: Bookcraft, 1996], 100)

Daily Living

ENDURE CHASTENING . . . BECOME SANCTIFIED.

ꟸ Chastening, whether through the Lord Himself (see Acts 9:3–7), by angels (see Mosiah 27:11–19), or by those who have stewardship, is a result of love—D&C 95:1–2

SEEK THE LORD AT ALL TIMES

In the day of their peace they esteemed lightly my counsel; but, in the day of their trouble, of necessity they feel after me.
D&C 101:8

The Lord helps those who have sought him early. (See D&C 54:10.) But those who haven't begun early in their religious life may resolve to seek the Lord more diligently. Through adversity we learn to recognize the Lord's hand in helping us. In hard times we have a chance to reevaluate and reorder our priorities in life. We learn what is most important to us. The way is open to strengthen faith and testimony.

(James E. Faust, *Reach Up for the Light* [Salt Lake City: Deseret Book, 1990], 80)

Daily Living

ALWAYS SEEK THE LORD IN TIMES OF JOY AND TRIAL.

- Our hearts and minds should always be on the things of the Lord in the sense that we seek to do His will and follow His counsels—Jacob 4:10
- When things are going well, we praise God with prayers of gratitude, but like Nephi of old we should continually pray and plead for the Lord's help in all things at all times—2 Nephi 4:17–35
- If we are constant in our prayers the Lord will be swift to hear our cries rather than slow—Mosiah 11:24
- If we fail to call upon the Lord we stand in jeopardy before the Lord—Ether 2:14

SUFFER PERSECUTION FOR THE LORD'S SAKE

And all they who suffer persecution for my name, and endure in faith, though they are called to lay down their lives for my sake yet shall they partake of all this glory.
D&C 101:35

Blessed are ye when men shall revile you and persecute and shall say all manner of evil against you falsely, for My sake. To suffer persecution as a follower of Christ is a privilege, "For great shall be your reward in Heaven." Persecution on Earth for the sake of the Lamb, entitles one to association with the innumerable company of glorious martyrs in Heaven.

(George Reynolds and Janne M. Sjodahl, *Commentary on the Book of Mormon*, arranged and edited by Philip C. Reynolds, 7 vols. [Salt Lake City: Deseret Book, 1961], 7:148)

Daily Living

SUFFER PERSECUTION FOR THE LORD'S SAKE AND RECEIVE GLORY.

- There can be no greater honor than to suffer persecution for the Lord's sake and the building up of the kingdom of God—3 Nephi 12:10–12
- In the fiery furnace of affliction and tribulation, one might suffer for the Lord, yet they will be strengthened, magnified, and blessed—D&C 121:7–8
- The pains we suffer for the kingdom will always be for our good—D&C 122:7
- Always pray for those who persecute and despitefully use you—3 Nephi 12:44

SALT OF THE EARTH

When men are called unto mine everlasting gospel, and covenant with an everlasting covenant, they are accounted as the salt of the earth and the savor of men; They are called to be the savor of men; therefore, if that salt of the earth lose its savor, behold, it is thenceforth good for nothing only to be cast out and trodden under the feet of men.

D&C 101:39–40

The "covenant of salt" (Lev. 2:13; Num. 18:19; 2 Chr. 13:5) indicates that anciently salt was a symbol of faithfulness, steadfastness, and purity. The word *savor* refers to the physical senses of tasting and smelling; it also means "to have experience of" and "to delight in." In some of his parables, the Savior referred to the righteous saints as "the salt of the earth" and as "the savor of men." How do we lose the savor that followers of the Lord should have? We lose it as we cease to serve Him, or even by becoming casual in our obedience. For example, if we become careless about attending our meetings, do we not lose some of the savor that good salt should have? If we neglect our prayers, our tithes and offerings, what becomes of our savor? . . . If we do not share the gospel with our neighbors, what becomes of our savor?

(Daniel H. Ludlow, *Companion to Your Study of the Doctrine and Covenants*, [Salt Lake City: Deseret Book, 1978], 246–247)

Daily Living

YE ARE THE SALT OF THE EARTH.

ꟹ To be the "salt of the earth" is a great responsibility and honor—3 Nephi 12:13

ABASE YOURSELF TO BE EXALTED

He that exalteth himself shall be abased, and he that abaseth himself shall be exalted.
D&C 101:42

As had been so strongly impressed on earlier occasions [Matt. 10:37; 18:3–4], excellence or supremacy in the apostolic calling, and similarly in the duties of discipleship or membership in the Church of Christ, was and is to be achieved through humble and devoted service alone; therefore said the Master again, "he that is greatest among you shall be your servant. And whosoever shall exalt himself shall be abased; and he that shall humble himself shall be exalted." [Matt. 23:12–13.]

(James E. Talmage, *Jesus the Christ* [Salt Lake City: Deseret Book, 1983, 513)

Daily Living

ABASE YOURSELF AND YE SHALL BE EXALTED.

- We abase ourselves as we become humble in all facets of life. We become humble when we come to understand our state in mortality—Mosiah 4:5
- We are totally dependent upon the goodness and mercy of God, and this surely helps us to be stronger in our humility as we fast and pray—Helaman 3:35
- When we understand our relationship with our Heavenly Father and our Savior, we are humble. We begin to experience the fruits of humility of being teachable, easily entreated, and submissive, willing to offer our all—Mosiah 3:19

THE CONSTITUTION

According to the laws and constitution of the people, which I have suffered to be established, and should be maintained for the rights and protection of all flesh, according to just and holy principles; That every man may act in doctrine and principle pertaining to futurity, according to the moral agency which I have given unto him, that every man may be accountable for his own sins in the day of judgment.

D&C 101:77–78

The Constitution of the United States is a glorious standard; it is founded in the wisdom of God. It is a heavenly banner; it is to all those who are privileged with the sweets of its liberty, like the cooling shades and refreshing waters of a great rock in a thirsty and weary land. It is like a great tree under whose branches men from every clime can be shielded from the burning rays of the sun. . . .We say that God is true; that the Constitution of the United States is true; that the Bible is true; that the Book of Mormon is true; that the Book of Covenants is true; that Christ is true.

(Joseph Smith, *History of the Church*, March 25, 1839, 3:304)

Daily Living

THE CONSTITUTION WAS ESTABLISHED FOR THE RIGHTS AND AGENCY OF MAN.

- The glorious Constitution has a divine origin. It is our responsibility to uphold and defend it at all costs. Our freedom depends upon it. It is through this freedom that the gospel has been able to go throughout the earth.

THE LORD BROUGHT FORTH WISE MEN

And for this purpose have I established the Constitution of this land, by the hands of wise men whom I raised up unto this very purpose, and redeemed the land by the shedding of blood.
D&C 101:80

The principles of that great instrument are to go forth to the nations, and the time will come when they will prevail, just as sure as the sun shines even when it appears to be in darkness and the clouds are over it. And the Lord says, concerning the works of those great men, "And redeemed the land by the shedding of blood." Shedding of blood! Does the Lord permit the shedding of blood and justify it? Yes, sometimes he does. Was not the war of independence of this country justifiable? . . . These principles are to go forth to *all flesh*. Don't forget it. The time will come when they will be carried to all the nations of the earth and they will be delivered from tyrants and oppressors.

(Charles W. Penrose, in Conference Report, April 1917, 20)

Daily Living

BE GRATEFUL FOR THE MEN THAT BROUGHT FORTH THE CONSTITUTION.

ꟿ Gratitude for the brave souls that fought for our freedom as a country and for establishing the blessed Constitution should fill our hearts. There is always a price to pay for freedom. The price our Lord and Savior Jesus Christ paid was for freedom from death and sin. The price those brave men and women paid was to redeem this land, even with the shedding of their blood. Now we must do all in our power to uphold our freedom and safety.

October 13

BE A LIGHT UNTO THE WORLD

For they were set to be a light unto the world, and to be the saviors of men; And inasmuch as they are not the saviors of men, they are as salt that has lost its savor, and is thenceforth good for nothing but to be cast out and trodden under foot of men.

D&C 103:9–10

I have seen a periodical recently in which it is stated that the only way in which we can become saviors on Mount Zion is to be baptized for our dead. . . . But there are a great many things in which we can be saviors. . . .We are to be saviors of men, too, in sending or carrying the gospel to every nation, kindred, tongue and people. That is imposed upon us; every Latter-day Saint, every man and woman and boy and girl born in the covenant or who has received it, is under obligations to do all that is possible for the sending forth of the word of the Lord to all nations of the earth. [Sec. 15:6; 18:10–16; 88:81–83.]

(Charles W. Penrose, in Conference Report, April 1918, 16, 18, 22)

Daily Living

BE A LIGHT UNTO THE WORLD AND THE SAVIORS OF MEN.

- We let our light, even the light of the Lord Jesus Christ, shine that others may see our good works and glorify our Father which is in Heaven—3 Nephi 12:16
- Remember we cannot hide our light, for we are to be a light unto the world—3 Nephi 12:14–15; 15:12
- We do for others that which they cannot do for themselves by assisting them in coming unto Christ—D&C 15:6; 128:15

LAY DOWN YOUR LIFE FOR THE LORD

Let no man be afraid to lay down his life for my sake; for whoso layeth down his life for my sake shall find it again. And whoso is not willing to lay down his life for my sake is not my disciple.
D&C 103:27–28

All that we possess of this world's goods has been given to us of the Lord, and we are to be regarded as but stewards over what we have received. We will have to give an account for our stewardship. In view of what the Lord has done for us, and given unto us, it is a small thing that He has asked of us in return, that we give to him one-tenth of what he has given to us. We have accepted the gospel as a gospel of sacrifice and self-abnegation. . . .

If we are not willing to lay down our lives for Christ's sake and His gospel's sake, we may not hope to receive the salvation which is God's greatest gift to man, and for which we have enlisted in His cause to obtain.

(George F. Richards, in Conference Report, April 1948, 19)

Daily Living

LAY DOWN YOUR LIFE FOR THE LORD'S SAKE.

- Discipleship comes with commitment. It is our honor and joy to be a disciple of Jesus Christ—3 Nephi 5:13
- Most of us will not have to give up our lives, but rather we are asked to live for the Lord and His work and glory that others might come unto Christ and be saved—Alma 29:9–10; 36:24; D&C 18:10–16
- Live for Christ. Live for others. Live for the establishment of Zion that all might be blessed—3 Nephi 12:33

DILIGENCE . . . FAITHFULNESS . . . PRAYER

All victory and glory is brought to pass unto you through your diligence, faithfulness, and prayers of faith.
D&C 103:36

I want to bear record . . . that there is no other way of retaining the spirit of this work and the fellowship of the Holy Ghost than through faithfulness and diligence in observing to keep the commandments of the Lord. The individual who will be humble all the day long and strive to keep the commandments of the Lord will never apostatize or become dissatisfied, but he or she will be preserved in the truth, and by and by will sit down in the mansions of the Father, to enjoy the blessings of eternal life. People who are spiritually-minded are devoted to the work. They pay their tithes and their offerings; they go to the ward meetings and to the stake meetings, and they are willing to devote their time, their talents and their all for the building up of the kingdom of God on the earth.

(Merriner W. Merrill, in Conference Report, April 1902, 40)

Daily Living

BE DILIGENT, FAITHFUL, AND PRAY WITH FAITH.

- The Lord expects us to do our part to receive the blessings associated with our requests—D&C 9:7–9; 1 Nephi 17:3, 16; Ether 3:1–6
- The Lord encourages us to exercise our prayers of faith, for through our prayers of faith we will be strengthened and have power to do all things that is expedient to the Lord—Moroni 10:23

STEWARDSHIP AND ACCOUNTABILITY

That every man may give an account unto me of the stewardship which is appointed unto him. For it is expedient that I, the Lord, should make every man accountable, as a steward over earthly blessings, which I have made and prepared for my creatures.
D&C 104:12–13

"Who then is that faithful and wise steward, whom his lord shall make ruler over his household, to give them their portion of meat in due season?" [Luke 12:42] The faithful steward is a good type of the apostles, individually or as a body. As stewards they were charged with the care of the other servants, and of the household; and as to them more had been given than to the others, so of them more would be required; and they would be held to strict accountability for their stewardship.

(James E. Talmage, *Jesus the Christ: A Study of the Messiah and His Mission According to Holy Scriptures Both Ancient and Modern* [Salt Lake City: Deseret Book, 1983], 409)

Daily Living

WE ARE ACCOUNTABLE FOR OUR TALENTS AND BLESSINGS.

- We will have to account to the Lord for what we have done with what we have been given—Luke 16:2; Romans 14:12; D&C 42:32; 20:71; 72:3
- We will be held accountable for our talents, gifts, thoughts, words, and deeds, as well sins of omission—D&C 10:23; 101:78; 134:1; Article of Faith 2; Matthew 12:36; 1 Peter 4:5

AGENTS UNTO YOURSELVES

For the earth is full, and there is enough and to spare; yea, I prepared all things, and have given unto the children of men to be agents unto themselves. Therefore, if any man shall take of the abundance which I have made, and impart not his portion, according to the law of my gospel, unto the poor and the needy, he shall, with the wicked, lift up his eyes in hell, being in torment.

D&C 104:17–18

Again, if others' blessings are not your blessings, others' curses are not your curses; you stand then in these last days, as all have stood before you, agents unto yourselves, to be judged according to your works.

(Joseph Smith, *History of the Church*, 1:282–83)

Daily Living

BE AGENTS UNTO YOURSELVES . . . MORAL AGENCY WITH ACCOUNTABILITY.

- Agency is a gift. The right to choose is necessary for our growth. We are a result of the use of our agency. Our choices and decisions determine our blessings or the consequences of our actions—2 Nephi 2:27
- Agency can operate because there is (1) opposition in all things, (2) knowledge of good and evil, (3) laws and commandments given by God, and (4) the freedom to choose—2 Nephi 2:11
- This gift of "free agency" is better referred to as moral agency, which connotes responsibility and accountability in regard to our choices—D&C 101:78

ZION AND THE CELESTIAL KINGDOM

And Zion cannot be built up unless it is by the principles of the law of the celestial kingdom; otherwise I cannot receive her unto myself.
D&C 105:5

The Zion the Lord seeks to establish through his covenant people . . . can be built up only among those who are the pure in heart, not a people torn by covetousness or greed, but a pure and selfless people. Not a people who are pure in appearance, rather a people who are pure in heart. . . . First, we must eliminate the individual tendency to selfishness that snares the soul, shrinks the heart, and darkens the mind. . . . Second, we must cooperate completely and work in harmony one with the other. There must be unanimity in our decisions and unity in our actions. . . . Third, we must lay on the altar and sacrifice whatever is required by the Lord. We begin by offering a "broken heart and a contrite spirit." We follow this by giving our best effort in our assigned fields of labor and callings. We learn our duty and execute it fully. Finally we consecrate our time, talents, and means as called upon by our file leaders and as prompted by the whisperings of the Spirit. . . .

(Spencer W. Kimball, *Ensign*, May 1978, 81)

Daily Living

ZION MUST BE BUILT UP BY THE LAW OF THE CELESTIAL KINGDOM.

ꟷ Seek to be a Zion person, family, and people by being pure in heart and living worthy of the celestial kingdom—D&C 76:51–55

LEARN OBEDIENCE

And my people must needs be chastened until they learn obedience, if it must needs be, by the things which they suffer.
D&C 105:6

It would take much of a lifetime for me to come to understand some of life's most important lessons about freedom and responsibility and maturity and discipline and submission and surrender and commitment and consecration. These lessons would be learned not just from a study of the written word but, perhaps more importantly, from life's reality tests and mortality's vicissitudes. Like Jesus and Melchizedek, we learn obedience by the things we suffer (Hebrews 5:8). As Cecil B. DeMille wisely pointed out, men and women cannot really break the Ten Commandments; they can only break themselves against the commandments (*Commencement Address*, 6).

(Robert L. Millet, *Alive in Christ: The Miracle of Spiritual Rebirth* [Salt Lake City: Deseret Book, 1997], 160)

Daily Living

LEARN OBEDIENCE THROUGH AND IN ALL THINGS.

- The Lord will do whatever it takes, including chastening, to help us learn to obey—Helaman 12:3–6
- We show our love of God through obedience—John 14:15
- Faithful obedience often precedes knowledge as demonstrated by father Adam—Moses 5:6
- We are blessed according to our obedience—D&C 130:20–21

TRIAL OF YOUR FAITH

But inasmuch as there are those who have hearkened unto my words, I have prepared a blessing and an endowment for them, if they continue faithful. I have heard their prayers, and will accept their offering; and it is expedient in me that they should be brought thus far for a trial of their faith.
D&C 105:18–19

Thus there ought to be expectations that in this laboratory of life we will actually see each other in the process of being remodeled. . . . We will obviously be aware of others who are also in the "furnace of affliction." However, we will not always have a smooth, ready answer to the question, "Why me?" "Why now?" "Why this?"—for as Moroni observed, "Ye receive no witness until *after* the trial of your faith" (Ether 12:6; italics added). As we see ourselves, and others, passing through fiery trials, the wisdom of Peter, who had his own share of fiery trials, is very useful: "Beloved, think it not strange concerning the fiery trial which is to try you, as though some strange thing happened unto you" (1 Peter 4:12).

(Neal A. Maxwell, *All These Things Shall Give Thee Experience* [Salt Lake City: Deseret Book, 1979], 44)

Daily Living

LIFE IS A TEST AND TRIAL OF FAITH.

- We are here on earth to prove ourselves—Abraham 3:25
- The great test of life is the test of faith—2 Nephi 26:9–11
- Seek to increase our faith —Romans 10:17; Helaman 3:35
- The witness can come after the trial of faith—Ether 12:6

MELCHIZEDEK PRIESTHOOD HOLDS THE KEYS

The power and authority of the higher, or Melchizedek Priesthood, is to hold the keys of all the spiritual blessings of the church.
D&C 107:18

Since the Melchizedek Priesthood holds the keys to spiritual blessings, spiritual influences are available from the heavens through the administration of that priesthood. Elders may call upon these powers to bless members of their families as they approach major events in their lives, such as school, missions, military service, marriage, etc.; to bless the sick; and to perform other ordinances of the gospel. While the Melchizedek Priesthood is upon the earth and operating in the lives of the members of the Church, its powers are for the benefit of both man and woman. By right of confirmation in the Church, all have the right to enjoy the gifts of the Holy Ghost.

(Roy W. Doxey, *The Doctrine and Covenants Speaks* [Salt Lake City: Deseret Book, 1970], 2:302)

Daily Living

THE MELCHIZEDEK PRIESTHOOD HOLDS THE KEYS.

ꟹ All spiritual blessings come from the priesthood that comes from our Heavenly Father through His Beloved Son Jesus Christ as inspired by the Holy Ghost. May we ever be mindful and sober concerning the sacred nature of the Melchizedek Priesthood and never do anything to debase or bring ridicule to the priesthood through our actions, for through it comes the ordinances and blessings of eternal life—D&C 84:34–40

DECISIONS IN RIGHTEOUSNESS

The decisions of these quorums, or either of them, are to be made in all righteousness, in holiness, and lowliness of heart, meekness and long suffering, and in faith, and virtue, and knowledge, temperance, patience, godliness, brotherly kindness and charity; Because the promise is, if these things abound in them they shall not be unfruitful in the knowledge of the Lord.
D&C 107:30–31

The genius of our Church government is government through councils. The Council of the Presidency, the Council of the Twelve, the Council of the Stake Presidency, or quorum, if you choose to use that word, the Council of the Bishopric, and the quorum or Council of the Quorum Presidency. I have had enough experience to know the value of councils. . . . In the spirit under which we labor . . . by counseling together, [we] can arrive at an accord, and that accord (the occasions are so negligible as not to be mentioned), and therefore I say that accord is always right. That accord represents the wisdom of the council, acting under the Spirit.

(Stephen L. Richards, in Conference Report, October 1953, 86)

Daily Living

MAKE DECISIONS IN RIGHTEOUSNESS.

ꕥ The attributes described above are part of the divine nature of Christ. When possessing this nature, we will do as Jesus would do, hence the leading quorums of the Church and all alike should make decisions based upon charity, for charity never faileth—2 Peter 1:3–12; Moroni 7:45–48

LEARN YOUR DUTY

Wherefore, now let every man learn his duty, and to act in the office in which he is appointed, in all diligence. He that is slothful shall not be counted worthy to stand, and he that learns not his duty and shows himself not approved shall not be counted worthy to stand. Even so. Amen.

D&C 107:99–100

We have been raised up of the Lord to take this kingdom and bear it off. This is our duty; but if we neglect our duty and set our hearts upon the things of this world, we will be sorry for it. We ought to understand the responsibility that rests upon us. We should gird up our loins and put on the whole armor of God. We should rear temples to the name of the Most High God, that we may redeem the dead. . . . Ours is no ordinary calling.

(Wilford Woodruff, *The Discourses of Wilford Woodruff*, ed. G. Homer Durham [Salt Lake City: Bookcraft, 1946], 128)

Daily Living

LEARN YOUR DUTY AND MAGNIFY YOUR CALLING.

ꟿ When one assumes or agrees to assume a responsibility, it becomes one's duty to follow through. Often duties are simply inherent within the office you occupy or the role you play. In the Scout oath, the words "On my honor, I will do my best to do my duty to God and my country" cast a guiding light over the full range of our human endeavor. Our duty is to God our Eternal Father—Ecclesiastes 12:13; Acts 5:29; Jacob 2:2; Alma 4:19; 7:22; D&C 20:68–69

STRENGTHEN YOUR BROTHERS AND SISTERS

Therefore, strengthen your brethren in all your conversation, in all your prayers, in all your exhortations, and in all your doings.
D&C 108:7

They meet together often to "teach one another the doctrine of the kingdom" (see D&C 88:77) and to fellowship and strengthen one another. . . . This spiritual fellowshipping and nurturing of one another is an essential part of the perfection of the Saints. All meetings and activities and practices of the Church should be designed to spiritually nourish the Saints and keep them in the "right way."

(Joseph Fielding McConkie and Robert L. Millet, *Doctrinal Commentary on the Book of Mormon*, 4 vols. [Salt Lake City: Bookcraft, 1992], 4:329)

Daily Living

STRENGTHEN YOUR BROTHERS AND SISTERS IN ALL THINGS.

- The excitement and joy within our very being, by helping one another, is illuminated by a heart that is at peace with the world and our fellow man. It is rejuvenating to the soul, and the fruits are precious when we seek to help others come unto Christ—Alma 29:9–10; 36:24; D&C 15:6; 18:10–16
- May we seek to serve and strengthen our brothers and sisters in every walk of life—Luke 22:32
- When we bless or serve anyone, we are blessing and serving the Lord Jesus Christ—Matthew 25:40

THE LORD'S HOLY HOUSE

And that all people who shall enter upon the threshold of the Lord's house may feel thy power, and feel constrained to acknowledge that thou hast sanctified it, and that it is thy house, a place of thy holiness.
D&C 109:13

All the gifts of the Spirit and of the holy priesthood mentioned in scripture have been manifest at one time or another in the spiritual outpourings attending temple dedications, including visions, revelations, healings, discernment, and prophecy; and likewise the fruits of the Spirit—love, joy, peace, long-suffering, gentleness, meekness, faith. For Latter-day Saints on such occasions it is as if the earthly and heavenly temples meet and as if the rejoicing of ancient worthies mingles with that of mortals.

(D. Arthur Haycock, *Encyclopedia of Mormonism*, 1–4 vols., ed. Daniel H. Ludlow [New York: Macmillan, 1992], 1456)

Daily Living

THE LORD'S HOLY HOUSE BRINGS POWER INTO YOUR LIVES.

- How do we feel when we enter the Lord's house? Do we sense the peace of the temple? Are we prepared to feel the spirit or are we just getting a session in? Is it just getting it done or do we understand the power of godliness being manifested in the ordinances in which we participate?—D&C 84:20
- Is gratitude felt for the goodness of God for his making possible these crowning blessings through temple ordinances? Consider well the power of the temple in your individual lives and the lives of those you serve.

THE TEMPLE—THE HOUSE OF GOD

And that this house may be a house of prayer, a house of fasting, a house of faith, a house of glory and of God, even thy house.
D&C 109:16

The words "the Lord's house" appear on each of the temples. A temple is the Lord's house, and when we enter his house, we enter as his guests. Thus, we should do everything possible to keep the Lord's house holy, unpolluted, clean, and sweet. . . . The house of the Lord is functional. Every element in the design, decoration, atmosphere, and program of the temple contributes to its function, which is to teach. The temple teaches of Christ. It teaches of his ordinances. It is filled with his Spirit.

(Spencer W. Kimball, *The Teachings of Spencer W. Kimball*, ed. Edward L. Kimball [Salt Lake City: Bookcraft, 1982], 534)

Daily Living

THE TEMPLE IS A HOUSE OF PRAYER, FASTING, FAITH, AND GLORY.

ꟈ Lest we forget, the temple is a place where the Lord reveals to His children great truths of everlasting life. The Lord also provides the temple to be "a place of thanksgiving for all saints, and for a place of instruction for all those who are called to the work of the ministry in all their several callings and offices; That they may be perfected in the understanding of their ministry, in theory, in principle, and in doctrine, in all things pertaining to the kingdom of God on the earth, the keys of which kingdom have been conferred upon you"—D&C 97:14–15

THE KEYS TO THE GATHERING OF ISRAEL

After this vision closed, the heavens were again opened unto us; and Moses appeared before us, and committed unto us the keys of the gathering of Israel from the four parts of the earth, and the leading of the ten tribes from the land of the north.
D&C 110:11

In the Doctrine and Covenants, the Lord has revealed many things associated with three aspects of the gathering of Israel in the last days.

1. The gathering of the dispersed of Israel to Zion. The great missionary program of the Church is an important part of this aspect of the gathering.

2. The gathering of the descendants of Judah to the land of Jerusalem. This aspect of the gathering has been emphasized for about one hundred years, but has greatly accelerated since May 15, 1948, when the modern country of Israel was established.

3. The return of the lost tribes. This aspect of the gathering is apparently still largely in the future.

(Daniel H. Ludlow, *A Companion to Your Study of the Doctrine and Covenants*, vol. 2 [Salt Lake City: Deseret Book, 1978], 2:107)

Daily Living

USE THE KEYS TO THE GATHERING OF ISRAEL—MISSIONARY WORK.

ᘓ As disciples of Jesus Christ, we have been foreordained to assist with this work. We are responsible to gather Israel by preaching and proclaiming the gospel of Jesus Christ—Jacob 5:70–75; Alma 13:3–7; Mormon 9:22; D&C 138:53–57

THE KEYS OF THE GOSPEL OF ABRAHAM

After this, Elias appeared, and committed the dispensation of the gospel of Abraham, saying that in us and our seed all generations after us should be blessed.
D&C 110:12

We know that the Lord called Abraham and made some very important promises to him and his posterity. His descendants through Isaac and Jacob, constitute the house of Israel, the people to whom the Lord entrusted the covenants and delivered his word through prophets for the guidance of the whole world. . . . The Lord has declared that Elias shall restore all things spoken of by all the holy prophets (D. & C. 27:6). This may have reference to all the prophets who were sent with keys of authority to Joseph Smith and Oliver Cowdery.

(Joseph Fielding Smith, *Church History and Modern Revelation*, 4 vols. [Salt Lake City: The Church of Jesus Christ of Latter-day Saints, 1946], 3:81)

Daily Living

THE KEYS OF THE GOSPEL OF ABRAHAM.

- We are responsible as the seed of Abraham for the building up the kingdom of God and the establishment of Zion, for perfecting of the Saints, redeeming the dead, and proclaiming the gospel—D&C 124:58

TURN THE HEARTS

After this vision had closed, another great and glorious vision burst upon us; for Elijah the prophet, who was taken to heaven without tasting death, stood before us, and said: Behold, the time has fully come, which was spoken of by the mouth of Malachi—testifying that he [Elijah] should be sent, before the great and dreadful day of the Lord come—To turn the hearts of the fathers to the children, and the children to the fathers, lest the whole earth be smitten with a curse.

D&C 110:13–15

The sealing power of Elijah makes it possible for this joining of the families, generation to generation, back to the beginning. . . . If Elijah had not come, we are led to believe that all the work of past ages would have been of little avail, for the Lord said the whole earth, under such conditions, would be utterly wasted at his coming.

(Joseph Fielding Smith, *Doctrines of Salvation*, 2:118, 121)

Daily Living

TURN YOUR HEART TO THE FATHERS AND TO THE CHILDREN.

℘ The sealing power restored by Elijah truly has changed the hearts of mankind. The spirit of Elijah inspires us to turn to those who have gone before and seek after them. In another important way, it has made family members turn to their immediate family in compassion and love. Part of the purpose of this existence is for us to experience family relationships and be bound through the ordinances of the temple. The question remains: Do we have the spirit of Elijah in our hearts?

THE SECOND COMING IS NEAR

Therefore, the keys of this dispensation are committed into your hands; and by this ye may know that the great and dreadful day of the Lord is near, even at the doors.
D&C 110:16

The Second Coming is near. Just as surely as Jesus was born in Bethlehem, just so surely will he come again, a resurrected, glorified being, and with him will come hosts, and there will be many spectacular changes. It will not be the end of the world in the sense of annihilation, but the end of its present relationships, and there will be many, many changes. Beginning with the bridegroom's coming will come the celestializing of this earth and tremendous changes which we can hardly think of or believe.

(Spencer W. Kimball, *The Teachings of Spencer W. Kimball*, ed. Edward L. Kimball [Salt Lake City: Bookcraft, 1982], 440)

Daily Living

PREPARE FOR THE SECOND COMING.

ꙮ How near is near? No one knows the day or the time. Our meeting may be at the end of our mortal probation. There is one important fact in regard to meeting our Savior—are we prepared? Let us satisfy our curiosity by being wise and looking for the signs of His coming—in order to get ready and make this day another day to prepare to meet God—Alma 34:32; LDS Topical Guide, "Second Coming," "Last Days," "Signs"

THE LORD THY GOD SHALL LEAD

Be thou humble; and the Lord thy God shall lead thee by the hand, and give thee answer to thy prayers.
D&C 112:10

The benefits of being humble must also give the answer to the need for this virtue (Mosiah 3:18–19). What, according to the revelations, makes of this quality the pathway to salvation? Obedience to the commandments is the first essential (Matt. 7:21). The Lord blesses the person of humility. In what ways? (1) He "shall lead thee by the hand, and give thee answer to thy prayers" (D&C 112:10). (2) The Lord's spirit enlightens the humble (*Ibid.*, 136:33). (3) "Let him that is ignorant learn wisdom by humbling himself" (*Ibid.*, v. 32). (4) The promise of seeing and knowing the Lord is made to the humble (*Ibid.*, 67:10). (5) His arm of mercy is extended to the humble in freeing them of bondage (Mosiah 29:18–20). (6) The weak are made strong and are thus able to fulfill other commandments (Ether 12:26–27). (7) The humble receive knowledge (D&C 1:28). (8) The blessing of assisting the Lord in his work comes to the humble (*Ibid.*, 12:8).

(Roy W. Doxey, *The Doctrine and Covenants Speaks* [Salt Lake City: Deseret Book, 1970], 2:336–337)

Daily Living

THE LORD THY GOD SHALL LEAD THEE BY THE HAND.

℘ The Lord can lead us if we are humble. Humility is a cardinal virtue—Alma 5:27; Ether 12:27; D&C 11:12; 12:8

NOVEMBER

And then, if thou endure it well,
God shall exalt thee on high;
thou shalt triumph over all thy foes.

—Doctrine & Covenants 121:8

November 1

AN EFFECTUAL DOOR SHALL BE OPENED

Wherefore, whithersoever they shall send you, go ye, and I will be with you; and in whatsoever place ye shall proclaim my name an effectual door shall be opened unto you, that they may receive my word.

D&C 112:19

Orson Pratt promised, "Brethren, I will prophesy that the power of the Lord God of Israel will be with you . . . and the way will be open before you, and the Lord will visit the hearts of the people before you arrive among them, and make manifest to them by visions and dreams that you are the servants of God, before they shall see your faces. And you will receive heavenly visions to comfort you, and dreams to give you knowledge of the things of God, if you prove faithful before him. I will prophesy this in the name of the Lord God of Israel."

(quoted in Rulon T. Burton, *We Believe* [Salt Lake City: Bookcraft, 1994], 580)

Daily Living

AN EFFECTUAL DOOR SHALL BE OPENED.

- Doors will be opened as you proclaim the gospel of Jesus Christ—D&C 84:88
- The Lord will provide will provide a way—1 Nephi 3:7
- The elect will hear His voice—D&C 29:7
- Through your faith all things shall be done, and it is expedient that people come unto Christ—Moroni 10:23

PURIFY YOUR HEARTS AND PREACH MY GOSPEL

But purify your hearts before me; and then go ye into all the world, and preach my gospel unto every creature who has not received it.
D&C 112:28

If our service is to be most efficacious, it must be accomplished for the love of God and the love of his children. . . . This principle—that our service should be for the love of God and the love of fellowmen rather than for personal advantage or any other lesser motive—is admittedly a high standard. The Savior must have seen it so, since he joined his commandment for selfless and complete love directly with the ideal of perfection. . . . "Be ye therefore perfect, even as your Father which is in heaven is perfect." (Matt.5:48) . . . Service with all of our heart and mind is a high challenge for all of us. Such service must be free of selfish ambition. It must be motivated only by the pure love of Christ. . . . I know that God expects us to work to purify our hearts and our thoughts so that we may serve one another for the highest and best reason, the pure love of Christ.

(Dallin H. Oaks, in Conference Report, 1984, 16)

Daily Living

PURIFY YOUR HEARTS—THEN PREACH MY GOSPEL.

- With a pure heart: Your motives will be righteous. You will be worthy of the Spirit. You will be at peace. You will have an overwhelming desire to bring others to Christ. You will have the image of Christ in your countenance—1 Timothy 1:5; Alma 5:19; 3 Nephi 12:8

NAMING OF THE CHURCH

For thus shall my church be called in the last days, even The Church of Jesus Christ of Latter-day Saints.
D&C 115:4

But I pray you consider what the real name means—"The Church of Jesus Christ of Latter-day Saints." We can understand, easily, what "Latter-day" means—modern day, this day; but what does the word "Saint" mean? By derivation, by acceptation, and by the best authority in the language, it means directly, used as an adjective, "holy," and when used as a noun "a holy one," and we, therefore, profess to be a body of holy men, holy women. We proclaim ourselves in the name of Jesus Christ to be the holy ones of the last days, a significant proclamation, blasphemous in the extreme if it be not justified.

(James E. Talmage, in Conference Report, April 1922, 72)

Daily Living

THE CHURCH OF JESUS CHRIST OF LATTER-DAY SAINTS.

ဢ The singing of a favorite Primary song brings joy to my soul. Ponder the words and think of those things you can and should do as members of the Church. "I belong to The Church of Jesus Christ of Latter-day Saints. I know who I am. I know God's plan. I'll follow Him in faith. I believe in the Savior Jesus Christ. I'll honor His name. I'll do what is right. I'll follow His light. His truth I will proclaim" (*Children's Songbook,* "The Church of Jesus Christ," 77).

ARISE AND SHINE FORTH

Verily I say unto you all: Arise and shine forth, that thy light may be a standard for the nations.
D&C 115:5

As defined by the Lord, the "light to the world" is the everlasting covenant, or, in other words, the fulness of the gospel of Jesus Christ as revealed through his church (D&C 45:9, 28). Isaiah wrote of a "standard" that was to be set up to the people of this world (Isa. 49:22; 1 Ne. 21:22). Elder Marion G. Romney identified the Church as that standard of which Isaiah spoke (CR, Apr. 1961, 119). . . . The charge to the Saints in all ages has been to dispel darkness with the light of the gospel (Matt. 5:14–16; 3 Ne. 12:14–16; D&C 115:42–5).

(Hoyt W. Brewster, Jr., *Doctrine and Covenants Encyclopedia* [Salt Lake City: Bookcraft, 1996], 325)

Daily Living

ARISE AND SHINE FORTH THE LIGHT OF THE LORD.

- Let your light shine forth that you might be an example of righteousness for all the world that others may come unto Christ—3 Nephi 12:16; D&C 103:9–10
- Pray for opportunities to share the gospel. Pray for people to serve—Matthew 25:40; D&C 123:12; Mosiah 2:17
- This can and will happen as you make this a priority in your life. Set some goals. Make some plans and be sure to set aside some time to ponder and pray so that there will be a time, a place, and a way to accomplish that which the Lord has commanded us to do—Mormon 9:22; Jacob 5:70–71

ADAM-ONDI-AHMAN

Spring Hill is named by the Lord Adam-ondi-Ahman, because, said he, it is the place where Adam shall come to visit his people, or the Ancient of Days shall sit, as spoken of by Daniel the prophet.
D&C 116:1

ADAM-ONDI-AHMAN was the place in which Adam blessed his descendants, three years before his death (Sec. 107:53). It is the place where he will sit in judgment, previous to the taking possession of the kingdom by the Saints (Daniel 7:9–14, 22). The Prophet Joseph, in a discourse delivered June 2, 1839, said: "Daniel speaks of the Ancient of Days. He means the oldest man, our Father Adam (Michael). He will call his children together and hold a council with them, to prepare them for the coming of the Son of Man. He (Adam) is the father of the human family, and presides over the spirits of all men; and all that have the keys must stand before him in this grand council. This may take place *before some of us leave this stage of action*" (*Journal of Discourses*, vol. VI., 237–8).

(Hyrum M. Smith and Janne M. Sjodahl, *Doctrine and Covenants Commentary* [Salt Lake City: Deseret Book, 1978], 743)

Daily Living

ADAM SHALL COME TO ADAM-ONDI-AHMAN.

ꝏ Adam-ondi-Ahman is indeed a sacred place where marvelous and wonderful things have occurred and will yet occur. One can only imagine the grandeur of the meetings held and planned for this sacred place—D&C 78:15

THE LAW OF TITHING

And this shall be the beginning of the tithing of my people. And after that, those who have thus been tithed shall pay one-tenth of all their interest annually; and this shall be a standing law unto them forever, for my holy priesthood, saith the Lord.
D&C 119:3–4

Tithing is so simple and straightforward a thing . . . it is a brief statement from the Lord, the payment left to the individual and motivated by faith. . . . By way of personal testimony, while speaking of the financial resources of the Church, we reiterate the promise of the Lord given anciently through the prophet Malachi that he will open the windows of heaven upon those who are honest with him in the payment of their tithes and offerings, that there shall not be room enough to receive the promised blessings. Every honest tithe payer can testify that the Lord keeps his promise.

(Gordon B. Hinckley, *Teachings of Gordon B. Hinckley* [Salt Lake City: Deseret Book, 1997], 654)

Daily Living

SEEK THE JOY AND BLESSING OF PAYING TITHES AND OFFERINGS.

ꝏ Tithes and offerings are used to build up the kingdom of God here upon the earth. We must remember that we owe our Heavenly Father everything; therefore, we should not withhold our oblations from Him. We pay our tithes and offerings not simply to receive God's blessings, but because we love Him and want to show Him our gratitude and obedience—Malachi 3:8; D&C 64:23; 85:3; 97:12

ADVERSITY

My son, peace be unto thy soul; thine adversity and thine afflictions shall be but a small moment; And then, if thou endure it well, God shall exalt thee on high; thou shalt triumph over all thy foes.
D&C 121:7–8

Adversity can be an effective teacher. . . . Freedom of choice in how we will react to adversity is essential to existence and to progression. When the testing is tough, faith in God's goodness may be all there is to go on for a time. But then, as we are reminded in 2 Ne. 2:2, "Thou knowest the greatness of God; and he shall consecrate thine afflictions for thy gain." We can learn from trial. We can . . . find the principle God has given to help us meet such a test and to gain great experience from it.

(Elaine Cannon, *Adversity* [Salt Lake City: Bookcraft, 1987], 41)

Daily Living

LEARN TO DEAL WITH ADVERSITY, TEMPTATION, AND OPPOSITION.

- Adversity and opposition are realities of life—2 Nephi 2:11
- It is present in all situations of life including temptation, willful disobedience, and even chastisement from the Lord or in a special trial He gives us for our particular tutoring and growth—Mosiah 3:19; D&C 29:39
- Often it comes as afflictions upon an innocent victim—Helaman 3:34
- How we view the situation is the key to dealing with adversity—Alma 62:41

KNOWLEDGE BY HIS HOLY SPIRIT

God shall give unto you knowledge by his Holy Spirit, yea, by the unspeakable gift of the Holy Ghost, that has not been revealed since the world was until now.
D&C 121:26

Latter-day Saints affirm the reality and effectiveness of learning by faith and revelation. The Lord's way of revealing himself and of communicating understanding about the doctrines and ordinances of his gospel is revelation by the Holy Ghost, the Spirit of God. Indeed, the prophet Jacob declared the impossibility of uninspired man's understanding God: "No man knoweth of his ways save it be revealed unto him; wherefore, brethren, despise not the revelations of God" (Jacob 4:8).

(Dallin H. Oaks, *The Lord's Way* [Salt Lake City: Deseret Book, 1991], 19)

Daily Living

GOD SHALL GIVE UNTO YOU KNOWLEDGE BY HIS HOLY SPIRIT.

- Gospel knowledge given by the Holy Spirit is life-saving knowledge, for it pertains to the plan of salvation and our eternal life—D&C 1:28; 68:3–7; 3 Nephi 5:20; 16:4
- We must seek this knowledge, for it is impossible to be saved in ignorance—D&C 131:6
- The knowledge of God the Father and our Savior Jesus Christ brings us life eternal—John 17:3
- The Holy Ghost teaches and inspires God's children with wonderful knowledge that becomes a blessing to His children here upon the earth—Alma 5:46; 3 Nephi 15:23

NOTHING WITHHELD FROM THE VALIANT

A time to come in the which nothing shall be withheld, whether there be one God or many gods, they shall be manifest. All thrones and dominions, principalities and powers, shall be revealed and set forth upon all who have endured valiantly for the gospel of Jesus Christ.

D&C 121:28–29

Furthermore, there had been revealed to Joseph seven years earlier the future of those not valiant in the testimony of Jesus (see D&C 76:79). That revelation can be juxtaposed to what the Prophet was told while in the jail: "endure it well," for glorious promises were given to those "who have endured valiantly for the gospel of Jesus Christ" (D&C 121:8, 29). Even if otherwise "honorable," those who are not valiant in the testimony of Jesus cannot be crowned in the celestial kingdom. A "good soldier" is "valiant" to the end.

(Neal A. Maxwell, *But for a Small Moment* [Salt Lake City: Bookcraft, 1986], 9)

Daily Living

Am I valiant in all things?

ဢ Elder Bruce R. McConkie offered specific counsel for evaluating how valiant we are. He taught, "Our doctrine is clear: its application sometimes seems to be more difficult. Perhaps some personal introspection might be helpful. For instance:

"Am I valiant in the testimony of Jesus if my chief interest and concern in life is laying up in store the treasures of this earth, rather than the building up of the kingdom?

"Am I valiant if I have more of this world's goods than my just needs and wants require, and I do not draw from my surplus to support missionary work, build temples, and care for the needy?

"Am I valiant if my approach to the Church and its doctrines is intellectual only, if I am more concerned with having a religious dialogue on this or that point than I am on gaining a personal spiritual experience?

"Am I valiant if I am deeply concerned about the Church's stand on who can or who cannot receive the priesthood and think it is time for a new revelation on this doctrine?

"Am I valiant if I use a boat, live in a country home, or engage in some other recreational pursuit on weekends that takes me away from my spiritual responsibilities?

"Am I valiant if I engage in gambling, play cards, go to pornographic movies, shop on Sunday, wear immodest clothes, or do any of the things that are the accepted way of life among worldly people?"

(Bruce R. McConkie, in Conference Report,
October 1974, 45–46)

WHY ARE THEY NOT CHOSEN?

Behold, there are many called, but few are chosen. And why are they not chosen? Because their hearts are set so much upon the things of this world, and aspire to the honors of men.
D&C 121:34–35

To seek the honors of men is to set aside the things of God and place priority upon the praise of the world (D&C 58:39). Nephi saw the wicked destroying the Saints of God for the praise of the world (1 Ne. 13:9). He also saw the practice of priestcraft whereby men preached for gain and the praise of the world rather than for the welfare of Zion (2 Ne. 26:29). Another ancient Nephite prophet indicated that seeking such praise cankers the soul and brings a misery which never dies (Morm. 8:38). Whenever the applause, accolades, and praise of the world take precedence over the things of God, one is seeking the honors of men.

(Hoyt W. Brewster, Jr., *Doctrine and Covenants Encyclopedia* [Salt Lake City: Bookcraft, 1996], 251–252)

Daily Living

BEWARE WHEN HEARTS ARE SET UPON THE THINGS OF THIS WORLD.

- If your heart is not pure and yielding it cannot receive the inspiration of the Holy Spirit as it should. The natural man will be manifest in all of its carnal desires, appetites, and passions, and will remain unrepentant and an enemy to God—Mosiah 2:38; 3:19; Helaman 3:35
- Charity and a pure heart with all its facets of goodness are the keys to a righteous life—Moroni 7:44–48; Mosiah 2:41

PRINCIPLES OF RIGHTEOUSNESS

That the rights of the priesthood are inseparably connected with the powers of heaven, and that the powers of heaven cannot be controlled nor handled only upon the principles of righteousness.
D&C 121:36

The priesthood can be "handled only upon the principles of righteousness." . . . He [God] has admonished all men who bear his priesthood to cultivate "charity towards all men, and to the household of faith, and let virtue garnish thy thoughts unceasingly; then shall thy confidence wax strong in the presence of God; and the doctrine of the priesthood shall distil upon thy soul as the dews from heaven." What a precious gift this bestowal of divine power is, and our Lord has generously made provision that every man who is worthy may receive and use it for the blessing of his fellow men.

(Stephen L Richards, *Where Is Wisdom?* [Salt Lake City: Deseret Book, 1955], 321)

Daily Living

SEEK THE PRIESTHOOD AND THE PRINCIPLES OF RIGHTEOUSNESS.

ꟷ Righteousness describes that state of being in which one is blameless, faithful, full of good works, and obedient to the commandments of the Lord. Righteousness is the oil in our lamps (see Matt 25:1–13), and righteousness is happiness (see 2 Ne. 2:13). Happiness is the design of our existence, and remember that faith in the Lord Jesus Christ is the foundation of all righteousness (see *Lectures on Faith* [Salt Lake City: Deseret Book, 1985], 1:1).

POWER AND INFLUENCE

No power or influence can or ought to be maintained by virtue of the priesthood, only by persuasion, by long-suffering, by gentleness and meekness, and by love unfeigned; By kindness, and pure knowledge, which shall greatly enlarge the soul without hypocrisy, and without guile.
D&C 121:41–42

Obviously this supernal spiritual style of leadership [see above] as thus set forth could not be sustained for long by anyone who was casual in his commitment or who was not making significant spiritual strides in developing the attributes of Jesus. This leadership style and attitude here made specific to priesthood bearers match[es] the attributes and qualities of a true Saint. . . .

(Neal A. Maxwell, *But for a Small Moment* [Salt Lake City: Bookcraft, 1986], 10)

Daily Living

LEARN THE RIGHTEOUS USE OF POWER AND INFLUENCE.

- Manner and motive determine the purity and effectiveness of one's work. You are magnified by the power of God as you demonstrate your purity of soul, the tenderness of your heart, and by esteeming them of great worth. Take upon you the divine nature of Christ—2 Peter 1:3–10
- Charity, which you can possess with no ulterior motives, duplicity, or hypocrisy of soul, qualifies you for the work and can be an influence for good wherever you are—D&C 4:5; 88:125; 1 Corinthians 8:1; 2 Nephi 26:30; Moroni 7:44–48; 8:17

REPROVING AND CHASTENING

Reproving betimes with sharpness, when moved upon by the Holy Ghost; and then showing forth afterwards an increase of love toward him whom thou hast reproved, lest he esteem thee to be his enemy; That he may know that thy faithfulness is stronger than the cords of death.

D&C 121:43–44

The purpose of reproving and chastening is to help people reform, repent, and purify their lives. Righteous chastening is always based on love for the individual. Sometimes the Lord uses external means such as famine, pestilence, and many other hardships (see Hel. 11:4–18) to bring us to a state of humility so that we can be taught and persuaded to change our ways. Through chastening we can grow—provided we are easily entreated and don't consider the chastening as punishment, but rather as a "course correction" to keep us on the right course. We must follow the counsel reproving (correcting) betimes (early on, without delay) with sharpness (with clarity) when inspired by the Holy Ghost and follow up with compassion and love. Never chasten or reprove if you don't have enough "Balm of Gilead" to heal and soothe the chastened.

(The authors, Ed J. Pinegar and Richard J. Allen, adapted from their book *Living by the Word* [American Fork: Covenant Communications, 2005], 40)

Daily Living

REPROVE AND CHASTEN BY THE HOLY SPIRIT WITH LOVE.

༄ Chastise only with love and only when moved by the Spirit.

November 14

CHARITY TOWARDS ALL MEN

Let thy bowels also be full of charity towards all men, and to the household of faith, and let virtue garnish thy thoughts unceasingly; then shall thy confidence wax strong in the presence of God; and the doctrine of the priesthood shall distil upon thy soul as the dews from heaven.

D&C 121:45

When you get the Spirit of God, you feel full of kindness, charity, long-suffering, and you are willing all the day long to accord to every man that which you want yourself. You feel disposed all the day long to do unto all men as you would wish them to do unto you. What is it that will enable one man to govern his fellows aright? It is just as Joseph Smith said to a certain man who asked him, "How do you govern such a vast people as this?" "Oh," says Joseph, "it is very easy." "Why," says the man, "but we find it very difficult." "But," said Joseph, "it is very easy, for I teach the people correct principles and they govern themselves"; and if correct principles will do this in one family they will in ten, in a hundred and in ten hundred thousand.

(John Taylor, *Journal of Discourses*, May 18, 1862, 10:57–58)

Daily Living

SEEK CHARITY AND EXPRESS CHARITY TO ALL MANKIND.

- Charity, the pure love of Christ, empowers one with many virtues and powers—Moroni 7:44–45
- Our feelings and sensitivity to others should be full of this caring and loving attitude. Giving and receiving of charity is transcendent, for it endows the giver and receiver.

LET VIRTUE GARNISH THY THOUGHTS

Let thy bowels also be full of charity towards all men, and to the household of faith, and let virtue garnish thy thoughts unceasingly; then shall thy confidence wax strong in the presence of God; and the doctrine of the priesthood shall distil upon thy soul as the dews from heaven.

D&C 121:45

Thoughts have a profound influence on the character, personality, and eventual actions of man. The Lord is concerned with our thoughts and warns us that we will be held accountable for them. Evil thoughts are a sin (Prov. 15:26; 24:9), and they frequently lead to further sinful action: "Out of the heart of men, proceed evil thoughts, adulteries, fornications, murders, Thefts, covetousness, wickedness, deceit, lasciviousness, an evil eye, blasphemy, pride, foolishness: All these evil things come from within" (Mark 7:21–23). Good thoughts can lead one to God by building faith and confidence. . . .

(Daniel H. Ludlow, *A Companion to Your Study of Doctrine and Covenants* [Salt Lake City: Deseret Book, 1978], 303)

Daily Living

LET VIRTUE GARNISH THY THOUGHTS UNCEASINGLY.

ঌ When virtue is within and placed upon all our thoughts, we indeed will change our attitude and behavior. Pure and holy thoughts dwelled upon create a desire that, when encouraged, results in action—Proverbs 23:7; 2 Corinthians 10:5; Mosiah 4:30; Alma 12:14; 37:36; D&C 6:36; 88:69; 100:5

DOCTRINE OF THE PRIESTHOOD

Let thy bowels also be full of charity towards all men, and to the household of faith, and let virtue garnish thy thoughts unceasingly; then shall thy confidence wax strong in the presence of God; and the doctrine of the priesthood shall distil upon thy soul as the dews from heaven.

D&C 121:45

An official explanation of this term appeared in print in 1961: "It is the doctrine that those who hold this power and authority will be chosen for an inheritance of eternal life if they exercise their priesthood upon principles of righteousness; if they walk in the light; if they keep the commandments; if they put first in their lives the things of God's kingdom and let temporal concerns take a secondary place; if they serve in the kingdom with an eye single to the glory of God" (*Improvement Era,* 64:115).

(Hoyt W. Brewster, Jr., *Doctrine and Covenants Encyclopedia* [Salt Lake City: Bookcraft, 1996], 141)

Daily Living

THE DOCTRINE OF THE PRIESTHOOD SHALL DISTIL UPON THY SOUL.

ஐ When we comprehend the doctrine of the priesthood as it distils upon our souls, it will bring a change in the way we view the priesthood. We will reverence the priesthood. We will honor the priesthood. We will come to realize that as we magnify our priesthood in righteousness, we will be an instrument in the hand of the Lord to bless others and also be blessed with all that the Father has . . . even eternal life—D&C 84:37–38

THE HOLY GHOST, THY CONSTANT COMPANION

The Holy Ghost shall be thy constant companion, and thy scepter an unchanging scepter of righteousness and truth; and thy dominion shall be an everlasting dominion, and without compulsory means it shall flow unto thee forever and ever.
D&C 121:46

The key to spiritual guidance is found in one word: worthiness. A comparison of D&C 63:16–17 with D&C 121:45–46 makes this point vividly: Those who look upon others with lustful hearts will not have the Spirit; they will experience fear; and they will deny the faith. In direct contrast, those who garnish their thoughts with virtue will have the Holy Ghost as a constant companion, they will feel confident in the Lord's presence, and the doctrine of the priesthood will distill upon their souls as the dews from heaven.

(Bruce C. Hafen and Marie K. Hafen, *The Belonging Heart: The Atonement and Relationships with God and Family* [Salt Lake City: Deseret Book, 1994], 281)

Daily Living

THE HOLY GHOST CAN BE THY CONSTANT COMPANION.

ꕤ Elder Rudger Clawson has suggested concerning the priesthood and the Holy Ghost, "Now, I ask you, what more could a faithful high priest receive than the promise of this blessing? Could he receive any more if he were an apostle? . . . Could he receive any more if he were the President of the Church, than a promise which gives to him a joint heirship in all things? No, he could not." (Quoted in Roy W. Doxey, comp., *Latter-day Prophets and the Doctrine and Covenants* [Salt Lake City: Deseret Book, 1978], 4:223–224.)

November 18

ALL THESE THINGS SHALL GIVE THEE EXPERIENCE

And if thou shouldst be cast into the pit, or into the hands of murderers, and the sentence of death passed upon thee; if thou be cast into the deep; if the billowing surge conspire against thee; if fierce winds become thine enemy; if the heavens gather blackness, and all the elements combine to hedge up the way; and above all, if the very jaws of hell shall gape open the mouth wide after thee, know thou, my son, that all these things shall give thee experience, and shall be for thy good.

D&C 122:7

Our human tendency is to forget the Lord, so adversity and afflictions are sometimes needed to put us in remembrance of Him. This should tell us how powerful and consuming the cares and pleasures of the world can become! And, also, how vital it is for us not to misread the role of affliction. Alma observed how the very poverty of one group of people actually had humbled them so that "they were in a preparation to hear the word." Paradoxically, we pray for peace, but in conditions of peace, some are so slow "to feel after" the Lord that the Lord's counsel is paid little heed. He who has called us His friends will not fail to tutor us as needed, whatever the conditions.

(Neal A. Maxwell, *Even As I Am* [Salt Lake City: Deseret Book, 1982], 107)

Daily Living

ALL THESE THINGS SHALL GIVE THEE EXPERIENCE.

℘ The tutoring of the Lord is forever present in our lives—Mosiah 3:19; Proverbs 3:5–6; D&C 19:23; 2 Nephi 11, 27

WE ARE THE FINDERS

For there are many yet on the earth among all sects, parties, and denominations, who are blinded by the subtle craftiness of men, whereby they lie in wait to deceive, and who are only kept from the truth because they know not where to find it.

D&C 123:12

Our whole souls should be filled with pity because of their condition (*those who know not God*), and we should sympathize with them because of their ignorance. . . . We should go forth among them with the sole desire in our hearts to manifest unto them that which God has revealed unto us, and carry to them that which has made us free and happy, and which has made us in very deed the Church and people of God. That should be the feeling of the Latter-day Saints (italics added).

(Hyrum M. Smith, in Conference Report, October 1903, 97)

Daily Living

SEEK TO FIND PEOPLE TO SHARE THE GOSPEL WITH.

- Do we truly care for the souls of mankind?—Mosiah 28:3
- Do we open our mouths?—D&C 33:8–11
- Do we pray and look for opportunities to share the gospel? Do we fast and pray for all those who know not God?—Alma 6:6
- Are we making a list of possible contacts that might be interested in hearing the gospel? We can do better. Pray for strength. Be bold but not overbearing. Remember the Lord will provide a way—1 Nephi 3:7

DUTY TO UPHOLD TO DEFEND THE TRUTH

Therefore, that we should waste and wear out our lives in bringing to light all the hidden things of darkness, wherein we know them; and they are truly manifest from heaven—These should then be attended to with great earnestness. Let no man count them as small things; for there is much which lieth in futurity, pertaining to the saints, which depends upon these things.

D&C 123:13–15

The fact is, we think we have a right to "life, liberty, and the pursuit of happiness," so long as we do not interfere with the rights of others; we therefore most decidedly object to being demolished; we do not like nor do we intend to be destroyed. Not that we presume to be able to defend ourselves unaided by divine power, against our numerous and unrelenting foes; but knowing in whom we trust, and the nature of the work in which we are engaged, we are not slow to believe, neither are we afraid to openly maintain that we were born to live and to uphold truth, to defend virtue, to establish righteousness, and to stand by the right, and by the help of God we intend to fill the measure of our creation.

(President Joseph F. Smith, *Journal of Discourses*, 26 vols. [London: Latter-day Saints' Book Depot, 1854–1886], 23: 74–75)

Daily Living

WE MUST UPHOLD RIGHTEOUSNESS AND DEFEND THE TRUTH.

ཊ We are the defenders of truth in mildness, meekness, and we uphold righteousness in all things—D&C 88:40, 66

DO ALL THINGS CHEERFULLY

Therefore, dearly beloved brethren, let us cheerfully do all things that lie in our power; and then may we stand still, with the utmost assurance, to see the salvation of God, and for his arm to be revealed.

D&C 123:17

The loss of life and property had been great, and as citizens of the state of Missouri and as American citizens, the Saints should have been protected by the laws of the land. But they had received no such protection and had, on the contrary, been the victims of heartless marauders. Thus, it was entirely proper to seek redress from the government of the state of Missouri. But the Prophet admonished the Saints to do so cheerfully.

So much energy is wasted in feelings of hatred and revenge, but when we can seek to set things right cheerfully. . . . When we harbor mean-spirited feelings of retribution, we are on the devil's turf; but when we seek redress cheerfully, the Lord is on our side.

(Spencer J. Condie, *In Perfect Balance* [Salt Lake City: Bookcraft, 1993], 168)

Daily Living

CHEERFULLY DO ALL THINGS THAT LIE IN OUR POWER.

ஐ Cheerfully do ALL that lies within our power, being on the Lord's errand and being asked to do all that we can do. Then, being full of faith and receiving the strength of the Lord, the power of God is revealed and extended to those in need—Alma 26:12; Ether 12:27; D&C 78:18

November 22

INTEGRITY OF YOUR HEART

And again, verily I say unto you, blessed is my servant Hyrum Smith; for I, the Lord, love him because of the integrity of his heart, and because he loveth that which is right before me, saith the Lord.

D&C 124:15

I would like to bear you my witness that unless the priesthood which we bear, and the Holy Ghost which has been conferred upon us, and our theological beliefs in God, in mortality, and in the Son of God—unless these things create in us meekness and humility of heart, integrity of mind and heart, and a deep love for our fellowmen, they are vain to us individually. This I believe with all my soul. The priesthood and the Holy Ghost were not given to honor us. They were given to us to make us men and to create in us the power to serve our fellowmen, to make us hungry for righteousness and for truth.

(Lowell L. Bennion, *The Best of Lowell L. Bennion: Selected Writings 1928–1988*, ed. Eugene England [Salt Lake City: Deseret Book, 1988], 261)

Daily Living

SEEK TO HAVE INTEGRITY OF HEART.

ꕤ Integrity of the heart (which is the center of the soul, the mind of man, the affections and decisions of your very being) is moral and pure, upright in all things. Indeed, one is honest with oneself and there is no hypocrisy. In all of the qualities of character and moral goodness everything hinges upon integrity and honesty, for if there be no truth there can be no trust—Hebrews 13:18

OFFERINGS AND INTENT ACCEPTED BEFORE THE LORD

Verily, verily, I say unto you, that when I give a commandment to any of the sons of men to do a work unto my name, and those sons of men go with all their might and with all they have to perform that work, and cease not their diligence, and their enemies come upon them and hinder them from performing that work, behold, it behooveth me to require that work no more at the hands of those sons of men, but to accept of their offerings.

D&C 124:49

In the accounts kept by the recording angels, figured out according to the arithmetic of heaven, entries are made in terms of quality rather than of quantity, and values are determined on the basis of capability and intent. . . . "For if there be first a willing mind, it is accepted according to that a man hath, and not according to that he hath not" [2 Cor. 8:12.] (JTC, 561–62).

(Daniel H. Ludlow, *A Companion to Your Study of the New Testament: The Four Gospels* [Salt Lake City: Deseret Book, 1982], 244)

Daily Living

OFFERINGS OF PURE INTENT ARE ACCEPTABLE BEFORE THE LORD.

℘ The Lord in His goodness and mercy only requires our very best effort. This includes our intent as well as our performance. Remember, He is the giver of all good and the power by which all things are done—Moroni 7:5–7; Matthew 6:1; Luke 6:45; Enos 1:9; D&C 4:5; 18:38; 88:67; 121:35, 45

November 24

PERFECTION THROUGH VICARIOUS WORK

And now, my dearly beloved brethren and sisters, let me assure you that these are principles in relation to the dead and the living that cannot be lightly passed over, as pertaining to our salvation. For their salvation is necessary and essential to our salvation, as Paul says concerning the fathers—that they without us cannot be made perfect—neither can we without our dead be made perfect.
D&C 128:15

This doctrine [baptism and work for the dead] presents in a clear light the wisdom and mercy of God in preparing an ordinance for the salvation of the dead, being baptized by proxy, their names recorded in heaven and they judged according to the deeds done in the body. This doctrine was the burden of the scriptures. Those Saints who neglect it in behalf of [the] deceased . . . do it at the peril of their own salvation.
(Joseph Smith, *History of the Church*, October 2, 1841, 4:426)

Daily Living

PERFECTION OF ALL COMES THROUGH VICARIOUS WORK FOR THE DEAD.

℘ To be a Savior on Mount Zion indicates doing work that includes vicarious service—the work that others cannot do for themselves. This type of work is supernal in nature as it has the attributes of Christlikeness within its service—Isaiah 52:7; D&C 138:54; 124:29; 103:9–10

DISCERNING OF MESSENGERS

When a messenger comes saying he has a message from God, offer him your hand and request him to shake hands with you. If he be an angel he will do so, and you will feel his hand. If he be the spirit of a just man made perfect he will come in his glory; for that is the only way he can appear—Ask him to shake hands with you, but he will not move, because it is contrary to the order of heaven for a just man to deceive; but he will still deliver his message. If it be the devil as an angel of light, when you ask him to shake hands he will offer you his hand, and you will not feel anything; you may therefore detect him. These are three grand keys whereby you may know whether any administration is from God.

D&C 129:4–9

There has never been a time when a doctrine has been presented to us by the servants of God that has appeared new or mysterious, but what the Spirit of God has been ready to bear testimony to the truth of the same . . . to be able to discern the right from the wrong in all cases that may come under our observation.

(Wilford Woodruff, *The Discourses of Wilford Woodruff*, ed. G. Homer Durham [Salt Lake City: Bookcraft, 1949], 62)

Daily Living

LEARN TO DISCERN MESSENGERS.

- Ask and it will be given—3 Nephi 27:28–29; D&C 4:7
- Be enlightened by the Spirit—D&C 11:13; 76:12
- Be obedient to the test—D&C 130:20–21

SOCIALITY THROUGH THE ETERNITIES

And that same sociality which exists among us here will exist among us there, only it will be coupled with eternal glory, which glory we do not now enjoy.
D&C 130:2

Mortal life may be a challenge, but immortality is assured through the atonement and resurrection of Christ the Lord. We may be beaten and bruised and battered on every hand by the vicissitudes of life, but we can glory in the assurance that life goes on hereafter and that for the faithful a refined and regenerated sociality will exist everlastingly. Like Job, we can exult in the sweet realization that body and spirit will be reunited (see Job 19:25–27), inseparably joined in the glorious resurrection.

(Joseph Fielding McConkie and Robert L. Millet, *Doctrinal Commentary on the Book of Mormon*, 4 vols. [Salt Lake City: Bookcraft, 1991], 3:23)

Daily Living

THE SOCIALITY WHICH EXISTS HERE WILL EXIST IN THE HEREAFTER.

ꕤ The joy of relationships with loved ones and friends will continue in the hereafter. This reminds us of things that matter most. What will you take to the hereafter? Your covenants, your knowledge of light and truth, your personal righteousness, your memories, and your relationships. If this is what we take with us, then probably these are the important things we should seek to improve here in mortality.

PRINCIPLE OF INTELLIGENCE

Whatever principle of intelligence we attain unto in this life, it will rise with us in the resurrection.
D&C 130:18

It is fair to conclude that spiritual and mental growth can be attained only by obedience to the laws on which they are predicated. If through diligence, observance of correct principles, discipline of the mind and of the spirit, a man attains to a fine development of personality in this life, surely it is not unreasonable to suppose that that will be his imperishable possession and glory in the life he enters upon after death. On the contrary, if through lethargy or sin his self-realization in this life is dwarfed, he shall be handicapped to that extent as he enters upon the new world.

(Albert E. Bowen, in Conference Report, October 1937, 86)

Daily Living

WE MUST SEEK LIGHT AND TRUTH, FOR IT WILL RISE WITH US.

- Light and truth come from God, which enlightens the soul to the gospel truths and covenants that will lead us back to His presence. We are commanded to bring our children up in light and truth—D&C 93:40–42
- Light forsakes the evil one—D&C 93:37
- That which is of God is light, and the more you accept, the more you will continue to receive—D&C 50:24
- When you are filled with light, you are able to comprehend all things—D&C 88:67
- If you abideth in the light, you will love your fellow men—1 John 2:8–11

INTELLIGENCE THROUGH OBEDIENCE

And if a person gains more knowledge and intelligence in this life through his diligence and obedience than another, he will have so much the advantage in the world to come.
D&C 130:19

Intelligence, then becomes but another name for wisdom. . . . Knowledge is one of the means by which such intelligence is attained; the use of knowledge is equally as important, for it gives life and direction to knowledge. The whole matter is much like faith and repentance—neither is complete without the other. When faith becomes active through repentance, man rises towards his God-like destiny. Faith itself, built upon human experience, conforming to God's will, is but a type of higher intelligence. . . . A person of limited knowledge but who earnestly and prayerfully obeys the law, rises to a higher intelligence or wisdom.

(John A. Widstoe, in Conference Report, April 1938, 50)

Daily Living

KNOWLEDGE AND INTELLIGENCE—DILIGENCE AND OBEDIENCE.

- The direction of the Liahona came from faith, diligence, and obedience—1 Nephi 16:28
- The blessings in your life come from giving heed to the word of God—Alma 37:44; 49:30
- The prophets rejoice when we give heed and diligence to their words—Alma 7:26
- Blessings are predicated on obedience—D&C 130:20–21

BLESSINGS PREDICATED ON OBEDIENCE

There is a law, irrevocably decreed in heaven before the foundations of this world, upon which all blessings are predicated— And when we obtain any blessing from God, it is by obedience to that law upon which it is predicated.

D&C 130:20–21

The perfection upon which exaltation hangs, I repeat, is an individual matter. It is conditioned upon the observance of celestial laws as they apply to earth life. The Word of Wisdom is one of them, so also are chastity, tithing, observance of the Sabbath day, prayer, honesty, industry, love of God and fellow men, patience, kindness, charity, and all the rest of the principles and ordinances of the gospel of Jesus Christ. Each individual who observes one or more of these laws shall receive the blessings predicated thereon, and each Church member who will, with all the energy of his soul, diligently strive to live them all, shall receive the blessings predicated upon such striving. (see D&C 93:1).

(Marion G. Romney, in Conference Report, October 1956, 15–16)

Daily Living

OBEDIENCE: THE LAW UPON WHICH BLESSINGS ARE PREDICATED.

- When you love the Lord, ye shall obey—Deuteronomy 30:20; John 14:15
- Obedience is better than sacrifice—1 Samuel 15:22
- The whole duty of man is to obey—Ecclesiastes 12:13
- Do the things the Lord has commanded—1 Nephi 3:7

November 30

THE NATURE OF THE GODHEAD

The Father has a body of flesh and bones as tangible as man's; the Son also; but the Holy Ghost has not a body of flesh and bones, but is a personage of Spirit. Were it not so, the Holy Ghost could not dwell in us.

D&C 130:22–23

God the Eternal Father and his Son Jesus Christ appeared to [Joseph Smith]. "I saw two Personages," he said, "whose brightness and glory defy all description." These two Personages spoke to him and called him by name. He heard their voices and asked them questions. They gave him answer (Pearl of Great Price, Joseph Smith—History 17). When he came out of that sacred interview he knew with certainty the nature of God. He had seen and conversed with him. From him he had received a personal introduction to his resurrected Son, Jesus Christ. In after years Joseph referred to God as an "exalted man," and said that both he and the Son were personages of flesh and bone, as tangible as man (D&C 130:22).

(Marion G. Romney, in Conference Report, October 1958, 96)

Daily Living

WORSHIP GOD AND KEEP THE COMMANDMENTS.

ℵ By understanding and appreciating the nature and perfections of the God the Father, our Savior Jesus Christ, and the Holy Ghost, we worship with reverence, follow in faith, and seek to always submit to the will of God. Remember, they are one in purpose, cause, and action.

DECEMBER

And continue thenceforth their labor as had been promised by the Lord, and be partakers of all blessings which were held in reserve for them that love him.

—Doctrine & Covenants 138:52

December 1

THE CELESTIAL GLORY HAS THREE DEGREES

In the celestial glory there are three heavens or degrees.
D&C 131:1

There are three divisions within the celestial, and the highest is that of exaltation. . . . To be exalted means to be raised above perfection of mortality—in other words, to be raised above everything, so that there cannot be anything higher than that of exaltation in the celestial kingdom . . . Exaltation automatically, by definition, implies that you have the power of reproduction, that you have the seeds eternally, and in order for that you have to have a companion. So in order to gain exaltation there must of necessity be the sealing of a husband and wife by the power of God or by an agent of God with his power given to him, so that it will be in effect after death and through all eternity, that you will be husband and wife even after the resurrection, and each of you being perfect with the power of reproduction that you might have continued increase in the worlds to come.

(Elder Eldred G. Smith, March 10, 1964,
BYU Speeches of the Year, 4–6)

Daily Living

GAIN EXALTATION.

ꝏ All has been done by God the Father and our Savior to provide us the opportunity of gaining exaltation. We must do all in our power to be worthy of this blessing by entering in the covenants in the holy temple and being true and faithful to those covenants—2 Nephi 31:20–21

THE HIGHEST CELESTIAL DEGREE —ETERNAL INCREASE

And in order to obtain the highest, a man must enter into this order of the priesthood [meaning the new and everlasting covenant of marriage]; And if he does not, he cannot obtain it. He may enter into the other, but that is the end of his kingdom; he cannot have an increase.

D&C 131:2–4

What do we mean by endless or eternal increase? We mean that through the righteousness and faithfulness of men and women who keep the commandments of God they will come forth with celestial bodies, fitted and prepared to enter into their great, high and eternal glory in the celestial kingdom of God; and unto them, through their preparation, there will come children, who will be spirit children. I don't think that is very difficult to comprehend and understand.

(Melvin J. Ballard, *Sermons and Missionary Services of Melvin J. Ballard*, ed. Bryant S. Hinckley, [Salt Lake City: Deseret Book, 1949], 239–40)

Daily Living

THE HIGHEST CELESTIAL DEGREE—ETERNAL INCREASE.

ꝏ Celestial marriage is the crowning ordinance in the Lord's house; this makes possible eternal families. This gives us eternal hope through the Atonement of our Lord and Savior Jesus Christ which makes all these ordinances and blessings possible in our lives. May we enter in the temple worthily, partake of the covenants and ordinances, and thus, through faithfulness, receive the blessings of exaltations.

THEN SHALL THEY BE GODS

Then shall they be gods, because they have no end; therefore shall they be from everlasting to everlasting, because they continue; then shall they be above all, because all things are subject unto them. Then shall they be gods, because they have all power, and the angels are subject unto them.

D&C 132:20

The great and grand secret of salvation, which we should continually seek to understand through our faithfulness, is the continuation of the lives. Those of the Latter-day Saints who will continue to follow after the revelations and commandments of God to do them, who are found to be obedient in all things continually advancing little by little towards perfection and the knowledge of God, they, when they enter the spirit world and receive their bodies, will be able to advance faster in the things pertaining to the knowledge of the Gods, and will continue onward and upward until they become Gods, even the sons of God.

(Brigham Young, *Journal of Discourses*, October 8, 1878, 18:260)

Daily Living

WE TOO CAN BECOME LIKE OUR SAVIOR AND HEAVENLY FATHER.

- We, having been spiritually born premortally of exalted beings, have the capacity through the magnificent plan of happiness to live a life like unto to our Heavenly Parents. Our Heavenly Father desires to give to us all that He has if we but keep the commandments and honor all of our priesthood covenants—D&C 84:38
- We become joint heirs with Christ—Romans 8:17

CONTINUATION OF LIVES

Verily, verily, I say unto you, except ye abide my law ye cannot attain to this glory. For strait is the gate, and narrow the way that leadeth unto the exaltation and continuation of the lives, and few there be that find it, because ye receive me not in the world neither do ye know me.

D&C 132:21–22

Every successful marriage in the Temple is based on faithfulness to the covenant of marriage there received. Every sin committed must be atoned for. Christ came into the world to atone for the sins of all those who truly repent and accept the Gospel; all others must pay the price of their own sinning. [2 Nephi 9:20–27.] No covenants or obligations will relieve the individual of punishment who is unrepentant, and there is nothing in the revelations of the Lord which holds out for any soul the hope that he may deliberately sin and escape the consequences. . . . The expression "continuation of the lives," means the right and power of eternal increase, or posterity. . . . To be denied posterity and the family organization, leads to the "deaths," or end of increase in the life to come.

(Joseph Fielding Smith, *Church History and Modern Revelation*, 1950, 4:161–62)

Daily Living

EXALTATION AND CONTINUATION OF LIVES.

℘ To qualify for eternal lives, we must come unto Christ, know God and Jesus Christ whom He has sent, and be true and faithful to our temple covenants—D&C 131:1–4

ETERNAL LIVES

This is eternal lives—to know the only wise and true God, and Jesus Christ, whom he hath sent. I am he. Receive ye, therefore, my law.
D&C 132:24

Know thee the only true God. It is one thing to know about God and another to know him. We know about him when we learn that he is a personal being in whose image man is created . . . when we learn that both the Father and the Son possess certain specified attributes and powers. But we know them, in the sense of gaining eternal life, when we enjoy and experience the same things they do. To know God is to think what he thinks, to feel what he feels, to have the power he possesses, to comprehend the truths he understands, and to do what he does.

(Bruce R. McConkie, *Doctrinal New Testament Commentary*, 3 vols. [Salt Lake City: Bookcraft, 1965–1973], 1:762)

Daily Living

ETERNAL LIVES—TO KNOW GOD AND JESUS CHRIST.

- Know the Father and the Son—John 17:3
- Possess charity, thus overcoming jealousy. Conquer fear and doubt with perfect love (see 1 John 4:18), increased faith (see Romans 10:17; Helaman 3:35), preparation (see D&C 38:30), knowledge, and experience. Grow strong in humility (see Mosiah 4:5; Ether 12:27; Helaman 3:35) and live the doctrine and know of its truthfulness (see John 7:16–18) and by doing these things you shall come to know God—D&C 67:10

SEND FORTH THE MISSIONARIES

Send forth the elders of my church unto the nations which are afar off; unto the islands of the sea; send forth unto foreign lands; call upon all nations, first upon the Gentiles, and then upon the Jews.
D&C 133:8

It is our duty, divinely imposed, to continue urgently and militantly to carry forward our missionary work. We must continue to call missionaries and send them out to preach the gospel, which was never more needed than now, which is the only remedy for the tragic ills that now afflict the world, and which alone can bring peace and brotherly love back amongst the peoples of the earth.

(Ezra Taft Benson, *The Teachings of Ezra Taft Benson* [Salt Lake City: Bookcraft, 1988], 180–181)

Daily Living

SEND FORTH THE ELDERS—MISSIONARIES ARE NEEDED.

- Revelations and commandments in the scripture give a clear mandate to the prophets and members concerning missionary work—Mormon 9:22; Matthew 28:19; Luke 24:47; Alma 37:33; Topical Guide, "Missionary work"
- Remember the joy and blessings of being a missionary—3 Nephi 5:13; John 13:34–35; Alma 29:9–10; 36:24; D&C 31:5; D&C 62:3; James 5:20
- Oh, the joy of being a missionary every day of your life as you seek to bring souls unto Christ—D&C 15:6; 18:10–16

GOSPEL PREACHED TO EVERY NATION

And this gospel shall be preached unto every nation, and kindred, and tongue, and people.
D&C 133:37

We have the gospel to preach to the nations, a message that the Lord has given unto us to promulgate to all peoples. . . . Our mission has principally been to preach the first principles of the gospel, calling upon men everywhere to believe in the Lord God of heaven, he that created the heavens and the earth, the seas, and the fountains of waters; to believe in his Son, Jesus Christ, repenting of their sins, to be baptized for the remission of the same; and then we have promised them the Holy Ghost. . . . And in regard to this I can say as Paul said on a certain occasion—"Ye are my witnesses," for this whole congregation, with few exceptions, know this to be true.

(John Taylor, *Journal of Discourses*, August 20, 1882, 23:235–236)

Daily Living

THE GOSPEL NEEDS TO BE PREACHED TO EVERY NATION.

ꟷ Presently the gospel is being preached in all the continents of the world in 350 plus missions with over 55,000 missionaries. In the year 2007, the Church had sent out its 1,000,000th missionary to the world with approximately 13,000,000 members, with over 125 temples dotting the earth on every continent. The Book of Mormon has been translated—in its entirety or in part—into 107 languages. You are part of this great work, this pruning of the vineyard, that is roiling forth to consume the earth that all might know and come unto Christ.

RIGHTEOUS GOVERNMENTS WERE INSTITUTED OF GOD

We believe that governments were instituted of God for the benefit of man; and that he holds men accountable for their acts in relation to them, both in making laws and administering them, for the good and safety of society.
D&C 134:1

Our Constitution and Bill of Rights guarantee to all our people the greatest freedom ever enjoyed by the public of any great nation. This system guarantees freedom of individual enterprise, freedom to own property, freedom to start one's own business and to operate it according to one's own judgment so long as the enterprise is honorable. The individual has power to produce beyond his needs, to provide savings for the future protection of himself and family. He can live where he wishes and pick any job he wants and select any educational opportunity.

(Ezra Taft Benson, *The Teachings of Ezra Taft Benson* [Salt Lake City: Bookcraft, 1988], 605)

Daily Living

RIGHTEOUS GOVERNMENTS WERE INSTITUTED OF GOD.

℘ We can choose to be a part of the governmental process with input to our elected officials, through volunteer efforts, and individual responsibilities as citizens. This we must remember, that freedom was bought with a price, and that we must do our part to insure our posterity the rights and freedoms that we enjoy with a constitution inspired by God. Never let apathy destroy your sense of values and caring for the well-being of our country.

RIGHTEOUS LAWS

We believe that no government can exist in peace, except such laws are framed and held inviolate as will secure to each individual the free exercise of conscience, the right and control of property, and the protection of life.

D&C 134:2

God is the author of righteousness. The framers of laws have, to a large extent, recognized that doctrine. The Gospel is the compilation, the aggregation of all principles of righteousness, and into the form of government which we uphold and support there have been woven the principles of individual and community righteousness which are underlain by truth which emanates from God himself . . . [in the Constitution of the United States]. You can't have a good government without good people, and goodness is a religious term. . . . I maintain that all true morality is supported by and finds its basis in religion.

(Stephen L. Richards, in Conference Report, October 1923, 47)

Daily Living

RIGHTEOUS LAWS ARE ESSENTIAL TO FREEDOM.

ᘓ Support and promote good legislation that continues to support the freedoms and protection we enjoy through the righteous laws of the land. When something comes up that threatens our well-being, we should do all within the framework of the law to insure that freedom and the rights of the people are not infringed upon.

LAWS MUST BE ENFORCED

We believe that all governments necessarily require civil officers and magistrates to enforce the laws of the same; and that such as will administer the law in equity and justice should be sought for and upheld by the voice of the people if a republic, or the will of the sovereign.

D&C 134:3

If they whose duty it is to enforce the law were whimsical or capricious, or if the laws were not administered and enforced with undeviating justice and equity, there would be confusion, defiance, and rebellion. With the average, normal person, force will not become necessary, but sometimes, for the safety of society, drastic measures must be employed. The Lord himself, though all powerful, refuses to use force to accomplish his purposes. Christ's obedience was always voluntary and love inspired.

(Hugh B. Brown, *Continuing the Quest* [Salt Lake City: Deseret Book, 1961], 228–229)

Daily Living

LAWS MUST BE ENFORCED—PEACE COMES THROUGH JUSTICE.

- Righteous laws are for the good of mankind. There are always blessings and consequences set for obedience or disobedience to the laws. We learn from the Book of Mormon, "by thus exercising the law upon them, every man suffering according to that which he had done, they became more still, and durst not commit any wickedness if it were known; therefore, there was much peace among the people of Nephi."—Alma 1:33

December 11

GOVERNMENTS PROTECT FREEDOM

We believe that religion is instituted of God; and that men are amenable to him, and to him only, for the exercise of it, unless their religious opinions prompt them to infringe upon the rights and liberties of others; but we do not believe that human law has a right to interfere in prescribing rules of worship to bind the consciences of men, nor dictate forms for public or private devotion; that the civil magistrate should restrain crime, but never control conscience; should punish guilt, but never suppress the freedom of the soul.

D&C 134:4

The Church believes that political and religious influence should be kept apart. It does not in any way desire to encroach upon the rights or privileges of the State. It only rises to defend encroachments upon man's right of conscience.

(John A. Widtsoe, *Program of The Church of Jesus Christ of Latter-day Saints* [Salt Lake City: The Church of Jesus Christ of Latter-day Saints, 1937], 100–101)

Daily Living

GOVERNMENTS MUST NEVER SUPPRESS THE FREEDOM OF THE SOUL.

ꕥ Agency can never be destroyed, for it is a gift from God. Freedom can be curtailed through unrighteous dominion and suppression of the soul. This we must never allow or tolerate. Charity does not have to accept abuse and coercion but rather, with a heart that is pure, seeks solutions to conflicts that endanger the freedoms of the soul.

GOVERNMENTS PROTECT OUR RIGHTS

We believe that all men are bound to sustain and uphold the respective governments in which they reside, while protected in their inherent and inalienable rights by the laws of such governments; and that sedition and rebellion are unbecoming every citizen thus protected, and should be punished accordingly; and that all governments have a right to enact such laws as in their own judgments are best calculated to secure the public interest; at the same time, however, holding sacred the freedom of conscience.

D&C 134:5

Saints are "bound to sustain and uphold" their "respective governments . . . while protected in their inherent and inalienable rights by the laws of such governments." D&C 98, verse 5, requires not only that the law support basic rights and privileges but that it must also be Constitutional. These conditions make the Saints' obligation to obey and sustain the law of the land more reasonable.

(Richard O. Cowan, *The Doctrine and Covenants, Our Modern Scripture* [Salt Lake City: Bookcraft, 1984], 204)

Daily Living

WE ARE PROTECTED BY OUR INHERENT AND INALIENABLE RIGHTS.

ꝏ We believe that government must protect our rights. Our war of independence was fought over our rights and freedoms. With the constitution we now enjoy, we have a system whereby we can act responsibly and with peace to bring about change when it is for the good of the people.

GOVERNMENT TO PROMOTE PEACE

We believe that every man should be honored in his station, rulers and magistrates as such, being placed for the protection of the innocent and the punishment of the guilty; and that to the laws all men show respect and deference, as without them peace and harmony would be supplanted by anarchy and terror; human laws being instituted for the express purpose of regulating our interests as individuals and nations, between man and man; and divine laws given of heaven, prescribing rules on spiritual concerns, for faith and worship, both to be answered by man to his Maker.

D&C 134:6

The duty of citizens is to honor and sustain laws and governments. . . . Governments are responsible "for the protection of the innocent and the punishment of the guilty"; citizens are to "step forward and use their ability in bringing offenders against good laws to punishment" (D&C 134:5–6, 8).

(*Encyclopedia of Mormonism*, 1–4 vols., ed. Daniel H. Ludlow [New York: Macmillan, 1992], 1104)

Daily Living

GOVERNMENT IS TO PROMOTE PEACE AND PROTECT ITS CITIZENS.

➻ The weaknesses of men and women can bring sorrow and misery to others who are independent of the government. As with all things on earth, everyone is accountable for their own actions and will be blessed or punished accordingly. Governments are accountable to the people for their actions.

APPEAL FOR REDRESS OF GRIEVANCES

We believe that men should appeal to the civil law for redress of all wrongs and grievances, where personal abuse is inflicted or the right of property or character infringed, where such laws exist as will protect the same; but we believe that all men are justified in defending themselves, their friends, and property, and the government, from the unlawful assaults and encroachments of all persons in times of exigency, where immediate appeal cannot be made to the laws, and relief afforded.

D&C 134:11

Men have come up from the oppression to overthrow coercive governments. The Declaration of Independence and the Constitution of the United States are examples of the declared rights of men and the protection afforded.

(Roy W. Doxey, *The Doctrine and Covenants Speaks* [Salt Lake City: Deseret Book, 1970], 2:432)

Daily Living

APPEAL FOR REDRESS OF ALL WRONGS AND GRIEVANCES.

ᘓ The right to overcome evil and wrongdoing is a responsibility and duty of the citizenry. Books are legendary upon the subject of negotiation, resolving conflict, and getting along. Simply remember to consider others as yourself. Be willing to listen and learn. Look to get along, not to always be right; in other words, seek to be a peacemaker rather than an adversary at war with yourself and others, lest we forget that charity does not have to tolerate abuse and victimizing of others.

PREACH THE GOSPEL TO THE NATIONS OF THE EARTH

We believe it just to preach the gospel to the nations of the earth, and warn the righteous to save themselves from the corruption of the world; but we do not believe it right to interfere with bond-servants, neither preach the gospel to, nor baptize them contrary to the will and wish of their masters, nor to meddle with or influence them in the least to cause them to be dissatisfied with their situations in this life, thereby jeopardizing the lives of men; such interference we believe to be unlawful and unjust, and dangerous to the peace of every government allowing human beings to be held in servitude.

D&C 134:12

Remember that your business is to preach the Gospel in all humility and meekness, and warn sinners to repent and come to Christ. Avoid contentions and vain disputes with men of corrupt minds, who do not desire to know the truth. [Sec. 10:62–63.] Remember that "it is a day of warning, and not a day of many words" [Sec. 63:58].

(Joseph Smith, *History of the Church*, 1:468)

Daily Living

PREACH THE GOSPEL TO THE NATIONS OF THE EARTH.

ဆ There is nothing in the gospel of Jesus Christ that is designed to bring about evil but, on the contrary, the gospel is designed to persuade mankind to do good continually. In fact, you have heard the quote by George Albert Smith: "Keep all the good that you have, and let us bring to you more good" (*Sharing the Gospel with Others,* comp. Preston Nibley, Salt Lake City: Deseret News Press, 1948, 12–13.)—Mormon 9:22

JOSEPH SMITH—THE GREAT RESTORER UNDER THE HAND OF GOD

Joseph Smith, the Prophet and Seer of the Lord, has done more, save Jesus only, for the salvation of men in this world, than any other man that ever lived in it. . . .

D&C 135:3

Within the space of that twenty years preceding his death, Joseph Smith set in motion a program for carrying the gospel to the nations of the earth . . . in times of dark adversity, men were called to leave their homes and families, to cross the sea, to proclaim the restoration of the gospel of Jesus Christ. His mind, his vision encompassed the entire earth. Seated in this hall [Salt Lake Tabernacle] today are those from North, Central, and South America; from the British Isles and Africa; from the nations of Europe; from the islands and continents of the Pacific; and from the ancient lands of Asia. You who have come from far and near, you are the flowering of the vision of Joseph Smith, the prophet of God. He was indeed a mighty seer, who saw this day and greater days yet to come as the work of the Lord moves over the earth.

(Gordon B. Hinckley, in Conference Report, April 1977, 96)

Daily Living

JOSEPH SMITH—THE GREAT RESTORER UNDER THE HAND OF GOD.

- Ponder and show gratitude to God for the life and works of the Prophet Joseph who, under the direction of Almighty God, restored the gospel and kingdom of God in this the dispensation of the fullness of times. For this and all that he has done, we are eternally grateful—D&C 21:4–6; 27:12–13; 124:125; 2 Nephi 3:11, 15

SEEK NOT TO BUILD UP YOURSELF

And if any man shall seek to build up himself,
and seeketh not my counsel, he shall have no power,
and his folly shall be made manifest.
D&C 136:19

Ego is so clever that it can persuade us we are serving a higher purpose by not being lowly! We are bound to notice offenses to ego. . . . However, there need never be a shrinkage in the circles of our spiritual significance if we are in the process of becoming men and women of Christ. . . . Almost all of us know what it is like to feel left out. Yet we are always within God's circle of concern! Blessed are the meek, for they are not so dependent on the praise of men. The meek know who they really are, and their real and lasting status will prevail. Mortal monuments, however pretentious, and the passing praise of the world, however lavish, do not really and finally matter.

(Neal A. Maxwell, *That Ye May Believe* [Salt Lake City: Bookcraft, 1992], 134–135)

Daily Living

SEEK NOT TO BUILD UP ONESELF BUT TO COUNSEL WITH THE LORD.

- Pride will destroy the soul and separate one from God. We must always remember the source of all good—3 John 1:11; Moroni 7:12–14
- Remember in your learning to counsel with the Lord—2 Nephi 9:28–29
- Never boast as to yourself—Alma 26:11–12; Helaman 4:13
- Always acknowledge the hand of God in all things—D&C 59:21

HONOR YOUR COMMITMENTS

Seek ye; and keep all your pledges one with another; and covet not that which is thy brother's.
D&C 136:20

To covet is to have an eager, extreme, and ungodly desire for something. The presence of *covetousness* in a human soul shows that such person has not overcome the world and is not living by gospel standards of conduct. Coveting is such a serious offense, and it is so imperative that man overcome all tendencies thereto, that the Lord condemned it in the Ten Commandments (Ex. 20:17; Mosiah 13:24).

(Bruce R. McConkie, *Mormon Doctrine* [Salt Lake City: Bookcraft, 1966], 156)

Daily Living

HONOR YOUR COMMITMENTS AND SEEK NOT TO COVET.

- Be honest with yourself—Alma 53:20
- Coveting occurs in relationships and the workplace primarily due to character flaws associated with the integrity of the heart. Our eyes are full of greediness—D&C 56:17
- Coveting begins with thoughts that are dwelled upon that result in lustful desires due to the supposed lack of or need for greater self-esteem that the world and things can bring. These desires eventually will become acted on if not bridled or controlled—Alma 38:12
- Cease to covet—D&C 88:123
- Be honest and upright in all things—Alma 27:27

SEEK NOT TO CONTEND

Cease to contend one with another;
cease to speak evil one of another.
D&C 136:23

In a recent conference message, Elder Russell M. Nelson expressed concern "that contention is becoming accepted as a way of life." In the press, on television, and in various aspects of political and public affairs, the *modus operandi* is contention. We live in an environment of contention. But, as Elder Nelson reminds us, contention is not the Lord's way: "How easy it is, yet how wrong it is, to allow habits of contention to pervade matters of spiritual significance, because contention is forbidden by divine decree: 'The Lord God hath commanded that men should not . . . envy; that they should not have malice; that they should not contend one with another'" (2 Ne. 26:32). The Savior is the "Prince of Peace," and the devil is the "father of contention" (3 Ne. 11:29).

(Dallin H. Oaks, *The Lord's Way* [Salt Lake City: Deseret Book, 1991], 150–151)

Daily Living

SEEK NOT TO CONTEND ONE WITH ANOTHER.

- ℘ Contention is of the devil—3 Nephi 11:28–29
- ℘ Peace is of the Lord—John 14:27; D&C 19:23
- ℘ Conflict and contention can be solved with humility and a pure heart, which will always be at peace—3 Nephi 12:9
- ℘ Pride must at all costs be avoided and the love of God be in your heart in order to overcome contention—4 Nephi 1:15–16

WE MUST BE TRIED AND TESTED

My people must be tried in all things, that they may be prepared to receive the glory that I have for them, even the glory of Zion; and he that will not bear chastisement is not worthy of my kingdom.
D&C 136:31

A commitment is a pledge, a vow, a determination, a promise, a resolution. Our understanding of and commitment to the covenants we have made with God are essential to our well-being now and in the eternities. . . .We should expect life to be difficult, because we are to be tried and tested in all things. It is in those very trials and tests that we discover and demonstrate the level of our commitment.

(Ardeth Greene Kapp, *Rejoice! His Promises Are Sure* [Salt Lake City: Deseret Book, 1997], 116–117)

Daily Living

WE MUST BE TRIED AND TESTED TO RECEIVE ETERNAL GLORY.

- We must be tried and tested—Abraham 3:25
- Remember, chastisement is to discipline us, thus providing a way for us to change and become more refined and purified. We must be tutored and mentored with instructions and chastisements of love—D&C 95:1–2
- We must never forget that true chastisement is inspired of the Holy Ghost—D&C 121:43
- We are here to prove ourselves worthy and prepare to meet God—Alma 4:32
- Endure to the end and receive eternal life—D&C 14:7

HUMBLE YOURSELF

Let him that is ignorant learn wisdom by humbling himself and calling upon the Lord his God, that his eyes may be opened that he may see, and his ears opened that he may hear.
D&C 136:32

Read again the account of Alma's mission to the Zoramites, found in Alma 31–35. Through him the humble and suffering people were taught to grow in faith in the word of God, which gives the answers to life's problems and the secret to spiritual growth.

Wanting help from God, instead of any other source, is at last the true solution. . . . Alma spoke of the blessing that comes from being compelled into humility because of life's circumstances. When we are humble, we are then ready to learn wisdom, to hear—really hear—the word of God. This learning through experience enhances our efforts to assist others.

(Elaine Cannon, *Adversity* [Salt Lake City: Bookcraft, 1987], 47)

Daily Living

HUMBLE YOURSELF AND LEARN WISDOM.

- Are we sufficiently humble?—Alma 5:27
- The fruits of humility are ever present as we seek to truly become like our Lord and Savior Jesus Christ. "I would that ye should be humble, and be submissive and gentle; easy to be entreated"—Alma 7:23
- In humility one can be exalted—Matthew 23:12
- Be humble without being compelled to be—Alma 32:16
- The Spirit will lead you to be humble—D&C 11:12

THE SPIRIT ENLIGHTENS THE HUMBLE

For my Spirit is sent forth into the world to enlighten the humble and contrite, and to the condemnation of the ungodly.
D&C 136:33

Spiritual food is as essential as material food, and yet many are starving themselves spiritually. In this latter day the Lord has reconfirmed that his "Spirit is sent forth into the world to enlighten the humble and contrite. . . ." (D&C 136:33.) . . . How do we receive this enlightenment? We must of course, be humble but we have also been instructed to "seek . . . diligently and teach one another words of wisdom; yea, seek ye out of the best books words of wisdom; seek learning, even by study and also by faith." (D&C 88:118.)

(Elder Franklin D. Richards, in Conference Report, October 1966, 70)

Daily Living

THE SPIRIT IS SENT FORTH TO ENLIGHTEN THE HUMBLE.

- The Spirit only works with the humble and faithful through fasting and prayer to the point that you can be sanctified—Helaman 3:35
- Sanctification comes by the power of the Holy Spirit—3 Nephi 27:20
- Remember, humility is vibrant and alive, not a station reached. It is an ongoing relationship with God.
- Seek enlightenment from the best books: the Book of Mormon, the Doctrine and Covenants, the Bible, and the Pearl of Great Price—D&C 88:118.

PONDER THE SCRIPTURES

I sat in my room pondering over the scriptures; As I pondered over these things which are written, the eyes of my understanding were opened, and the Spirit of the Lord rested upon me, and I saw the hosts of the dead, both small and great.
D&C 138:1, 11

There are special gifts and endowments reserved for those who study and ponder the scriptures; for those who treasure up the Lord's word; for those who fast and pray and seek knowledge by the power of the Spirit. They receive guidance and enlightenment that can be gained in no other way. They become men of sound understanding. They gain the spirit of revelation and of prophecy and teach and speak with power from on high.

(Marion G. Romney, *Learning for the Eternities* [Salt Lake City: Deseret Book, 1977], ii)

Daily Living

PONDERING INVOKES THE POWER OF REVELATION.

- The power of pondering and meditating invokes the power of faith in the Lord Jesus Christ. Faith works through mental exertion (see *Lectures on Faith* [Salt Lake City: Deseret Book, 1985], 7:3).
- The windows of heaven are opened, and you receive revelation—1 Nephi 11:1; Helaman 10:2–3
- If we are to feast upon the word of God we must ponder and pray to understand and appreciate the scriptures and then liken them to our lives—1 Nephi 19:23
- The word is the greatest power to cause change—Alma 31:5

PONDER ON THE LOVE OF GOD

And reflecting upon the great atoning sacrifice that was made by the Son of God, for the redemption of the world; And the great and wonderful love made manifest by the Father and the Son in the coming of the Redeemer into the world.
D&C 138:2–3

Finally, while pursuing our individual submissiveness, we are helped immensely when we ponder the infinite Atonement. God did not spare His Beloved Son from the anguish of these perfecting experiences. Jesus Christ has been, is, and will be our empathic Advocate with the Father. Not only is He our Advocate, but He helps us through our individual ordeals. By His own suffering He was perfected, including in His capacity to help us with our individual suffering (Alma 7:11–12).

(Neal A. Maxwell, *Not My Will, But Thine* [Salt Lake City: Bookcraft, 1998], 3)

Daily Living

PONDER ON THE ATONEMENT AND ON THE LOVE OF GOD.

- The infinite and eternal Atonement is the center and key to the gospel. This makes possible the overcoming of death and sin. We can be resurrected, forgiven, and gain exaltation through obedience to the laws and ordinances of the gospel and enduring to the end—2 Nephi 31:20–21
- Realize our plight without the Savior—2 Nephi 9:6–9
- This infinite Atonement is what draws all mankind to our beloved Savior Jesus Christ—3 Nephi 27:13–14
- By pondering the Atonement we become filled with gratitude to the Lord—the catalyst for change.

December 25

HOPE OF DELIVERANCE

All these had departed the mortal life, firm in the hope of a glorious resurrection, through the grace of God the Father and his Only Begotten Son, Jesus Christ. I beheld that they were filled with joy and gladness, and were rejoicing together because the day of their deliverance was at hand. They were assembled awaiting the advent of the Son of God into the spirit world, to declare their redemption from the bands of death.

D&C 138:14–16

What have we to console us in relation to the dead? We have reason to have the greatest hope and consolation for our dead of any people on the earth; for we have seen them walk worthily in our midst, and seen them sink asleep in the arms of Jesus; and those who have died in the faith are now in the celestial kingdom of God.

(Joseph Smith, *History of The Church*, 6:315)

Daily Living

HOPE IN CHRIST MAKES AN ANCHOR TO OUR SOUL.

- Hope, which cometh of faith, makes an anchor to our souls—Ether 12:4
- True hope is based upon the Lord Jesus Christ and upon the concept of eternal life—Titus 1:2
- Hope provides us with a sense of confidence in looking forward in righteousness. A life without hope is empty, and sin lies at our doors. A life filled with hope is a life filled with light and meaning.

GOSPEL PREACHED IN THE SPIRIT WORLD

But behold, from among the righteous, he organized his forces and appointed messengers, clothed with power and authority, and commissioned them to go forth and carry the light of the gospel to them that were in darkness, even to all the spirits of men; and thus was the gospel preached to the dead.
D&C 138:30

This key of knowledge, I say, gives enlarged views of the mercies of God, and reveals the fact that every man, both in time and eternity, will always have the privilege of doing right, and reaping the reward of his righteousness. . . . it gives us to understand that in the spirit world the Gospel is preached to the departed spirits of men, that is, to those who have departed from this life and that they are instructed in the way of salvation.

(B. H. Roberts, *The Gospel and Man's Relationship to Deity* [Salt Lake City: Deseret News, 1901], 243)

Daily Living

THE GOSPEL TO BE PREACHED TO ALL THOSE IN THE SPIRIT WORLD.

ꟸ The love for all of God's children is exemplified by the plan which affords all mankind the privilege and right to return to the presence of their Heavenly Father regardless of the time and space in which they lived here upon the earth. The prophet Joseph said, "After all that has been said, the greatest and most important duty is to preach the Gospel" (*History of the Church*, 2:478). This is why we preach the gospel to every nation, kindred, tongue, and people on both sides of the veil.

CHOICE SPIRITS TO COME FORTH

The Prophet Joseph Smith, and my father, Hyrum Smith, Brigham Young, John Taylor, Wilford Woodruff, and other choice spirits . . . were reserved to come forth in the fulness of times to take part in laying the foundations of the great latter-day work.
D&C 138:53

I am convinced that the Lord has reserved us as his choice spirits to come forth in this time to become leaders in his kingdom—a kingdom far greater than this world has known. It is up to us to increase our understanding, to use our time profitably and to have a firm resolve to keep all of God's commandments. In this way, the task before us will become a joy.

(John H. Vandenberg, January 7, 1964,
BYU Speeches of the Year, 10)

Daily Living

CHOICE SPIRITS TO COME FORTH TO DO THE LATTER-DAY WORK.

ꝏ All blessings come from righteousness. We came endowed with blessings, as well as some cautions for our earthly existence, from premortal earth life. Sometimes these may be given within our patriarchal blessings. Alma records concerning some of those endowed with favored blessings due to their faithfulness, "being called and prepared from the foundation of the world according to the foreknowledge of God, on account of their exceeding faith and good works"—Alma 13:3–5

BUILDING OF THE TEMPLES IN THE LATTER-DAY

Including the building of the temples and the performance of ordinances therein for the redemption of the dead, [who] were . . . in the spirit world.
D&C 138:54

I hope you are using the temple constantly, because you will gain blessings there that you cannot gain anywhere else on the face of the whole earth. . . . It stands as a statement that we as a people believe in the immortality of the human soul. . . . It speaks of the importance of the individual as a child of God. It speaks of the importance of the family as a creation of the Almighty. It speaks of the eternity of the marriage relationship. It speaks of going on to greater glory. It is a place of light, a place of peace, a place of love where we deal with the things of eternity. If there is any man here tonight who is not worthy to go into that holy house, I urge you to put your life in order so that you may go there and partake of the unique and wonderful blessings that we have there.

(Gordon B. Hinckley, *Teachings of Gordon B. Hinckley* [Salt Lake City: Deseret Book, 1997], 623–624)

Daily Living

SEEK THE BLESSINGS OF THE TEMPLES IN THE LATTER-DAY.

- The great work of proclaiming the gospel, perfecting the Saints, and redeeming the dead through vicarious temple ordinances is the great work of this last dispensation. Our exaltation is dependent upon our searching after our dead and performing the ordinances they cannot perform for themselves—D&C 128:15

PREPARED TO COME FORTH IN DUE TIME

Even before they were born, they, with many others, received their first lessons in the world of spirits and were prepared to come forth in the due time of the Lord to labor in his vineyard for the salvation of the souls of men.
D&C 138:56

Every man who has a calling to minister to the inhabitants of the world was ordained to that very purpose in the Grand Council of heaven before this world was. I suppose that I was ordained to this very office in that Grand Council.

(Joseph Smith, *History of The Church*, 6:364)

Daily Living

WE'VE BEEN PREPARED TO COME FORTH IN THE LATTER-DAY.

- We were prepared to come forth in these the latter days. What an honor and privilege to serve the Lord in these days of the restoration of the gospel in the dispensation of the fullness of times and to taste the joy—Alma 36:24
- Remember this, the bringing of souls to Christ is of the greatest worth—D&C 15:6
- We will joy with the souls we assist to come to Christ, now and in the hereafter—D&C 18:10–16
- This is the last time the vineyard will be nourished by the Lord and His servants—Jacob 5:70–71
- The message in the Doctrine and Covenants is clear: prepare the way of the Lord for His Second Coming by bringing souls to Christ.

PREACH IN THE SPIRIT WORLD

I beheld that the faithful elders of this dispensation, when they depart from mortal life, continue their labors in the preaching of the gospel of repentance and redemption, through the sacrifice of the Only Begotten Son of God, among those who are in darkness and under the bondage of sin in the great world of the spirits of the dead.
D&C 138:57

Now, all those [who] die in the faith go to the prison of spirits to preach to the dead in body, but they are alive in the spirit; and those spirits preach to the spirits that they may live according to God in the spirit, and men do minister for them in the flesh; and angels bear the glad tidings to the spirits, and they are made happy by these means.

(Joseph Smith, *Encyclopedia of Joseph Smith's Teachings*, eds. Donald Q. Cannon and Larry E. Dahl, [Salt Lake City: Bookcraft, 1997], 644)

Daily Living

FAITHFUL ELDERS PREACH IN THE SPIRIT WORLD.

ॐ Missionary work and preaching the gospel never stops. The spirit world is absorbed and engrossed in the work of bringing souls to Christ. Jesus Christ is the only name given whereby mankind can be saved. Through preaching the gospel and doing vicarious work for the dead, the lifesaving principles and ordinances will be brought into their lives as they choose to accept them. The joy is felt on both sides of the veil as the work proceeds in bringing souls to our Savior Jesus Christ thus qualifying them to return to the presence of out Heavenly Father.

THE DEAD REDEEMED

The dead who repent will be redeemed, through obedience to the ordinances of the house of God.
D&C 138:58

To liberate themselves, then, the unrighteous must accept the gospel preached to them by the Lord's spirit missionaries. Then, they must repent and accept responsibility for their sins and take advantage of Christ's atoning sacrifice. And finally, since they no longer possess physical bodies, they must wait for others to perform vicarious ordinances for them on earth.

(Victor L. Ludlow, *Principles and Practices of the Restored Gospel* [Salt Lake City: Deseret Book, 1992], 224)

Daily Living

THE DEAD WHO REPENT WILL BE REDEEMED.

- The Lord seeks that all the children of our Heavenly Father be given every opportunity to return to His presence. This overwhelming love and devotion to the children is captured in the expression of Nephi when he wrote concerning our beloved Savior Jesus Christ, "He doeth not anything save it be for the benefit of the world; for he loveth the world, even that he layeth down his own life that he may draw all men unto him. Wherefore, he commandeth none that they shall not partake of his salvation"—2 Nephi 26:24–33
- May we press forward with faithful diligence to proclaim the gospel to all mankind.

INDEX

ꙍ

About the Authors

ED J. PINEGAR

Ed J. Pinegar is a retired dentist and long-time teacher of early-morning seminary and religion classes at Brigham Young University. He taught at the Joseph Smith Academy and has served as a mission president in England and at the Missionary Training Center in Provo, Utah. He has been a bishop twice and a stake president and is a temple sealer. Ed and his wife, Patricia, are the parents of eight children. He and his wife are currently serving a full-time mission.

RICHARD J. ALLEN

Richard J. Allen is a husband, father, teacher, and writer. He has served on several high councils, in several stake presidencies, and as a bishop. Richard's teaching assignments in the Church have included service as a full-time missionary, instructor in various priesthood quorums, Gospel Doctrine teacher, and stake institute director. He has served as a faculty member at both Brigham Young University and the Johns Hopkins University. Richard has coauthored many articles, manuals, and books and has served on a number of national educational boards. He and his wife, Carol Lynn Hansen Allen, have four children and five grandchildren.